Gender and Organized Crime in Italy

Gender and Organized Crime in Italy

Women's Agency in Italian Mafias

Ombretta Ingrascì

BLOOMSBURY ACADEMIC
LONDON • NEW YORK • OXFORD • NEW DELHI • SYDNEY

BLOOMSBURY ACADEMIC
Bloomsbury Publishing Plc
50 Bedford Square, London, WC1B 3DP, UK
1385 Broadway, New York, NY 10018, USA
29 Earlsfort Terrace, Dublin 2, Ireland

BLOOMSBURY, BLOOMSBURY ACADEMIC and the Diana logo
are trademarks of Bloomsbury Publishing Plc

First published in Great Britain 2021
This paperback edition published by Bloomsbury Academic in 2023

Copyright © Ombretta Ingrascì, 2021

Ombretta Ingrascì has asserted her right under the Copyright,
Designs and Patents Act, 1988, to be identified as Author of this work.

For legal purposes the Acknowledgements on p. xii constitute an
extension of this copyright page.

Series design by Adriana Brioso
Cover image: Sicily, Italy. (© DeAgostini/Getty Images)

All rights reserved. No part of this publication may be reproduced or
transmitted in any form or by any means, electronic or mechanical,
including photocopying, recording, or any information storage or retrieval
system, without prior permission in writing from the publishers.

Bloomsbury Publishing Plc does not have any control over, or responsibility for,
any third-party websites referred to or in this book. All internet addresses given
in this book were correct at the time of going to press. The author and publisher
regret any inconvenience caused if addresses have changed or sites have
ceased to exist, but can accept no responsibility for any such changes.

A catalogue record for this book is available from the British Library.

A catalog record for this book is available from the Library of Congress.

ISBN: HB: 978-1-3501-5078-2
PB: 978-0-7556-4206-9
ePDF: 978-1-3502-3883-1
eBook: 978-1-3502-3882-4

Typeset by RefineCatch Limited, Bungay, Suffolk

To find out more about our authors and books visit
www.bloomsbury.com and sign up for our newsletters.

To Petra

Contents

Foreword *Donald Sassoon*		ix
Acknowledgements		xii
Note on the Text		xiii
Introduction		1
1	Cosa Nostra and the 'Ndrangheta	9
	Violence, power and business	9
	Organizational structures and rituals	11
2	Women in Italian Society	23
	The labour market	23
	Social customs and women's rights	29
3	Mafia Control Over Women	37
	The code of honour	37
	Female oppression	42
	Honour killings	48
	Blood alliances through marriages	56
4	Conformist Agency: Performing Soft Power	63
	Education	63
	Vendetta	72
5	Compliant Agency: From Margins to Delegated Power	81
	The drug trade	81
	Economic crimes	93
	From Hermes tasks to leadership positions	101
	Female agency meets mafia organizational needs	119
6	Transformative Agency: Searching for Autonomous Paths	127
	The strength of vulnerability	127
	Speaking out	131
	Following their own children	151
	The ethical impact	154

Appendix: Lea Garofalo's letter to the President of the Italian Republic	161
Notes	165
Bibliography	195
Judicial Sources	207
Index	209

Foreword

Donald Sassoon

The Hollywood treatment of the mafia has largely been centred on male roles. Women existed, if at all, as sexy decoration, dutiful wives, very occasionally as reluctant accomplices, rarely as rebels. They seldom participated in the actual organization and development of the criminal business. Ombretta Ingrasci's path-breaking study engages the reader in a far more complex perspective. Her fascinating account shows how women succeeded in breaking the 'glass ceiling' even in a traditional criminal organization such as the Italian mafia. This is bound to raise eyebrows. It shows that the mafia and 'its' women have managed both to build on their traditional values (the so-called 'code of honour', the misogynistic commitment to 'family values') while at the same time adapting to major social and cultural changes.

For historians, criminal organizations constitute a problem. When gangsters meet they do not keep minutes, do not write down their plans, avoid anything that might leave traces, and, outside of their circles, try to disguise their accomplishment. The secret services may prevent historians from examining their own archives for thirty, fifty, even one hundred years, but, eventually, when everyone concerned is dead, archives are open and (some) truth comes out. Even some terrorist groups keep documents in the hope that history will 'absolve' them or glorify them. But mafiosi do not keep archives. Direct observation cannot be used, for obvious reasons. So what are the sources? Luckily for historians, the police and the judiciary intercept conversations, extract confessions, put criminals up for trial, convene witnesses and, once the criminals are in prison, keep up the surveillance. So far so good, but what is needed is to unveil the even less visible face of the mafia, what goes on in the family, the language mafiosi speak, the feelings they have. This can only be done through oral sources, by interviewing witnesses and those who collaborated with the law. Ombretta Ingrasci comes up with the goods, and admirably so.

She has been able to use long interviews, and not just with women but also with the mafiosi themselves, as well as with lawyers, politicians, journalists and social workers, during a period of more than twenty years. Her 'prize witness' was a woman 'Rosa N.' whom she first interviewed in 1998, who used to belong to the 'Ndrangheta, the Calabrian mafia, and who had spent many years in jail.

Two factors facilitated the increasingly important role of women in the Italian mafia:

1. The success of police operations over the last thirty years has meant that many mafiosi have ended up in prison and others have been forced on to the run. The absence of men has led to the advancement of women. The process is similar to that which occurred during the two world wars when women entered, though often only temporarily, the work force to replace men who had been drafted into the armed forces. In an organization were trust is essential, vacancies cannot be filled by 'normal' recruitment. The job must be done by someone you can rely on, someone you can trust, a member of the 'family'. When the godfather is away or dead, the godmother can take over.
2. Over recent decades the mafia has moved from extortion rackets to the drug trade and the laundering of money. Extortion required aggressive and violent men able and willing to threaten shopkeepers, entrepreneurs and politicians. Drug dealing and money laundering, however, are jobs that required brain more than brawn; they can thus be perfectly well done by increasingly educated women (some even become qualified accountants), able to take advantage of freedom of movement (which they did not have in the past) and better able than men to appear inconspicuous and thus less likely to be investigated by the authorities. As Ombretta Ingrascì explains: 'the development of the role of women in the mafia cannot be understood without taking into consideration the bigger picture, i.e. the general changes in the condition of women which have occurred in Italy since 1945'.

The author (who maintains an admirably dispassionate tone throughout the book) also eschews the cliché of women as permanent victims: many played a crucial role passing on the mafia code within mafia families – just as they often do in society at large, especially in religious-minded groups. There is a certain female complicity in teaching gender inequality. Many women consider violent and oppressive male behaviours 'normal' and correct: they have been socialised to accept the entire cultural ideology of male dominance.

Traditionally, in southern Italy having a working woman in the family was regarded as embarrassing: it showed that you were poor. Besides, once women were out and about you could not control them. If mafiosi used their wives and daughters for work once belonging exclusively to men it meant the clan was weak. But even the mafia has had to adapt to new times. The ridiculously named 'honour code' – 'gangster rules' would be a better label – had to be modified.

None of this should imply that, somehow, 'women's lib' has reached the mafia. Fathers, brothers and even cousins continue to control women and are the perpetrators of 'honour' related violence. If you can't trust a woman to be faithful to her husband, you can't trust her not to go to the police.

Take the case of Lea Garofalo, who was killed in 2009 at the age of 35 by her husband, drug boss Carlo Cosco. In 1996 he was arrested by the police and Lea took advantage of the situation to run away with her daughter, hoping for a better and less dangerous life. Carlo Cosco could not accept her decision, not because he loved her but because Lea's behaviour had brought him shame and ridicule. As soon as he left prison, he busied himself with organizing her murder. Fearing for her life and for that of her daughter, she sought the help of the police, but she made the mistake of believing in Carlo's promise that he would take care of their daughter economically and agreed to meet him. She was killed and her body dissolved in acid.

Another woman, Francesca Bellocco, had an extra-marital affair with an 'Ndrangheta member. She was killed by her own son, Francesco, who was following a 'family tradition'. This murder contributed to the Bellocco family's prestige as local criminals. Francesco is now in prison, probably still convinced that he had upheld the family 'honour' by killing his own mother.

'Godmothers' can be involved in drug trafficking as couriers, dealers and even bosses while the appalling treatment of women continues, just as in wider society we can have women prime ministers coexisting with a lamentably high level of domestic violence, abuse and murders.

Yet women involved in the mafia, as this engrossing book shows only too well, are not always victims. 'Godmothers' may well end doing what 'godfathers' do: killing to protect the 'business' and pass on to their children the mafia culture within which they have grown. After all, escaping one's past, one's environment, one's family has never been easy.

Acknowledgements

Many thanks to all the key observers I met during the years of my research. In particular, thanks go to the magistrates who furnished me with valuable judicial sources and pivotal information. Special thanks to Nicola Aiello, Marco Alma, Maurizio Bonaccorso, Alessandra Cerreti, Caterina Chinnici, Salvatore Dolce, Alessandra Dolci, Simona Ferraiuolo, Nicola Gratteri, Paolo Guido, Gaetano Paci, Flavia Panzano, Annamaria Picozzi, Michele Prestipino, Maurizio Romanelli, Elio Romano, Massimo Russo, Lia Sava and Laura Vaccaro.

Many thanks to the collaborators with justices who generously offered me the account of their lives; to journalist Salvo Palazzolo for sharing with me unique insights into Cosa Nostra; to Tomasz Hoskins, Nayiri Kendir, Juliet Gardner, Sophie Campbell and Merv Honeywood for managing the editorial process with great professionalism; to Brent Waterhouse who carried out careful proofreading on this book; to Ilaria Favretto for her precious advice; to Monica Massari for the generous and inspiring conversations; to all my friends, ready to help me at any moment (warm thanks especially to Gigi); to Anna and Sergio for their extraordinary capacity to listen to me; to my dad, Gianni, who transmitted me the interest in the Mafia, and to my wonderful mum, Graziella, whose soul is always with me; to my sister Marina for her infinite support, and to her beautiful family; to Petra, my sweaty and funny girl; and, finally, to Matteo, who travels in life with me.

Note on the text

Some of the cases analysed in this book regard people whose criminal trial has not yet been completed or who have been acquitted. Their stories have been reported for knowledge purposes and therefore they have a mere historical-documentary value that goes beyond any judicial evaluation.

Some names of persons mentioned in the book have been substituted with pseudonyms for security or privacy reasons.

Introduction

Public representations of mafia women tend to portray them either as 'godmothers' or as victims. This volume aims to question these two stereotypical views by reconstructing a more complex picture. For this purpose, it will understand mafias as organizations involving not only criminality, but also economic, social and cultural aspects; it will avoid compressing mafia women's experiences into static and homogeneous analytical categories; and, it will treat gender as the product of both sociocultural structures and unconscious processes.

In Italy, four mafia-type organizations exist, referred to as Cosa Nostra, the 'Ndrangheta, the Camorra and the Sacra Corona Unita. Originating in the south – respectively in Sicily, Calabria, Campania and Apulia – they later spread to Northern Italy, as well as abroad.

These underground organizations are made up of various clans, show different structures – from hierarchical to horizontal, use violence and corruption to control a given territory, and are totally embedded within their surrounding socioeconomic and cultural context. Among the lower classes, they easily appeal to a great number of workers by offering job opportunities. At the political level, they bind themselves tightly to administrators by threatening them or offering them electoral votes in exchange for public resources. In financial and business milieus, they are welcome because they bring illegal funds to launder.

One of the main assets of mafia associations is their ability to maintain traditional values and at same time adapt to wider economic and sociocultural changes.[1] This is quite evident from the ability shown by mafias in keeping traditional ideology – grounded on the law of silence, the code of honour and vendetta – alive and well, while taking on the entrepreneurial features required to enter new criminal and legal markets.

When referring to these associations, their multifaceted nature, as briefly described above, suggests we use the expression 'mafia system'.[2] This allows us to grasp the main fabric of mafia associations, i.e. an integration between criminal, socio-economic and cultural dimensions, and a corresponding combination of ideological and organizational traits. Women's condition, roles and functions make this interweaving quite explicit. This is because on the one hand they have played historically important functions in the household, which is the context where the cultural aspects of the organization are nurtured, and on the other they have been increasingly employed in the criminal sphere. Basically, they occupy the space between the family and the clan's affairs, which in mafias tends to be blurred.

Despite this twofold, crucial position held by women within the mafia system, they cannot be considered as a specific group of people. Following the intersectionality approach, it is important to remember that women's experiences are shaped not only by gender, but also by other social identity categories.[3] In the case of mafia women, differences in their condition depend on socioeconomic and demographic variables, as much as on other factors including, for instance, the criminal organizations to whom they belong, their family origin, the types of kinship they have with male mafia members and the latter's degree in the ranks of the organization and, no less important, their own personality.

For these reasons the stories and lives related in this work must be read as biographies that are fundamentally unique and thus cannot be treated as paradigmatic cases.[4] However, we can recognize that they share some *practices in situations*[5] that, being recurrent, enable us to grasp and illustrate certain tendencies, dynamics and mechanisms that seem to characterize the mafias in terms of gender norms, functions and relationships, and are also revealing in terms of women's acts and feelings.

In order to maintain a fecund and dynamic relation between the single life history and the general conditions of women in the mafia system, one would do well to give the utmost importance to the following warning: 'it is a mistake to picture attributes like gender as toxic capsules full of norms and interpretive schemas that individuals swallow whole and that lodge intact in their psychic structure ... But it is also a mistake to picture attributes like gender as systems of social and economic opportunities, constraints, rewards, and penalties that never impinge upon individual identity.'[6]

Avoiding these two mistakes is necessary when exploring the nexus between gender and agency in relation to women's experiences in the mafia system. Indeed, it is advisable to employ a balanced approach that allows us to represent mafia women as subjects who are neither totally autonomous nor passive. This work has identified different kinds of agency performed by mafia women, including conformist, compliant and transformative ones. Women express the former agencies by supporting the mafia through enhancing its ideology and carrying out pivotal activities for the organization's survival or growth, and display the latter type of agency by abandoning the mafia system.

Exploring the inner side of the mafias – where women largely remain – is a challenging undertaking. Direct observation is out of the question because mafia groups are secret and criminal. The main sources available are those produced by law enforcement institutions, including investigative reports and judicial files (indictments, acts and rulings). They contain many primary sources (i.e. transcriptions of intercepted conversations and electronic surveillance carried out within the prison system) that are highly useful in reconstructing these *practices in situations*. However, analysing these primary sources, drafted by police officers and magistrates, has to be done with caution, insofar as they show an institutional view of the mafia that is aimed at underlining the criminal aspects of the phenomenon.[7]

Moreover, life within the household and its cultural foundations emerges very rarely in judiciary sources, because acts in the private sphere are not criminally chargeable. To reveal the more invisible face of the mafia, one must turn to oral sources, including interviews with witnesses and collaborators with justice.[8]

The main source of this work is an interview with a woman, Rosa N.,[9] who used to belong to a family that was part of the 'Ndrangheta organization. I interviewed her in 1998, five years after she decided to turn state's evidence at the age of thirty-six. Her tale revealed in advance many issues related to the condition and role of women in the 'Ndrangheta that were later confirmed by other testimonies that emerged in the 2000s. I also interviewed men who collaborated with justice, in order to grasp both perspectives, female and male.[10]

In conducting the interview with Rosa N., which was an 'open-ended dialogue',[11] I was not only a researcher aware of creating and producing a document based on a life story, but also a woman listening to the story of another woman. This dual identity of the researcher is not a drawback in collecting oral sources, but rather an advantage because it allows one to create 'the conditions in which the object of research enters into the process as an active subject'.[12] By recognizing 'the objects of the research as subjects in their own rights', the researcher is able to use life stories and life histories for academic purposes without making 'the research relationship an exploitative one'.[13] Such an approach enabled me to develop a collaborative and interactive relationship with Rosa N.[14] The way I carried out the interview was conditioned by my concern over the ethical dilemma of treating a life story as one of the sources of my research, as was my interpretation. However, my moral doubts allowed me to remain an observer who takes nothing for granted and shows respect when interpreting the words offered by the informer.

This internal information was combined with that contributed by experts on the topic, including public prosecutors, politicians, local journalists, lawyers, priests and social workers, who I interviewed during a period of time covering twenty years.[15]

This book is set out in six chapters. The first will trace the main characteristics of the two organizations on which this volume focuses, Cosa Nostra and the 'Ndrangheta. It will look into their methods, activities and different structures and will furthermore highlight those aspects that are most relevant in understanding the functions and condition of women within these two organizations. Cosa Nostra and the 'Ndrangheta's activities developed along quite similar lines. Since the 1970s, their criminal operations have moved mainly towards drugs, a business that enabled them to gather a considerable amount of capital. This financial accumulation brought about a need to launder the money and enter legal markets. Both the drug trade and these economic investments opened up jobs for women, who were considered useful since being female made them inconspicuous and less likely to be discovered by the police. Additionally, the fact that they were increasingly educated and had more freedom of movement than in the past, as a consequence of the wider process of female emancipation, made them precious pawns for the criminal organizations. Indeed, the development of the role of women in the mafia cannot be understood without taking into consideration the bigger picture, i.e. the general changes in the condition of women which have occurred in Italy since 1945. The second chapter will thus outline two areas of change that proved pivotal for the transformation of female positions in Italian society, the labour market and social customs. In Italy, women's presence in the workplace increased during the Second World War and went through a phase of decline from 1945 until the late 1960s. A new period of growth occurred in the 1970s. Interestingly, the legitimate world and the mafia system show many similarities in their use of the female workforce.

This chapter will stress the contradictions emerging from the process of women's emancipation undergone by Italian society, marked both by gender equality achievements in terms of education and rights, and by high level of violence against women, especially in the domestic environment.

The mixture of change and continuity characterizing the path taken by women in Italian society after the Second World Word had an impact on mafia organizations. This is because Mafia associations are not detached from society. Basically, changes and continuity in the position of women in terms of the labour market and social customs had a twofold influence on women belonging to the mafia system. On the one hand, they facilitated female participation in the criminal arena. On the other, they made women more aware of their subordinate condition, thus driving them to distance themselves from the system. Changes in the field of the female labour market and in social customs provided women with the means to perform the types of agency mentioned above, whether conservative and compliant – which contributed to perpetuating mafia organizations – and transformative – which led women to oppose the male mafia system.

After these two introductory chapters, the volume starts to look specifically at female involvement in the mafia system. Although women cannot hold formal positions in mafia-type associations, they have been engaged indirectly and directly, as Chapters Three, Four and Five will explore.

The third chapter deals with indirect female participation influenced by the code of honour, which requires women to behave correctly in order to preserve men's respectability, which in turn has a significant effect on male mafia careers. The regime of honour under which some mafia women fall not only indicates what behaviour and attitudes are male or female, but also sets out how one should act, and what one cannot do. If women deviate from honour rules, they must be punished. The 'Ndrangheta might call for the death penalty for women who drift from its code of honour (i.e. if they have an extra-marital affair or talk with the police). The solution of honour killing is a path used to restore a family's reputation after an event that has tarnished its name. In other words, if deviant female behaviour has dishonoured the family, it has the duty to prove to the entire community that it can defend its own pride, whatever the cost, even if this involves sacrificing its own daughters, sisters or wives.

Above and beyond their representative nature, restrictive and violent honour-related practices make it clear that the female body is used by members of mafias to display the power of the organization and its ability to control and punish those who breach the rules.

Indirect female participation is also evident when women are objects exchanged in arranged marriages. The third chapter will thus also illustrate the relevance of the policy of marriages within mafia culture and organizational strategies. The female participation reconstructed in Chapter Three seem to characterize the 'Ndrangheta more than Cosa Nostra, and the past more than the present.

The fourth and fifth chapters will deal with the direct participation of women, respectively, in the private sphere and the criminal arena. Women play crucial roles in transmitting mafia principles within mafia families, along with the other members of a kinship group. The son-mother and the daughter-mother relationships will be investigated emphasizing female complicity in teaching gender inequality and the law of the Father. The family will be understood as a pivotal device for a mafia organization, which contributes to shaping men and women's mentality and behaviours into ones that serve the association's activities aimed at wealth and power. Direct female involvement is also clear when looking at their engagement with vendetta practices, which women traditionally tend to support.

Both transmitting mafia codes and reigning over the custom of vendetta gives women a sort of 'soft power', that is, the female authority in using cultural tenets as weapons for enhancing the ideology underpinning the mafia system.

It is impossible to identify when women started to exercise soft power, since this is linked to the private sphere, which is more difficult to study as it does not leave written sources. It is easier to explore the criminal involvement of women, which leaves judiciary traces, even though for many years the police neglected the presence of women in mafias. According to these sources, the involvement of women in the criminal sector of the mafias begun at the time of the mafias' engagement with drugs, and developed with their increasing need to launder illicit money. Chapter Five analyses the stories of specific women working in the drug business across all levels of the organization, and then looks at the stories of women whose names were used in establishing front companies and registering property and bank accounts, since women generally had no criminal records and were less monitored. It will also deal with stories of women engaged in more sophisticated functions related to money laundering, managing the cash of the clan and carrying out extortion. Finally, it will describe female participation inside the core of the mafia, which ranges from acting as words-couriers between bosses to running mafia clans. This 'advancement' has marked Cosa Nostra more than the 'Ndrangheta.

Since the late 1980s, positions of leadership in the mafia have also been delegated to women. As so often before in women's history, taking over of traditional male jobs occurs out of necessity, in emergency situations. In the last thirty years the Italian government has fought organized crime more efficiently from a penal perspective. As a consequence, many mafia bosses were captured and others forced to live on the run. This depleted the ranks of Cosa Nostra, that needed to recruit not only more people but, above all, trustworthy ones, able and willing to fill the 'vacancies' created at the top of the criminal association. As a result, some women became mafia bosses on behalf of their male relatives (husbands, brothers or fathers). The chapter will discuss what kind of power women held when men delegated them with leadership tasks and question whether this delegation had an impact on gender relationships.

Women's direct participation, both in the private sphere and in the criminal one, is the result of a type of agency that is conformist and compliant, and as such it has brought about changes but with morphostatic results, insofar as the male chauvinist order persists. Women, however, as mentioned earlier, were also able to express another kind of agency, which has proven to be transformative. The last chapter will investigate this form of female agency, whose results were profoundly innovative. To understand the choice of women rebelling against the mafia system, this work will use the concept of vulnerability, which in recent decades has occupied significant space within feminist debate in the field of philosophy of law, politics and sociology. It is a cogent concept containing different theoretical suggestions and interpretations, and thus it shows some ambiguities. However, it has proved to be particularly valid in understanding the new paths taken by mafia women who, subjugated to their family and husbands, have found a way to eradicate kinship constrictions. The final chapter will thus illustrate the force of vulnerability through the stories of women who decided to collaborate with justice or follow their children in Youth Court programmes implemented as a consequence of the removal of the father's authority. This chapter will discuss the ethical impact that their choice has brought at different levels, including individual and social.

This book is based on lengthy research on mafia women that started in the late 1990s for my master's thesis and continued with my PhD research, carried out in the early 2000s.[16] The result of this work appear in the book *Donne d'onore. Storie di mafia al femminile*, published in 2007.[17] At that time, my theoretical aim was to see whether or not the change in women's roles in the mafia indicated a process of female emancipation. My findings suggested that mafia women's passage from marginality to leadership positions could be defined as a process of *pseudo-emancipation*. In the last twenty years, although it has become clear that the notion of female emancipation is a theoretical trap that limits the understanding of the subjective nuances of women's experience, the model of interpretation constructed in my previous work proved capable of understanding long-term historical processes. In other words, further evidence confirmed that general indicators did exist – the persistence of patriarchal relations and women's economic dependence, temporary allocation of power to women during periods of emergency, use of female labour in low-profile jobs, and exclusion of women from career opportunities – which suggested that the increasing public presence of women in the mafias, beyond mere supportive and private roles, was the result of a process of female pseudo-emancipation. At the same time, it seems that the above definition could not be extended to a single subject whose relation to female emancipation was personal and might therefore not be understood by social scientists. This is to say that the pseudo-emancipation model was valid at the macro level, yet failed to wholly explain the micro level.[18]

Given the fact that many female behavioural patterns have been seen in the mafias, and that women have many unique and internal reasons to either support or refuse the mafia system, the above model has been integrated with a more fluid theoretical understanding, in order to give greater consideration to the subjectivity of women's experiences in the mafias. Exploring the different qualities of agencies performed by mafia women[19] and uncovering the layers of their vulnerability has allowed me to overcome the conundrums involved in questioning emancipation in relation to women in the mafias, which is a dead end both theoretically and empirically.

In conclusion, this work does not claim to know what women, belonging to the mafia system or leaving it, think or feel. To avoid this risk, I have reduced references to women's private and intimate sphere to a bare minimum, and I have tried to respect these life histories, and above all 'the pain of others',[20] as much as I could.

1

Cosa Nostra and the 'Ndrangheta

Violence, power and business

Cosa Nostra and the 'Ndrangheta, just as other mafia-type organizations, are made up of secret criminal groups that carry out activities aimed at accumulating wealth and power.

Mafia methods call for violence, as much as corruption and complicity with wider society. The mafia's recourse to violence, both inflicted and threatened, is due to military, economic and symbolic reasons.[1] Violence is a resource allowing mafiosi to exercise control over a given territory; to handle conflicts either internally or externally; to obtain dominant positions in markets, both illegal and legal; and to achieve a 'good' reputation that contributes to enhancing the mafia identity associated with 'men of honour'.

The various degrees and forms of violence perpetrated by mafias depend mainly on their structures.[2] Inter-organizational conflicts characterize associations with a horizontal structure to a greater extent than those with a vertical one. Generally speaking, the mafia's use of violence tends to be frugal. Only when strictly necessary do they use violence in a spectacular manner. After the early 1990s, both Cosa Nostra and the 'Ndrangheta have reduced their recourse to visible violence, in order to avoid attracting law enforcement's attention and the hostility of citizens – especially of those living in areas more recently colonized by the mafias.[3] Thus they have opted for less visible and more subtle forms of violence.

The professional use of violence is pivotal for achieving the two objectives of mafia associations, power and business.[4] On the one hand, violence and intimidation allow mafia groups to extort money from legitimate businesses. The 'mafia tax' (*pizzo*) is requested in exchange for 'protection', the need for which is created by the mafia itself through other crimes, like fire attacks or robberies.[5] Through this crime, mafias not only get money, but can above all exercise their control and govern a given territory.

On the other hand, violence is essential for participating in illegal and legal markets. Cosa Nostra and the 'Ndrangheta have undergone a similar evolution as 'enterprise syndicates'. They have both proven able to adapt to the modernization of Italian society. By passing from an agrarian to an urban phase and then becoming increasingly involved in drugs and financial activities, they both undertook a transformation parallel to that of Italian society, which has brought about changes in terms of needs, consumption and mentality.[6] During this transformation, the two organizations have entered various illegal and legal markets, proving their ability to take advantage of the opportunities emerging both from underdeveloped and advanced socioeconomic contexts.

As of the beginning of the process of industrialization and the expansion of building work, mafiosi focused their interests on the construction sector. At first, mafia groups transferred the method of control used in the agricultural sector, in small farms (i.e. the so-called *guardania*), into construction sites, i.e. imposing manpower and the supply of materials. Later, they directly obtained public contracts and subcontracts for public and private construction projects by corrupting politicians and entrepreneurs.[7]

At the same time, in the 1970s, mafia clans also started to participate in the drug trade. The Sicilian mafia became involved in this business by using the routes traditionally employed for trafficking tobacco and citrus fruit, and by investing the money accumulated in the construction sector. The 'Ndrangheta entered the drug market using the money coming from the ransom of the numerous kidnappings they perpetrated between the late 1960s to the early 1990s.[8]

In the 1980s Cosa Nostra played a prominent role in drug trafficking, while in the late 1990s this role was taken over by the 'Ndrangheta. Since the 1980s drug trafficking has grown significantly, allowing the elite 'Ndrangheta families to make great profits.[9] In recent decades, moreover, 'Ndrangheta groups have increased their arsenal of arms, leading investigators to define the organization as 'a military power'.[10] The combination of this military capacity with their great financial resources opened up significant opportunities in the economy and in politics.[11]

Both in Cosa Nostra and 'Ndrangheta clans, the earnings from extortion and drug trafficking activities tend to flow into a common fund that is meant to fuel the welfare system.[12] Mafias provide social protection for their members. The outflows from the fund are devoted not only to wages, sustaining detainees' families and legal assistance, but also go to mobility and communication, work tools (i.e. technology, weapons, corruption), health emergencies and housing.[13]

Not surprisingly, the welfare system offered by the mafias plays a significant role in attracting new candidates and also in increasing the members' attachment to the organization. Indeed, it is 'one of the main forms of control exerted by leaders over their members',[14] establishing loyalty and affection towards the criminal association.

The huge amount of money accumulated through narcotics led to the need to launder it. Both Cosa Nostra and 'Ndrangheta clans have invested their illegal capital in various sectors, including retail, construction, health care, food services, tourism, clubs, etc. They have also increased their interest in the usury market. This crime allows them not only to launder money, but also to exercise control over their territories.[15] Mafiosi have exploited the negative economic conditions seen in Italy since 2008, and the consequent need for liquidity experienced by entrepreneurs and citizens. Some 'Ndrangheta groups' great availability of cash alongside society's need for money has created a perfect match between demand and supply, leading this economic crime to spread widely.[16]

To achieve their power and entrepreneurial aims, mafias have used not only violence, but also social capital. This has been a key resource for building networks of relationships in the 'legal' world, useful for expanding connections with politics and businesses.[17] Both Cosa Nostra and the 'Ndrangheta have shown great expertise in developing partnerships with politicians and professionals. Close relationships with some politicians, both locally and nationally, have facilitated mafia actors in obtaining impunity and being awarded public contracts. Reciprocal and fruitful links with professionals (i.e. lawyers, accountants, architects) have been consolidated due to the growth of the mafia's involvement in the legal economy.[18]

Organizational structures and rituals

When analysing mafias' structures it is necessary to distinguish two levels: the basic organizational unit and coordination bodies,[19] and intra-organizational and inter-organizational dynamics.[20] The above distinctions are crucial in order to understand female involvement in the mafias, insofar as women take part, even if not officially, in the first level but not in the second. Indeed, the presence of women has emerged more in the criminal investigations that have disarticulated the basic units of the organization rather than in those that have hit the higher-level organizational bodies.[21]

Moreover, it is worth remembering that mafia-type organizations, like ordinary ones, tend to adapt their structure to the changing needs produced by the context in which they are embedded.[22] Not surprisingly, both Cosa Nostra and the 'Ndrangheta have adopted different forms of structure in the course of their organizational life.[23] The balance between centralization and a looser composition, as well as between a hierarchical and a horizontal structure, has changed according to the external and internal circumstances. These are often interrelated. For example, when conflicts ripen within clans belonging to the same organizations, it is likely that law enforcement agencies find space to act. Organizational responses to these interwoven internal and external negative circumstances might push the clans to reinforce their compartmentation in order to increase secrecy and thus minimize risks; or they might entrust significant roles to persons that are trustworthy, even if they do not occupy official positions, like women.

As we will see, in the last three decades Cosa Nostra's configuration has moved towards the 'Ndrangheta's structural model and vice versa. In other words, as Sciarrone observes:

> The 'Ndrangheta seems to have imitated Cosa Nostra in providing itself with a unitary organ of coordination, but paradoxically, at the same time, the Sicilian mafiosi—to protect themselves from collaborators of justice and from more efficient repression strategies used by the investigative apparatus—have shown a tendency to reorganize themselves according to a model that is similar to the Calabrian one, segmenting families and groups in order to render the association more impenetrable.[24]

Mafias' members call themselves *uomini d'onore* ('men of honour'), because the code of honour, along with the institution of vendetta and the law of silence, shapes their 'ideology', which serves their organizational/criminal aims.

The process of recruiting members is delicate and complex, insofar as the organization needs people who are ruthless and able to keep secrets. This process may be kin-based, or it may result from a selection that occurs after a period of observation, or a combination of the two.[25] Once selected, a man is made part of the organization through an initiation ceremony during which he must swear eternal faith to the syndicate.[26] Once he has entered, the new member learns through the 'practicing community', which facilitates and promotes the exchange of knowledge, discourses and practices, both criminal and relational.[27] Following the group's veterans and spending time with one's companions in the field is how the ability to work in the mafia environment is acquired. When the clan corresponds to the family of the new member, the latter consolidates and develops what he has already acquired during his primary socialization.

The initiation ceremony is strictly banned to women both in Cosa Nostra and the 'Ndrangheta. Being male is one of the requirements for gaining mafia membership. Only the 'Ndrangheta has seen a few cases of affiliated women, dating to the early 1900s, as has emerged from trial documents from the time. The reasons for the conviction of the members of a criminal organization based in Palmi, a small town in Calabria, and the surrounding area, include a specific reference to women:

> In this association of criminals ... women were also admitted, dressed as men, that took part in thefts and other crimes. The women admitted to having to take an oath while pricking the little finger of their right hand to produce blood, and swearing to keep the aforementioned secret. Everybody commonly carried pistols and daggers.[28]

According to police sources from the early 1900s, the clan of Santo Stefano D'Aspromonte in Calabria even had a female section, while in Nicastro, another small town in Calabria, the boss' sister-in-law, 'armed and dressed as a man', accompanied him by night in his criminal activities.[29]

In the 'Ndrangheta, rituals mark not only the entrance into mafia groups, but also other career passages. The large number of rituals serves to make members more attached to the organization.[30] Indeed, through their symbolic force, rituals are crucial in building a sense of belonging and enhancing mafioso male identity.[31]

Women do not need ceremonies to participate in the mafia, because their role is not formal and official. It takes place within the family and thus does not require rituals, only close bonds of trust with the male members of the clan. Just as rituals are a means to make men dependent on the organization, so are family ties for women.

Cosa Nostra

The confession of mafia boss Tommaso Buscetta, given to judge Giovanni Falcone in 1984, sparked off a Copernican revolution in understanding the structure of the Sicilian Mafia.[32] Up to then, most scholars believed the mafia was composed of loose, unconnected criminal groups.[33] Therefore, they focussed their interest primarily on cultural aspects, i.e. mafia behaviour based on the code of honour and vendetta. Scholars shifted their perspective after Buscetta revealed the mafia as a hierarchical organization, called Cosa Nostra, composed of different mafia groups coordinated by a single commission.[34] Evidence of a structured and coordinated organization did exist before Tommaso Buscetta's testimony, but public opinion tended to overlook or even deny it.

Historian Salvatore Lupo reported evidence of some trials in the late nineteenth century against hierarchically organized associations such as the *Fratuzzi* from *Bagheria* and the *Stoppaghieri* from *Monreale*.[35] Lupo's thesis is also confirmed by a report written by Palermo Police Chief Ermanno Sangiorgi.[36] The presence of an organized association was furthermore verified in 1937, when boss Michele Allegra confessed the mafia was divided into groups called Families led by a chief.[37] Giuseppe Luppino gave a similar confession in March 1958, recorded in a 1950s ruling I discovered in a 1990s trial document.[38] Not only did Luppino tell the police he was initiated by mafiosi, but he also described in detail the structure of the mafia, just as Buscetta did thirty years later. In the mid-1960s, Judge Cesare Terranova pointed out that the danger of mafia families lay in their capacity for coordination.[39] A few years before Buscetta's confession, Leonardo Vitale reported information about the structure of Cosa Nostra. However, police considered him insane and confined him in a mental institution. When he was released from it, he was killed.

According to Buscetta's outline, the basic group of the organization is called a 'Family', and corresponds to a certain controlled territory, which is highly important for mafia identity since the Family takes its name from there.[40] At the bottom of the pyramid, there are fifty to three hundred *soldati* (soldiers), *uomini d'onore* from each Family, who elect the *rappresentante* (representative) from the Family, who then in turn appoints a *vicerappresentante* (deputy representative). Between the representative and the soldiers lies the *capodecina*, who leads ten *soldati*. In the province of Palermo, a level called the *mandamento* (district) also exists. This is made up of three Families from contiguous territories led by the *capo-mandamento* (district head), who is elected by the Families' representatives. In other Sicilian provinces (including Agrigento, Trapani, Enna, Caltanissetta and Catania), the representatives from the Families elect the representatives from the province who comprise the *commissione regionale* (regional commission).

The basic rule of the organization is that every Family must control the activities in its territory, where soldiers cannot operate without permission from the Family's representative. Families are independent in terms of local activities, yet are compelled to follow the general strategy decided by the *Cupola*, or coordinating commission. This hierarchical structure proved to be successful, so much so that it became a model imitated internationally by other criminal organizations.

To understand the relationship between structure and context, it is worthwhile to go back to the late 1950s, when the organization started to show the need for coordination bodies. As mentioned above, at that time the mafia became involved in new and larger businesses including drug trafficking. These new operations created new requirements including greater coordination among individual clans. The Sicilian Families set up the *Cupola*, which was composed of representatives from the various Sicilian provinces, and was established during a meeting between American bosses, such as Joe Bonanno and Frank Coppola, and Sicilian bosses, such as Genco Russo and Vincenzo Rimi, at the Hotel 'Delle Palme' in Palermo on 12 October 1957.[41] As of that time, the mafia employed the name Cosa Nostra that had previously been attributed only to the American mafia.[42]

Despite the establishment of a coordinating body, a climate of warfare reigned among mafia *cosche* (clans) between the late 1950s and early 1960s. Increasing economic competition due to drug trafficking ended the peaceful division of illegal markets. This mafia warfare concerned in particular Corleone (a small town near Palermo) and Palermo, the heart of mafia Families and the oldest mafia territory.[43] In Corleone, the boss of the main mafia Family, Michele Navarra, director of the local hospital and head of the local Christian Democratic party, was murdered in 1958 by Luciano Leggio, known as Liggio, who then became the *capo mafia* of Corleone.[44] The two main members of Liggio's faction were Totò Riina and Bernardo Provenzano, who would become protagonists in later developments in the history of the mafia.[45]

In 1963, Palermo mafia Families, who covered sixteen territories in the city, began disagreeing about the boundaries of their respective dominions. Warfare developed and a great number of murders were committed on both sides between 1961 and 1963. The state took countermeasures and the mafia Families and their coordinating body apparently went through a period of fragmentation. However, after a brief period of instability in the late 1960s, following the exile of many important bosses to Northern Italy,[46] Cosa Nostra began flourishing again in the 1970s.[47] In 1973, Stefano Bontade and Gaetano Badalamenti, representatives of the Palermo Families, and Totò Riina, representative of the Corleone Family,[48] set up a triumvirate, leading once again to the constitution of a provincial commission, the *Cupola*. This central body set strict rules to prevent Families from making important decisions, such as murdering a public official, without first consulting Cupola members.[49] In other words, in the early 1970s Cosa Nostra changed from a well-coordinated federation of Families, based on common rules and strategies, to a central, hierarchical structure.[50]

Drug trafficking required more money to be invested, and profits from the real estate business were insufficient. This encouraged the Corleonesi to engage in kidnapping. However, the Cupola had banned this criminal activity since key alliances would have been ruined with politicians, entrepreneurs, magistrates and sections of social groups that supported and colluded with the mafia, thus damaging the equilibrium between mafia, business and politics in Palermo. In spite of this, and given the fact that those leaders who considered kidnapping counterproductive (Gaetano Badalamenti and Stefano Bontate) were in prison at that time, the Corleonesi started kidnapping wealthy people.[51] Moreover, in 1971 the first murder was committed of a representative of a state institution, the Chief Prosecutor of Palermo, Pietro Scaglione. In the early 1980s, the Corleonesi's challenge to the rules of the Cupola intensified and competition resulting from the sudden increase in wealth destroyed the balance between mafia Families.[52]

Corleonesi boss Totò Riina began to build his power through the boundless use of violence and the art of introducing spies and allies into other Families. Gradually, many Families from other areas (Trapani, Palermo, San Giuseppe Jato, Partinico, Mazara del Vallo) joined Riina's ranks. The rest of the mafia commission, worried about Riina's increasing power, held secret meetings that were spied on by Riina's ally, boss Michele Greco, nicknamed 'the Pope'. Many *pentiti* described Riina as a clever man who was able to pit commission members against each other. In early 1979, Stefano Bontate, understanding the great danger in Riina's cunning methods, ordered two of Riina's lieutenants and Riina himself to be killed; he was however warned by Michele Greco, and went on the run. These events were the seeds of the second mafia war, which took place in Palermo between 1981 and 1983, when the rank and file of the Palermo Families clashed with those from Corleone. In the course of the feud, around 600 'people lost their lives in what became an unstoppable slaughter'.[53]

As a consequence of this conflict, the mafia's compact structure started to weaken, giving criminal investigations more room for action. The investigations carried out by the so-called Pool of Palermo, in which judges Giovanni Falcone and Paolo Borsellino gave a pivotal contribution, led to the Palermo 'maxi-trial'. The main instrument of prosecutors was article 416bis, introduced in 1982 by the Rognoni-La Torre law. It defined the offense of association for criminal purposes specifically related to the mafia.[54] This meant that being a member of a mafia association was a crime, whether or not one had committed any particular offence.[55] The discovery of a broad, structured organization, confirmed by the testimony of Tommaso Buscetta, enabled the Palermo antimafia team to put many Cosa Nostra members on trial, from the lowest levels to the Boss. On 16

December 1987, verdicts from the 'maxi-trial' found 114 defendants not guilty and 344 defendants guilty (with sentences totalling 2,655 years in prison).[56][57]

Not surprisingly, over the course of the late 1980s and 1990s, the mafia showed signs of vulnerability, partially due to the 'maxi-trial' and its loss of political protection.[58] The latter was caused by the serious crisis undergone by major Italian political parties as a result of what the media called the 'collapse of the First Republic', followed by criminal investigations by the Milan Public Prosecutor's Office into the corrupt system of public contract management.[59] Moreover, in 1992 the verdict of the Supreme Court confirmed the previous decisions of the 'maxi-trial'. Cosa Nostra's reaction was harsh. First, it decided to murder Christian Democrat Salvo Lima since he was no longer able to guarantee mafiosi impunity. Then it showed its power against the state by killing judges Giovanni Falcone and Paolo Borsellino (on 23 May 1992, and 19 July 1992, respectively), and later, in 1993, by organizing bomb attacks against monuments and even killing civilians. This climate of terrorism led the state and civil society to react. The former passed significant legislation to tackle mafia associations, such as the witness protection programme and Article 41bis of the penitentiary code related to maximum-security prisons.[60] These new measures were extensively implemented, to the point that many mafiosi were captured, including Totò Riina, and many were compelled to go underground. This power vacuum was partly filled by women, as we will see in the following chapters.

The antimafia context forced Cosa Nostra to rethink its structure. The difficulties experienced by Totò Riina led to the emergence of Bernardo Provenzano's structural model. Although Provenzano took part in Riina's attack against the state in the early 1990s, at the same time he drew up a parallel strategy. In developing crucial links with the legitimate world, Provenzano concentrated not only on the traditional construction business, but also on new ones, including the health and waste sectors. When Leoluca Bagarella, Totò Riina's substitute, was arrested in 1995, Provenzano became the boss of bosses and, as such, opted to give Cosa Nostra a new direction. His plan proved successful in making the boundaries between the organization's legal and illegal activities more and more indistinct. He managed to do this because, learning from the ruinous strategy of terror perpetrated by Riina, he decided to reorganize the association and to reduce the use of violence. Provenzano's new order envisaged a 'new Cupola', made up of the oldest *capi-mandamento*. As Alessandra Dino explained, 'the new ruling system combined the structure of a network ... with centralised decision-making processes and control of information'.[61] The selection of people that went through the initiation rite to become 'men of honour' became more rigid.

Provenzano, moreover, decided to reintroduce a 'common fund', which had to be filled by the contributions coming from each district.

In the 2000s the incisive action taken against the Sicilian mafia led to the arrest of Provenzano, which obviously had an impact on the structure's organization. Cosa Nostra went through another period of fragmentation, in which the families became more autonomous and some of them had to face financial problems. Nowadays, the individual units of the organization are apparently 'waiting for a new leader'.[62] In 2006, for a short period of time, Salvatore Lo Piccolo, representative of the Tommaso Natale territory, covered this role in the area of Palermo. In 2008, mafia groups planned to reconstitute the Commission. However, disagreements among families hindered this project. Even the representative of the Province of Trapani, Matteo Messina Denaro, one of the most powerful bosses of Cosa Nostra, despite his charisma, popularity and authority, has not replaced Totò Riina. He is aware that his designation requires the consensus of the Commission, in order to be accepted by the whole organization.[63]

'Ndrangheta

At present, law enforcement agencies consider the 'Ndrangheta one of the most powerful criminal organizations worldwide.[64] Its success comes not only from the lack of attention paid to it by institutions in the past,[65] which proved to be a great advantage in their competition with other mafia-type organizations, but above all from its peculiar structure, based on kinship.

The basic unit of the 'Ndrangheta is called an 'ndrina and its internal structure is hierarchical. Most of its members are bound by kinship and its name stems from the surname of the *capobastone*, the head of the unit. A certain number of geographically contiguous 'ndrine form a so-called *locale*, which takes its name from the territory it governs.[66]

Generally speaking, the *locale* is made up of a 'minor society' and a 'major society': the former is obliged to account to the latter, which is made up of seven affiliates who have the high title of *santista* (see Table 1 referring to the 'Ndrangheta's positions and titles).

Each *locale* has a leader, an accountant who manages the group's finances, and a so-called '*crimine*' who deals with the organization of illegal activities. There are also other positions and ranks, that were designed to foster a hierarchy of knowledge. This means that each affiliate's level of knowledge about the organization is different and depends on his degree and position. Basically, the higher levels are the repositories of knowledge that is not accessible to the lower levels. Each rank (also called dowry or flower) is acquired by merit or by seniority and remains for life. The positions, which indicate the functions performed by the individual affiliates, are attributed on the basis of the ranks owned and are temporary.[67]

According to some collaborators with justice, the structure of the 'Ndrangheta includes an official position for some women, called *sorella d'omertà* (sister of silence). However, investigations have not revealed empirical evidence of this position, with the exception of one case.[68] The position of *sorella d'omertà* was mentioned by collaborator with justice Antonio Zagari during a judicial hearing in 1995 in the trial following the *Isola Felice* investigation. He provided a symbolic depiction of the 'Ndrangheta, including its positions, ranks, hierarchy and other issues regarding ritual and symbolic matters. Zagari had already talked about *sorelle d'omertà* in his autobiography, asserting that:

> 'Ndrangheta, rules do not consider female members a possibility; but if a woman is particularly deserving, she can become an associate with the title of *sorella d'omertà*; without taking an oath, which is obligatory for men. However, very rarely is this title given to those who are not already wives, sisters, fiancées, or related in some way to men of honour.[69]

Collaborator with justice Calogero Marcianò also made reference to the *sorella d'omertà*, mentioning the only case that had been dealt with by magistrates: Maria Morello.

> This position, which exists in every region, is given to a woman, who in the case of Lombardy is Maria Morello. This woman is responsible for assisting members of the association who are in hiding. In the case of Morello ... I can say that she is fully part of the association and holds the position of *santista*, which is the highest rank a woman can have in the 'Ndrangheta. I would also mention that there can only be one female member of the clan in a region, who has the position of *santista* and carries out, as I was saying, the tasks of a *sorella d'omertà*.[70]

In the history of 'Ndrangheta clans, the ritual practices related to positions, degrees and titles have remained constant, albeit with some variants.[71] Most of them were already part of the nineteenth-century organizational model. The clan's sharing of this symbolic apparatus has offered an image of the organization's unity both to the individual criminal groups and to the external perception. In recent times, this symbolic unity has reflected an increasing correspondence in terms of structure on the interorganizational level, given that the association underwent a process of centralization.

In the past, each 'ndrina could always operate autonomously. Only for the most important strategies would they operate together, thereby composing a sort of federation or criminal consortium.[72] This horizontal intra-organizational structure had advantages and drawbacks: on the one hand, it offered flexibility to the single criminal unit, allowing them to adapt easily to the demands of the criminal market; on the other hand, it led to many conflicts between 'ndrine, as shown by the numerous feuds that have occurred over the history of the organization. These feuds attracted the attention of law enforcement, which led to negative consequences in the lucrative businesses in which they were increasingly involved. The solution was to enhance the federative nature of the organization and also its centralization. And so, after the second 'Ndrangheta war, which occurred between the late 1980s and the early 1990s, the 'ndrine of the Reggio Calabria area developed a 'central structure of coordination and composition of conflicts'.[73] They organized a body of consultation with the function of 'managing the conflicts and co-managing the most important businesses'.[74] The body was composed of the main bosses belonging to the two coalitions that fought during the war, including Giuseppe de Stefano, Pasquale Condello and Pasquale Libri. In spite of this tendency toward centralization, the association remained a confederation of criminal groups related to each other through a 'reticular and cooperative model'.[75]

A series of antimafia investigations revealed this tendency towards a centralized, unitary model. Judicial files concerning the operation known as *Arca* and *Cosa mia*, regarding the infiltration related to the modernization of the A3 Salerno-Reggio Calabria motorway, have proved the existence of a system of subdivision through which the construction work was managed by the 'Ndrangheta's clans.[76] The latter, who controlled the various areas crossed by the motorway, shared the racket money requested from the companies involved in the infrastructure work. Significantly, one emissary of the 'Ndrangheta collected it and split it up among the representatives of the 'ndrine. The *Meta* investigation was also able to detect unitary features in the organization's actions in the city of Reggio Calabria, as regards the extortion sector. The magistrate noted that it was

> an organization that needs new tools and shared hierarchies ... and that evolves, updating itself, on the basis of shared principles. This organization has an authoritative head that coordinates criminal actions and does not make any exceptions, which finds broad legitimacy in the generalized awareness of the criminal weight of its leaders. The latter are no longer simply the recognized heads of the respective territorial divisions, but are the expression, the result of

precise agreements, made within a mafia-like organization that has abandoned its anti-historical rationale based on establishing boundaries, to become increasingly influential, functional and recognizable.[77]

This tendency towards unity was required to overcome conflicts and also to offer an external image of unity and thus of strength. Indeed, the magistrate underlined that 'in this way, civil society and entrepreneurs receive a clear message: the period of wars is over, the 'Ndrangheta tends to be cohesive and to enhance itself internally and also externally, expecting its part in every economic activity'.[78]

In 2010, the *Crimine-Infinito* investigation reconstructed in detail the structure of the 'Ndrangheta, observing, above all, elements of unity.[79] One magistrate wrote: 'the 'Ndrangheta is a unitary organisation governed by a vertical body, la *Provincia*',[80] which 'by strictly respecting the rules and procedures, leaves wide room for autonomy to the external bodies'. The *Provincia* is directed by the *capocrimine*, which is the highest office of the organization, and is made up of three districts (*mandamenti*): the Centro (the city of Reggio Calabria), Jonica and Tirrenica (Piana and the coast).[81]

According to the rules that emerged in this investigation, each 'ndrina does not account to the neighbouring *locale* but, when necessary, to the main *locale* or to the province. Another body that exists is called the ''ndrina *distaccata*', which is a group of members that to be detached from the *locale* to which they belong.

The image of the 'Ndrangheta as a unified organization, which is quite common in public opinion, risks seeing this association simply as a monolithic organization, neglecting the autonomy that individual clans can still exploit in relation to many activities and the alliances they make with each other. To contrast this image, scholars have underlined that the 'Ndrangheta is 'a plural and multifaceted phenomenon under the same collective name'.[82] Moreover, they have underlined the heterogeneity characterizing the different clans, especially in terms of their economic resources.[83]

2

Women in Italian Society

The labour market

Like women in many countries, during the Second World War Italian women were recruited to do the male combatants' former jobs.[1] The number of employed women, however, decreased in the aftermath of the war.[2] Among the causes for this decrease was the return of men from the front, who claimed back their jobs. In other words, during the difficult years following the war, men's and women's interests clashed due to the shrinking labour market.[3] As a result, most women were expelled from the labour market and confined to the domestic sphere. This reinforcement of the sexual division of labour was supposed to help families cope with post-war economic shortages. Indeed, female labour was expended mainly within the household to sustain the family, in a period during which the income of many Italian families failed to cover basic necessities.[4]

The war spurred the growth of women's awareness despite their subsequent expulsion from public life. Women had demonstrated their ability to do certain traditionally male jobs, refuting popular notions that men were more skilled at them. Through their involvement in traditionally male fields, women had to some extent revealed that their previous exclusion was mere gender discrimination, usually justified on the basis of supposed physical and psychological inability. In addition, women who fought in the Resistance experienced historically new responsibilities and freedom, thus becoming an important model of emancipation for women of the next generation.[5] The award given to women for their fundamental contribution to the nation's liberation from Nazi occupation was the right to vote. This in itself was of course insufficient to improve women's position in society. In fact their presence in the labour market started to decline. Formally speaking, the Constituent Assembly, elected in 1946, passed an article stating that 'the working woman must have all the rights that the working man has and equal wage for equal work'.[6] In practical terms, women had many long battles ahead before achieving any real implementation of those rights.

The mobilization of women during the war and their dismissal thereafter showed that the female presence in the labour market was permitted and accepted as long as it was needed. As economist Francesca Bettio observes: 'The role of women in the labour market was traditionally conceived as a labour reserve, as easy to mobilise as to dismiss.'[7]

Throughout the 1950s, the exclusion of women from the labour force was endorsed by intense political propaganda grounded on a negative image of working women and a positive one of the mother and wife. The ideological alibi that only certain jobs were suitable for women helped to support the sexual division of labour and at the same time to disguise the underlying female subordination.

Between the 1950s and the mid-1960s, although previously based largely on the agricultural sector, Italy became one of the most industrialized countries in the West. The period of economic growth between 1958 and 1963 became known as the 'economic miracle'.

However, this sudden boom did not last, since it stemmed from two unstructured factors – cheap labour and low technological investment. These only made Italy competitive until Third World countries entered the market, offering greater availability of these same factors. And so the Italian economy moved from boom to bust in the mid-1960s. The solutions undertaken to tackle this critical economic moment included restructuring of the factory system and concentrating on high-quality and fashion goods. Solutions such as these had devastating effects on female employment because they resulted in the expulsion of female workers, whose numbers had increased during the euphoric growth of the economic miracle, into marginalization.[8] The relation between expulsion and marginalization is quite clear: the expelled labour force was reutilized externally within the same productive process but in a marginalized form, i.e. as informal labour (paid 'under the counter'). The so-called *ristrutturazione* that occurred between 1963 and 1968 implied new working hours, based on overtime and premiums, and the decentralization of production with a distribution of labour outside the factory.[9] As a consequence of the first implication, industries looked for a physically strong working class and thus women, along with old people, were referred to as the '*quote deboli*' ('weak part') of the supply.[10] Indeed, within an overall decline in employment, the number of employed men increased and that of women decreased.[11] In other words, male workers replaced female ones in order to accelerate production.

The second implication, i.e. the decentralization of production, entailed external work which involved more women than men. Locked out of the official market, women were employed externally without any sort of regulation. This type of employment took on different forms such as domestic labour and temporary or part-time work.¹² For example, domestic labour, which reduced the expenditure of industry due to low wages and high flexibility, was above all a female activity that often used the free collaboration of other family members. As a consequence, there was an unavoidable correspondence between work and family activities.¹³ Parallels with the mafia can be traced in this respect since, as will be explored later on, most of the work carried out by mafia women in drug trafficking occurred in the household. The management of illegal activities by mafia families, particularly in some stages of drug trafficking, might be defined as a form of domestic labour.

To sum up, the crisis of the mid to late 1960s led women to be expelled from the official labour market due to the reorganization of work within industries and the decentralization of production. As a consequence, women were employed by small factories. This type of employment was a form of segregation. In Flavia Pristinger's words: 'The massive use of female labour by small factories could be considered a peculiar form of female job segregation. It is clearly a system of sexual allocation of labour that "favours" characteristics and work methods "typical" of women (i.e. availability for temporary employment, short hours and low wages), which are in reality conditioned by family life.'¹⁴ This use of female labour marked the beginning of a hidden but significant situation that has characterized female labour for many years.

The difficulties experienced by women in entering and remaining within the official labour market were caused by more than just the above-mentioned economic factors. Cultural elements, such as the widespread negative conception of female work, also affected women's participation.¹⁵ In southern regions of Italy, having a working woman in the family was considered shameful, since women were not controlled when outside the home for work, and it publicly revealed the family's need for female wages. That is why domestic labour was an ideal solution because it allowed families to both control women and at the same time satisfy the necessity of hiding female labour.¹⁶ Similarly, male underestimation of female labour has been at the core of the formal exclusion of women from the mafia. A collaborator with justice from the 'Ndrangheta told me that if men used their women for male tasks it meant their mafia clan was weak. He maintained women were the 'weaker sex' and as such must be protected and not work.¹⁷ However, as will be seen later, the necessity of employing even women has led mafia men to betray this conviction.

The 1960s were years of massive urbanization; workers moved from the countryside to the city in order to find jobs in the industrial sector. In most cases, their wives, previously engaged in activities linked to the countryside, ended up being housewives in the city. Relegating women to the house was complementary to the progress of Italian society towards a model of mass consumption.[18] In terms of the labour market, the increase in the number of women as housewives implied a decrease in female involvement in the productive sphere. However, scholars caution us not to believe the figures that emerged from the official data of the 1960s, which stated women were either employed in the official labour market or happy housewives.[19] The reality was much more complex since, as already shown, women were likely to be employed in the hidden and informal sector. In studying the female labour force, it is fundamental to take into account the existence of this hidden reality, which made official figures misleading.[20] These hidden features marked women's history in almost all fields, including the mafia. The presence of women in the mafia has been a masked reality and as such, unlikely to be accurately portrayed by criminal statistics.

The typical characteristics of female labour (including marginalization, segregation and exploitation) analysed so far have not been contingent on any specific context. Yet, they must be considered as the most significant hallmark of female participation in the labour market, as well as in mafia activities.

From 1972 to 1989, the number of employed women increased from 27.4% to 34%. Post-industrial society facilitated women's access to the labour market. The growth of the service sector and development of automation and computers were both crucial to this. These transformations, marking post-industrial society, created new spaces of activity and job opportunities for women. Since the 1970s, the rise of female employment in all European countries has been proportional to the expansion of the service sector; women were over-represented 'especially in retail sales, banking, and public and private services, whereas they were a minority in manufacturing, mining, construction, public works, and transportation'.[21] Theoretically, the tertiary sector allowed women to reconcile their roles as mothers, wives and workers since many occupations in the tertiary sector offered the opportunity, in terms of schedules and flexibility, to dedicate time to child rearing and management of the household. Moreover, technological development affected the distribution of jobs between the sexes. On the one hand, it reduced the importance of physical strength in the workplace and, on the other, facilitated domestic work. This argument is also valid in explaining the increase in women's participation in mafia activities, in part caused by the financial modernization of the mafia that occurred as of the 1980s. In Chapter Five we will see that the emerging financial tasks opened up job opportunities for women within the mafia, since they were removed from most of the violent work of the underworld, for which, due to physical and cultural reasons, women were not as well-equipped as men.

Two further factors contributed to the increase in women's presence in the labour market since the 1970s: the rise in female education and a decrease in the birth rate. The latter reflects the greater number of women employed in the public sphere and the smaller number of women devoted to the home.

Previously, women could be kept outside the labour market partly because of the increase in male wages, which made female wages unnecessary. From the late 1960s, however, fewer family members meant families were deprived of earnings, thus prompting the need for female wages. This was particularly accentuated with the arrival of the consumer society, where buying consumer goods became indispensable. At the same time, society also expected women to fulfil their traditional role in the household, a role that became even more demanding with the development of a mass consumption society.[22] Despite increased convenience in the household, domestic tasks were not reduced for two interrelated reasons: the Italian welfare state did not offer solid support in terms of social services; concurrently, Italian society continued giving great importance to the role of the mother and wife, while underestimating that of the working woman. In other words, women were neither aided with material support nor facilitated from an ideological point of view. As a result, women were torn in conflicting directions: not only were they required for the labour market, they were also reclaimed for the household without any aid. Even in rare cases where the welfare state worked, women still had to deal with bureaucratic procedures, compelling them to perform 'the function of unpaid agents of the welfare state'.[23] Hence, it is easily understandable that most women looked for more flexible jobs that enabled them to fulfil their role as mothers simultaneously. So they were likely to be employed in temporary jobs, which implied low wages and no guaranteed legal protection. Many occupations in the tertiary sector offered these related opportunities and disadvantages. In the service sector, women were employed mostly in lower-paid or less secure jobs.[24] Consequently, women often looked for jobs in the public sector, in order to secure welfare benefits, such as a pension or paid maternity leave.[25] In southern Italy, the situation was worse than in other regions because the tendency for women to be excluded from the official market and employed in 'informal labour' was particularly pronounced.[26]

From the 1970s, the rise in education enabled women to be employed in better paying professional jobs. However, they were likely to remain at the bottom of the profession.[27] Even in cases where women achieved leading positions, they were confined to special activities and still received lower wages than men.²⁸ And when they entered traditionally male jobs, they were mostly confined to those fields related to tasks conventionally considered belonging to women (i.e. doctors tended to specialize in paediatrics, maternity, mental illness, hygiene and prevention – all less remunerative than surgery; lawyers in family law more than corporate law).²⁹ It is not trivial to recall the close relationship existing between gender education and types of jobs.³⁰ This situation was affected by gender differential education and social expectations: 'If education encouraged women to seek work, it also steered them toward already feminised sectors of the economy, which consequently became even more feminised.'³¹

Over the last four decades, women have sought to reconcile their presence in the labour market with that in the household. The term *doppia presenza* (dual role) is the hallmark of women's identity in postmodern society.³² However, this dual role is a difficult model to live up to. Women manage to fulfil this role only when they can afford to employ outside help or have a supportive family network. Only these circumstances leave women free to work, since they provide help in managing the home and childrearing.³³ This is because in Italy, female participation in the workplace has not been balanced by improvements in social services or the organization of work in terms of scheduling.³⁴ Moreover, the parallel presence of men in the household has still remained minor.³⁵ The result of this kind of situation is that often women have to choose between a job and their family. Thus the shift from the model characterizing the 1960s and 1970s – marginalization – to the one that has marked Italian society since the 1980s – dual roles – has been partial and incomplete.

Despite the significant changes seen in the labour market due the advancement of technologies that have been facilitators for female working experience, there have still been structural factors and restraints – coming from both the family and the market – that have hampered a balance between the private and the public spheres. Economic politics oriented towards the deregulation of the labour market have had a negative impact on young women's employment, especially in the south (the rate of female occupation in 2016 was 31.7%).³⁶ In the 2000s, Italian women still experience high levels of unemployment, lower wages compared to men even in executive positions, work segregation,³⁷ a low level of presence in politics, while in their careers they come up against the so-called 'glass ceiling'.³⁸

The fragility of female employment also reflects a traditional mentality about whether it is appropriate for women to work, shared by both men and women belonging to the lower class and living in the south. According to a survey, 54% of men and 39.9% of women from the south (aged eighteen to twenty-four and belonging to less privileged social groups) agree with the following affirmation

"For the sake of the family, it is better that men devote themselves mainly to economic needs and women take care of the home".[39] In the north, the percentage of men and women with this same belief was, respectively, 37.2% and 22.8%.

Social customs and women's rights

Italian society has constantly been influenced by the Catholic Church, especially as concerns social customs and habits related to the private sphere.[40] What is more, conservative Catholic principles were supported by the policies of the party that governed the country from the Second World War to the early 1990s (during the so-called 'First Republic'), the 'Christian Democrats'. Even the Communist party showed caution toward questions regarding morality and sexuality.[41] Its interest in women's issues was mainly confined to matters related to the workplace. Italian society, however, produced a powerful feminist movement, which, while remaining outside its institutions,[42] was able to achieve fundamental goals and thus counterbalanced the influence of the Catholic Church on Italian society.[43]

In the aftermath of the Second World War, gender relations were in turmoil due to the return of men from the front. During their absence, women had also taken on the role of fathers, thereby challenging the traditional father's authority.[44] Confusion in gender relations emerged in the letters collected by journalist Anna Garofalo, who in the late 1940s ran a radio programme called *Parole di donne* (Women's Words). These letters by many women of various ages and social backgrounds were brought together in a book published in the early 1950s.[45] This book is a valuable source, insofar as it gives insight into the common feelings of the generation of women in the late 1940s.

Generally speaking, after a period of strong participation in the public sphere, the return to the private sphere created frustration, since it was perceived as unfair and even paradoxical, considering the war had weakened the myth of masculinity. As Garofalo metaphorically wrote: 'The effects of war are reflected even in human relationships and love; and so the myth of male infallibility collapsed along with bridges and houses.'[46] As already mentioned, the right to vote did not imply a great advancement in women's conditions. The letters sent to Garofalo showed that women were glad to vote but, being politically unaware, needed men's help in order to make their political choices.[47]

A sort of disappointment regarding the hopes raised by the Second World War emerges in Garofalo's letters:

> I am afraid that during the fight for liberation and the return of democracy, we were under the illusion we could also establish more modern customs in our country and bring the progress of law into the fields of individual morality, and relationships within the family and between the sexes.[48]

During the late 1940s and early 1950s, legislation failed to meet individual expectations. Civil rights and the new needs of women were not included in the political agenda. The state and church did not acknowledge social changes in customs and mores; on the contrary, they dragged society back to the pre-war period.[49] Relentless propaganda glorified the sexual division of labour and suffocated the seeds of a modern identity for women.[50] Central to this campaign was the exaltation of virginity. The condition of virginity was considered a woman's most important value since it attributed her with a social identity, insofar as it permitted her to achieve the status of wife and consequently mother. The everlasting cult of Mary, virgin and mother at the same time, and the revival of the hagiographic myth of Maria Goretti were essential in this propaganda.[51]

The above mentioned pressure on women towards a patriarchal system did not interrupt the development of female consciousness toward liberation.[52] Indeed, a 'silent revolution' occurred in the 1950s, paving the way for the student demonstrations and feminist movements of the late 1960s. Gabriella Parca's book *Le italiane si confessano* (*Italian Women Confess*), a collection of letters sent to women's magazines by women from various backgrounds, showed examples of women challenging the moral behaviour expected by society in the 1950s.[53] Many letters were confessions of premarital sexual experiences, which led them to feel guilty because they ran against the Catholic precepts permeating Italian society. As Parca observed: 'the deep contradiction between the morality of the environment and its practices emerges from the ease with which, despite the fear, she gives up this 'valuable good' (virginity)'.[54]

Undoubtedly, the dichotomy between social expectations and individual desires in relation to sexual issues caused frustration and confusion. However, 'subordination for matrimonial ends continues to be the only means for giving her own availability recognition and citizenship'.[55]

Between the 1950s and the late 1960s, Italian society underwent pivotal changes, caused partly by the economic boom that occurred between 1958 and 1963. This economic growth was fast and short-lived, thus bringing about 'a number of grave structural imbalances'.[56] The most dangerous among these was 'the distortion of consumption patterns'. As Paul Ginsborg noted, 'the economic "miracle" served once again to emphasise the importance of the individual family unit within Italian civil society'.⁵⁷ The family reduced its members and became more and more a consumer unit; as a result, the nuclear family prevailed over the extended one.⁵⁸ Industrialism, urbanism and secularism influenced family functions whose transformation affected women, who performed their social role mostly in the private sphere. Women became the target of the new market connected to the domestic appliance and food industries. The prevailing image of women in the 1960s was as both beautiful housewives and efficient household managers who were still able to care about themselves in terms of aesthetic appearance.⁵⁹ This latter aspect took on enormous importance, inasmuch as it opened up a new field of consumption that included cosmetics, hygiene and clothing.⁶⁰ Changes in consumption related to the body, home and transport also influenced women's lives. Not surprisingly, the number of women's magazines emphasizing consumerism increased.⁶¹ The female model presented by the 'hidden persuaders' of advertising in the 1960s was one of 'a household woman committed to managing and polishing her nest'.⁶² At the same time women were supposed to be 'submissive and sweet; the attention women paid to their bodies was also completely aimed at pleasing men, in accordance with a model of beauty which could be neither too provocative nor too eccentric, but pleasant and reassuring instead'.⁶³

There is little doubt that the above changes were more concerned with the body and fashion than civil rights. Bikinis, mini-skirts and new hairstyles marked the modern Italian woman in the early 1960s. However, she was still bound to male power and struggled to enter the labour market. Changes in consumption entailed 'a modification of women's lifestyles and their self-presentation in everyday life: going out, walking in public, travelling, smoking, and questioning sexual mores'.⁶⁴ Yet, this novelty did not translate into action.⁶⁵ Resistance to changes in traditional patterns of gender relations emerged from a research study on Italian men carried out in 1965 by Gabriella Parca. Her survey, later turned into a book called *I sultani* (The Sultans), showed that 81% of Italian men missed whorehouses and 61% of them wanted to marry a virgin. Most of them also stated that women must be beautiful and tidy, but not intellectual.⁶⁶

Years of contradictions, the early 1960s marked an important moment of transition. Ginsborg observed: 'The Italy of the boom was still a society full of taboos about sexual behaviour. The restrictive code of official morality was deeply intertwined in the South with codes of honour.'⁶⁷ At the same time, it is to the 1960s that one must look when searching for the seeds of the great transformation in terms of sexual attitudes that occurred in the 1970s. Indeed, these seeds date to the years of protest, i.e. the two-year period between 1968 and

1970. Student movements and working-class protests contributed greatly to modifying Italian social customs. These modifications concerned the patriarchal system in terms of parental control. Young people could experiment with new freedoms. Furthermore, signs of transformation in gender relations came from the increase in the number of separations in the mid to late 1960s; this increase made divorce one of the most important issues debated in Italian society.[68]

The period of 1968–9 was a turning point in women's liberation as well, partly as a result of their participation in the student movement and the 'autunno caldo' ('hot autumn') of September and October 1969. These latter political experiences made women more conscious of their rights and the possibility of claiming them. The student movement exploded and questioned the relations grounded on authority in the factory, the school and the family, including gender and parental relationships.[69] However, there was evidence that even women in the movement ended up experiencing a sort of sexual division of labour, since tasks and activities were defined by sex.[70] Once again women were confined to minor activities and excluded from decisional roles that were considered male. Since this discrimination happened within a group that claimed it was attacking the patriarchal system, women became more willing to create feminist groups.[71]

Moreover, female consciousness spread beyond the elite as a result of the creation of mass education.[72] Many formal and informal barriers to higher education were removed.[73] As a consequence of higher educational opportunities, 'a new type of woman started coming into being; generally urbane, young, unmarried, and well-educated'.[74]

In the late 1960s, the move towards anti-conformist styles and fashions reflected the social transformation taking place; women refused elegant dresses, make-up and high heels and shifted to boots, sandals and trousers.[75] Sex became a crucial issue as young people claimed more freedom to express their sexuality. Adult society tried to hinder this transformation. To give an example, the film *Theorema* by director Pier Paolo Pasolini was banned on grounds of sexual obscenity.[76]

In 1966, chemistry created the contraceptive pill, but it could only be prescribed for medical reasons. This was the period when Pope Paul VI published his encyclical *Humane Vitae*, condemning sexual intercourse not aimed at procreation.[77] For this reason, the Church condemned the use of contraception. This meant condemning the instrument that, by stopping women's fear of undesired pregnancy, enabled women to express their sexuality as freely as men.

In the 1960s Italy seemed to be modern, yet its transformation was partially obstructed by society. A traditionalist mentality prevailed. An illuminating example of the difficulty of social progress was the social reaction in 1968 after the elimination of Article 559, which charged women, and not men, with adultery.[78] According to common belief at the time, this article kept women from cheating on their husbands.[79] Therefore, most Italians wanted to keep the article in the legal code even though it legalized a double morality in terms of adultery and discriminated against women. Such a puritanical reaction is good evidence in support of the idea that Italian society was still retrograde at the time as regards sexual morality.

In conclusion, Italian society showed a modern side embodied by economic growth and the proliferation of consumer goods. Yet, this growth was so rapid it overwhelmed a poor population from the austere 1950s. Italian society could not absorb the profound forms of modernity stemming from the society of mass consumption. However, we cannot deny that gender relations started to be challenged in the 1960s. The outcome of this process would occur in the 1970s with changes in legislation and gender identity.

During the 1970s, 'important achievements in terms of legislation (including divorce, family law reform and abortion) affected women's social and individual identities'.[80] In 1974, feminists directed their efforts towards keeping the divorce law because Catholics wanted to change it through a popular referendum. This eventually did not modify the divorce bill, resulting in an important achievement for women's rights. Moreover, it became clear that there was a need to reform family law, which seemed anachronistic and far removed from the reality of most Italian families. The new family law finally passed in 1975; it stated that father and mother were equal in terms of duties and rights within the household: no longer paternal control, but parental control, was the basic principle of the family. The last of the important transformations in legislation seen during the 1970s occurred in 1978 and was the most important achievement for women in practical and symbolic terms: the legalization of abortion.[81] In 1981, Catholics tried to abolish Law 194 through a referendum; however, it was saved also thanks to a strong feminist campaign.[82]

On a general level as well as in practical terms, the above achievements brought more freedom into the lives of women, especially with respect to self-determination. This brought about changes in the way they made fundamental choices regarding their private lives. In other words, legal protection led to an increase in female consciousness when facing crucial life decisions.

Another factor that contributed to liberating women, by giving them time and strength to engage in public activities, arose in the 1970s when domestic products became products of mass consumption. Therefore, the opportunity to reduce housework stopped being a privilege enjoyed only by women belonging to the upper class.[83]

As mentioned above, two significant indicators of changed conditions for women appeared in the 1970s and developed over the following decades: the increase in female education and the fall in the birth rate. These correspond to a decline in the number of married women; indeed marriage rates in the 1970s and 1980s dropped in line with European trends.[84] For some women, marriage stopped being perceived as the only way to fill a recognized social role.[85]

These transformations concerned northern Italy more than southern Italy, still dominated by the patriarchal model.[86] Even in the 1990s, as shown by research carried out in the provinces of Agrigento and Caltanissetta in Sicily, the endurance of a patriarchal ideology not only emerges clearly but was also perceived by women as right and proper. Empirical data indicated that women were in marginal positions and excluded from decision-making and power roles and interviewees stated that they felt completely self-fulfilled in being overloaded by paid labour and household work, and that they were proud to transmit this model to their daughters.[87] As concerns women in the south, it is also necessary to recall that their situation was worsened by the patronage system:[88] they had to deal with services that were less effective than those in the central and northern Italy, due to the mafia's presence and widespread corruption.[89]

Over the last forty years, women have benefited from the progress made in the 1970s in terms of rights. However, it has become evident that their path towards emancipation, understood not only in terms of gender equality but also in terms of gender relations, has been full of obstacles.

In recent decades, women's status and identity has shown highly contradictory features. These were partially dependent on the different speeds shown by legislation, social mentality and technological transformation influencing society. While on the one hand women have gained freedom in terms of movement and, to a more limited degree, in terms of social expectations, on the other the threat of male violence and the lesser opportunities available to women, due to the lack of social welfare, have challenged these achievements.

In Italy, the number of cases of rape has increased.[90] This could be explained in part by a parallel increase in reports and thus a decrease in hidden cases. However, this does not eliminate the essential issue of restriction in women's freedom of movement due to the lack of progress in male sexual behaviour.

What is more, the Italian state has been very slow in facing issues related to violence against women. The social belief that women were somehow guilty of being raped underpinned legislative ineptitude.[91] In the 1980s, to combat this kind of prejudice, women in street demonstrations sang the sarcastic slogan '*Scusaci, maschio, di averci stuprate, siamo noi che ti abbiamo provocato*' ('Forgive us, men, for raping us, we were the ones who provoked you'). Feminists in the 1980s also directed their efforts toward the campaign to change rape laws. The discussion on altering the laws against sexual violence in order to change rape and sexual harassment from crimes against morality to crimes against personal integrity lasted for years.[92] Regretfully, this modification occurred only in the late 1990s.[93]

Concerns with pornography and its consequences increased. Progress in gender relations should have led to an increase in male respect for women's sexuality and the female body. However, an increase in sexual violence that simulates the sexual behaviour suggested by violent pornography has indicated a contrary trend.

It is more and more evident that violence against women occurs mainly in the household. According to data concerning the period going from 2001 to 2016, those responsible for most femicides are relatives of the victims, partners or ex-partners.[94] Between 2007 and 2017, 1,740 women were murdered in Italy. 71.9% of them were killed within their family, and the 67.6% within the couple; 26.5% by their former partner. In particular, from 2005 to 2015, the murders that occurred within a couple had a passionate motive in 40.9% of cases, and in 21.6% they originated from quarrels or disagreements. In 2018 as well, the highest amount of femicides was committed within the couple (65.6%);[95] a negative trend characterized by the situation in Calabria,[96] where in some circumstances the violence against women develops within a mafia context.

In conclusion, recent decades have witnessed an ambiguous situation. On the one hand Italy has shown significant progress in terms of gender equality, as is demonstrated by the fast increase of its score within the Gender Equality Index, even if it still remains low compared to other advanced European countries. On the other hand, the data concerning violence against women, along with media representations of women as mere objects, show clear setbacks in the development of gender relations.[97] Moreover, it is quite evident that Italian women still struggle for equal opportunities and experience increasing difficulty in integrating reproductive and productive functions. According to several social and cultural indicators, the female identity embodied by the 'dual role' is more a myth than a reality. As pointed out earlier, the term *doppia presenza* (dual role), conceived by sociologist Laura Balbo, was intended to describe the new female identity resulting from women being in the labour market as well as the household.[98] It embraces the public and private dimensions without considering them as dichotomies. This would mean eliminating the gap between the two spheres, historically considered separate, of public and private activities, workplace and household, and the political and personal realms. The consequences in terms of female identity would involve overcoming the two extreme images that have labelled women, showing them either as housewives and mothers, devoted to childrearing, or working women, possessing male characteristics.[99] Instead of achieving this *doppia presenza* (dual role), women over the last few decades have ended up experiencing 'dual jobs'.[100] As pointed out in dealing with the female labour market, this resulted from a lack of aid to women when they entered the workplace.[101] In Italy, the increase in female employment has not been balanced by a parallel extension of social services and male participation in the domestic realm.[102]

The contradictions and complexity emerging from the above picture on female participation in the labour market and on social customs concerning gender, as seen in Italian social history, is the context in which to read the multifaceted condition of women in the mafia system, that we will explore in the next chapters.

3

Mafia Control Over Women

The code of honour

Mafia members control women tightly, in order to show their ability to exercise protection and thus power. The main means used to discipline women is the code of honour that regulates the mafia system.[1] Honour-related controlling practices characterize both Cosa Nostra and the 'Ndrangheta. The latter is still particularly attached to the honour code today, while Cosa Nostra is less so than in the past. In these two organizations the honour system affects women's lives. This seems less the case with the Camorra, in which women, according to some studies, are more liberated sexually and follow a model that is 'not the feminine one of modesty and reserve (shame), but the manly one based on "respect", arrogance and threat'.[2] According to other studies, instead, female subjugation driven by a patriarchal mechanism and by men's concern for their male reputation is also seen in the criminal organization based in Campania.[3]

Generally speaking, then, the regulation of family/mafia groups through a code of honour is found across different criminal organizations and historical periods, and affects women belonging to different age groups.

Defining and conceptualizing the code of honour is a challenging exercise. Anthropologist Carmelo Lisòn Tolosana observed that when we analyse the 'complex syndrome of Honour-Shame ... we enter one of those peculiar anthropological labyrinths from which it is difficult to emerge without a sensation of vertigo and confusion, such is its historical polymorphic density'.[4] Adopting a long-term perspective facilitates our understanding of this thick concept.[5] In Europe, the code of honour was widespread in aristocratic circles from the fifteenth to the eighteenth century and was adopted by the bourgeoisie in the nineteenth century. Traditionally, this was a code of behaviour grounded mainly on outward characteristics, such as bravery and violence, and was aimed at regulating social conflicts. An honourable person was one able to defend his land and women. Thus, the sexual behaviour prescribed for women – virginity and chastity – was crucial to guaranteeing respect for men in the surrounding social context. 'Proper' female sexual behaviour gave a good reputation not only to men, but also to families, clans, towns and countries.[6] This link may still be found in some areas of contemporary Italy. In 2003, Rosa, a young woman from Africo, a village on the Ionian coast of Calabria, told me: 'My mother-in-law is really glad her son got married to me, because I come from Africo and women from Africo have good reputation compared to those from other Calabrian towns'.[7]

To avoid any loss of honour, men exercised strict control over women's bodies, considered family property.[8] In other words, to save their reputation, men protected women with the aim of preventing any female act that might question their honour and punished women if they violated the prescribed norms, in order to regain respect from the community.

Scholars identify the erosion of the honour code as one of the hallmarks of a modern society, in which supposedly 'there is no longer any need to maintain group markers', since 'ascribed status and institutionalised role behaviour have lost their social significance'.[9] Theoretically, contemporary societies no longer need honour-related violent conduct for regulating conflicts. Therefore, the honour code could be expected to shift to a value system linked more to inner qualities and 'the cultivation of one's dignity'.[10] In practice, this transformation has only occurred partially. Honour norms, entailing violent sanctions if transgressed, have persisted in 'societies with weak mechanisms for organizing and controlling endogenous violence'[11] and demand for deterrence. This is the case of a criminal environment which is characterized by an endemic lack of trust and where it is not obviously possible to appeal to the State to resolve disputes.[12] In mafia organizations, for example, having a 'good reputation' remains linked to the cornerstones of the honour code, including force, violence and virility. The mafias inherited the code of honour from the past due to its organizational and binding functions.[13] Mafia groups and individuals, operating in an unstable environment, as is the case with criminality, require guiding principles both outside and inside the organization. Externally, the mafias have exploited the code of honour in order to disguise their criminal motivations related to power and money, showing honourable intentions to avoid moral condemnation. Ultimately, they have manipulated the code's original meaning for their own ends. The image of the mafioso as a man of honour is paradoxical, considering that the traditional notion of honour, while encompassing the use of violence, also entailed generosity, altruism and greatness of soul. The mafia's criteria for a 'good' reputation, which allows men to acquire honour, consist in the ability to murder and keep secrets, and to 'correct' women's sexual behaviour.[14] However, the association between mafia and honour has helped lead the mafia not to be identified with a specific criminal organization, allowing it to enjoy a certain consensus based on its reputation as an 'honourable society' (*società d'onore*) in areas where it was widely spread.[15]

Internally, the use of the honour code has offered the mafias' members a solid ideological apparatus. Honour, indeed, shapes mafia identity. Becoming a man of honour involves acquiring a specific identity associated with virility, power and money. Therefore, for someone who feels anonymous in society, mafia membership is perceived as a chance to obtain social recognition. A number of state witnesses, who used to belong to mafias, confessed that before becoming men of honour they felt like '*nuddu ammiscatu con nente*' ('a nobody mixed with nothing'). Norms of honour contribute to enhancing a feeling of belonging. Following shared rules and being aware that violating them will be punished contributes to perceiving the organization as a whole. The group benefits from a control mechanism grounded on the members' awareness that the loss of honour caused by one of the group's members might have an impact on the entire organization.[16]

Moreover, honour can serve as an individual mafioso's alibi, in order to justify his brutal conduct. It is a sort of neutralization's technique,[17] aimed at facilitating the commission of violent crimes like murder.

Norms of honour are particularly powerful since 'once adopted, they are relatively resistant to extinction, and thus regardless of whether they are ultimately social or moral/personal they can be internalized to the extent that individuals follow them in an unconditional way'.[18]

Given that affiliation to a mafia organization is reserved to those who are considered honourable, and that the man of honour's traditional characteristics include the ability to guarantee the sexual integrity of women (wifes, daughters and sisters), women are involved in men's initiation into the mafia. They become a male vehicle for gaining a good reputation and credibility and thereby becoming a proper candidate for entering mafia groups. Through their appropriate sexual behaviour, women are a source of male prestige.[19] By showing their ability to protect female sexuality from other men, mafiosi demonstrate their skills in protection and thus improve their reputation.[20] The latter is a pivotal resource in an illicit environment dominated by a deeply rooted lack of trust and where economic transactions are risky.

In mafia groups, thus, the consequences of female loss of honour affect manliness, similarly to traditional honour cultures across the globe.[21] Becoming a cuckold is the worst offence for a man in an honour-based culture. Women's misbehaviour affects masculine identity, or more specifically men's virility, and thus the way they are seen by the community.[22] In the mafia this has negative consequences on the man's career. Collaborator with justice Antonino Belnome, who led a *locale* of 'Ndrangheta in Giussano, a small town close to Milan, in the notes he wrote in prison, explained this mechanism:

> Among affiliates, family reputation is very important because mothers and sisters bring honour. He will have to be very careful and take care of this aspect personally, because it can affect his career in the 'Ndrangheta. Disrespectful behaviour by mothers and sisters, especially if any family member would complain or cooperate with the law, is unacceptable. For an affiliate, these things are inadmissible. He will have to find the most appropriate way to try to save his honour, otherwise he will be sidelined without hesitation or decisions will be made that may (it also depends on the severity of the facts) even involve death.[23]

How female sexual behaviour can influence male careers in Cosa Nostra is shown by events involving Margherita Petralia, which dates to the early 1980s. A soldier, Gaspare Sugamiele, who worked for Margherita's husband and was charged with following and controlling Margherita, told judges about the expulsion of Margherita's husband and father-in-law, since she had an extra-marital affair:

> In the early 1980s, Vito and Gaspare Sugamiele were 'put in their place' because of decisions made on the provincial level following the fact they had not taken radical steps in regards to Gaspare's wife, Margherita Petralia, who was involved in an extra-conjugal relation that had come to public knowledge following a check made by the Carabinieri at Sugamiele's house, on which occasion the woman was caught by surprise in the company of her lover.[24]

Mafia women's virtuous sexual conduct increases men's symbolic capital, which is crucial for recognition and thus domination,[25] especially in the men's path towards their own affirmation in the mafia organization. Since mafias are criminal organizations aimed at increasing their own power, they need to demonstrate dominance. Controlling and punishing women's 'misconduct' is one of the ways mafias can make their power visible. Upholding patriarchal gender power relations, based on the subjugation of women, is a mafioso's instrument to maintain social order inside the organization and to affirm their power in the eyes of the community. Acquiring and maintaining these two assets is crucial for carrying out criminal business smoothly. And this explains the legitimation of violent male, and sometimes female, conducts towards women.

In analysing the mechanisms of an honour-based society, it is crucial to take into account that a person's respectability may not correspond to his honourable qualities. Indeed, honour is a category of public evaluation, insofar as the ascription of honour is given by others. What matters is public recognition. What the community thinks about an individual is more important than his/her true qualities.[26] In the space between what is known publicly (appearance) and reality (being), the rules of the honour code may be negotiated.[27] That is why social practice often does not correspond to the model of behaviour prescribed by the norms of honour. In mafia organizations, a deep gap exists between theory and practice. Economic reasons often lead mafiosi to put questions of honour aside and thus negotiate the rules prescribed by the code. In some circumstances mafia organizations consider it more convenient to reconcile two people in a conflict involving honour rather than seek revenge. In other words, it is often better to avoid a feud, even one that may be sparked off by a point of honour. In the terms used by mafias, this negotiation of the behavioural model prescribed by the code of honour is called '*ragionamento*' (reasoning); showing that in the mafia, convenience prevails over ideology.[28]

Negotiating the rules of honour is an opportunity often reserved to men, rather than women. In the mafias, a double standard involving gender exists in terms of the sexual rules of honour, much as in other honour-based communities.[29] This different possibility of negotiating the rules of honour is due to the fundamental role of female sexual conduct in influencing how honour is attributed to men and therefore their mafia membership and career. Some observers have pointed out that in blackmail, women have a strong weapon they may use against their male relatives.[30] They sustain that 'honour legitimizes female power', given the fact that women have the possibility to subtract men's symbolic capital through their 'misconduct'. It is self-evident that this might be valid for cases in which there is space of negotiation even for women, namely when the dishonourable act does not become public or punishing the woman would be not convenient from a strategic and economic perspective.

Unlike most women, men of honour might not follow some rules of conduct theoretically established by the code of honour, for example restricted sexual behaviour. Violation of norms, like the prohibition of having relationships with fellow mafiosi's women or with mistresses, might not be punished for the sake of the organization. As depicted masterfully in the film *Angela*, directed by Roberta Torre and based on a true story, a young mafioso has an affair with the wife of his boss but is not punished and is allowed to remain in the criminal group, because he is clever and ruthless, and as such useful to the organization.[31]

The double 'morality' regarding gender is evident as concerns the possibility of having a love affair outside marriage. Women betraying their men are heavily punished, when the circumstances do not offer space for negotiation. But for a men, having a mistress, or more than one, is considered a sign of virility, which is crucial in the 'men of honour's' self- and hetero-perception. Betraying a wife is part of the attribute of the mafia's 'hegemonic' masculinity. What is important is to avoid falling in love with the mistress and leaving the wife. Belnome explains this: 'A man who belongs to the 'Ndrangheta is allowed to have a "lover", but he must absolutely not leave his wife for any another woman, because as long as his wife keeps his honour perfectly intact she will always be a privileged person.'[32]

Unlike male betrayals, female ones are often punished and can cause feuds to erupt. That is why it is a taboo subject. For example, those who turn state witness, when talking with authorities, tend to avoid referring to female sexual conduct, since it is deemed highly risky. They have the courage to talk about their crimes, even murders, but do not want to face issues related to the sexual lives of women related to mafiosi.[33] Even some prosecutors treat this subject with caution. For example, they avoid transcribing conversations revealing female betrayals, because they know that, if they become public, these women might be condemned for their 'misbehaviour'.[34]

Female oppression

Female relatives of 'men of honour' live under male and female control resulting in oppression and often in male violence. Especially in the 'Ndrangheta, the code of honour becomes a military-like control system reducing women to objects belonging to the men and the family, as much as its territory. In a society structured around honour, the objectification of women serves to render 'them disposable once they are perceived to have committed a transgression, since they are deemed to lack worth if they are no longer 'honourable'.[35]

Some women growing up in an 'Ndrangheta family are subjected to segregation as of their adolescence. One woman, who later turned state's witness, confessed:

> I was born and raised in a very strict family, and I was not allowed to go out. They did not let me study; when I reached second grade they told me that it was not necessary to continue because, clearly, the most important thing was to be at home, work in the home and, thus, school was of no use. But if I didn't need school, I also didn't need to smuggle cigarettes, and yet I had to do it.[36]

Male bloods relatives, including fathers, brothers and even cousins, control women and are the perpetrators of honour-related violence. In particular, brothers have the task of monitoring their sisters, in order to protect the family's honour. That is why they may be possessive and even violent. Giuseppina Pesce, collaborator with justice, who belonged to an important 'Ndrangheta family of Rosarno in Calabria, was profoundly worried about her brother's reaction to her betrayal. She stated to magistrates:

> As long as my brother is alive, I will be condemned to death, because he is the one who has to carry out the sentence for my betrayal ... He would have killed me, because women who betray are killed. It's a law. It's happened so many times in the past, because here in Calabria that's how they think. It's their mentality.[37]

Not only her brother, but also her cousins started to monitor her as soon as they knew about her love affair.

> Before I was arrested, one day my uncle ... took me to one side and told me to be careful, because an alarm had gone off over me and sooner or later I would be blocked, and my cousins were watching me.[38]

Even in Cosa Nostra, there have been examples of women strictly controlled by their brothers. Giuseppina Vitale, head of the Partinico criminal group in the 1990s when her brothers were in prison, grew up under her male relatives' surveillance. During childhood she learnt to obey to their brothers and experienced their violence. In her autobiography she wrote:

> It happened so many times that I was beaten by my brothers. There were so many reasons for it: because I had left without permission, because maybe I was leaning out the window to see who was passing by ... once Nardo gave me a kick in the butt that prevented me from walking for three days.[39]

The brothers' panoptical control resulted in prohibitions related to many spheres of her life. Control practices were a means for the two brothers to preserve their reputation as protectors:

> What burned him was that people thought he couldn't keep me down. And if he didn't know how to keep under control the *fimmines* (women) of house, what kind of man was he? What kind of honourable man was he? Yes, because Nardo was advancing in his career in Cosa Nostra and something like that was not needed at the time. People thought that, if his sister made him look like a fool, then others could too.[40]

Men's control over their sisters' sexual lives might result also in condemning homosexuality, as occurs in other honour-related communities.[41] Emilio Di Giovine, in the 1980s, had a plan to kill his lesbian sister, as he told me:

> I also wanted to kill another sister. Because she was a lesbian. Rumours circulated first, then we discovered it and I was about to have her killed. What an ugly person I was. How disgusting! My uncle saved her. In my opinion, she had to die. It was too much for the family, we were traditional, from Calabria. I was sexist, worse than racists. I had blinkers over my eyes. Like a horse, I saw nothing but that.[42]

A specific category of women experiencing gender discrimination due to the application of the honour code is made up of widows, who are compelled to remain faithful to their dead husbands or even their dead fiancés. Behind the prohibition of other love affairs lies the fear of losing the family's honour. 'There were people whose husband had died and they had to remain like my mother-in-law, my ex-mother-in-law now … her husband was dead and she couldn't even look at another man',[43] collaborator with justice Giuseppe C. explained to me. Totò Riina's sister, who was engaged to Calogero Bagarella, murdered during the '*strage di Viale Lazio*' in the 1960s, could not have another love affair after the death of her fiancé.

This rule was valid even in the 'Ndrangheta, as shown by the solution found by the Papalia family against the risk in terms of honour caused by having a widow inside. State witness Saverio Morabito once told the following story:

> The widow of Papalia, killed by a friend (because of a vendetta) … later got married to one of the dead man's brothers, Domenico Papalia. He married her because she was a widow with a daughter and, there in Platì, she would never have found anybody who would have married her; who is going to marry a woman that already has a kid? Nobody, because the mentality is that everybody wants a virgin bride … But if a woman becomes a widow while she's still young, either she finds somebody who'll remarry her immediately, and that is difficult, or she just runs wild; she's at the mercy of anybody, and all those vultures circle around her till everybody is talking about it. So to avoid that kind of thing happening in their family, they decided that Domenico Papalia would marry the widow. It's all part of ancient customs.[44]

In more recent times, a woman totally segregated after her husband's death was Elisa,[45] born in 1978 to a couple of farmers living in Rosarno. Her husband, the son of a boss of a well-known 'Ndrangheta family in the area, was psychologically vulnerable and addicted to drugs and alcohol. He was violent with his wife and daughters, so much that Elisa expressed the wish to separate from her husband. And yet, her father-in-law prohibited the conjugal separation, because it would have brought dishonour to the entire family.

The boss felt ashamed of his son's weakness and therefore did not involve him in mafia affairs, unlike the other male family components. Elisa's husband was so psychologically unstable that he committed suicide in 2005. His family blamed his wife for his suffering that led him to commit suicide, and after the tragic event compelled her to move into their house with her children. In her in-laws' house she could not go out, unless accompanied, and was treated roughly. Sadly, she passed from the domestic violence perpetrated by her husband to that exercised by her in-laws. After one year she was able to run away, helped by her father who, despite the fear instilled by her daughter's father-in-law, found the courage to go the police and brought a letter written by Elisa denouncing the unbearable conditions in which she was compelled to live. Prosecutors later condemned the entire family (father, mother, two sons, one daughter and one son's wife), for oppression and abuse.

In the sentence, they wrote that her relatives:

> exercise over . . . (Elisa), through violence and threats, a power that corresponds to the right over property, reducing her to a state of continuous subjection. In particular: by threatening her with death and giving her responsibility for her husband's suicide . . .; Submitting her to a continuous series of moral harassments; Preventing a life with normal relationships; Preventing her from freely leaving home without their presence; Preventing her from accompanying their minor daughters to school; Preventing her from choosing her own doctor; Preventing her from moving to her parents' home after her suicide attempt on 11.02.2006; Preventing her from exercising parental powers over their minor daughters; Taking away and looking after her minor daughters against her will. With the aggravating circumstance of having committed these crimes through abuse of domestic relations and cohabitation. And with the power of intimidation deriving from belonging to a mafia association.[46]

This case shows also the active female involvement in women's oppression. Victims of violence themselves, it is not rare for older women to endorse male controlling practices by helping men in monitoring other women. Elisa's mother-in-law, for example, suffered her husband's betrayals and violent behaviour in addition to her son's verbal violence. At the same time however, she was very tough with her daughter-in-law. Women's 'complicit' participation in male control practices or even violent actions towards other women has also been observed by scholars studying cultures with honour-based value systems, who wonder whether this can be interpreted as a form of female empowerment.[47] Some scholars maintain that women's involvement in male control over women, as emerges in mafia groups more attached to the rules of honour, is the result of coping mechanisms invented by women to bear male symbolic and sometimes physical violence. Sustaining the male model is a way of finding recognition within a context dominated by men.[48]

Various reasons may lead women to be complicit with men and sustain male subjugation, 'bargaining with patriarchy'[49] or assuming indirect power. Nevertheless, what is crucial is the fact that women consider violent and oppressive male behaviours towards themselves 'normal' and correct, since they have been socialized within the cognitive and cultural framework of male dominance.[50]

One category particularly affected by male control in mafia contexts consists in the wives of imprisoned mafiosi, whose families depended economically on the criminal association and thus became the property of the entire organization.[51]

Maria Stefanelli was not only forced to visit her husband in prison accompanied by her husband's brother,[52] but was also compelled to live with her mother-in-law. Born in a small town in the area surrounding Reggio Calabria, in 1990 she married a 'Ndrangheta boss, because she wanted to escape from the sexual violence perpetrated by her uncle, who married her mother after her husband's death. Her husband belonged to the Marando family, which operated in Volpiano, a small town in Northern Italy, in the field of racketeering, drug trafficking, and videopoker. The woman was beaten so much by her husband, that when he died, she perceived his death as a liberation.[53]

During the detention of her husband she was constrained to live with her little daughter in the house of her mother-in-law who, as she narrated:

> profited from my polite behaviour towards her – which I forced myself to do, so we could live in peace – and used it as a pretext to make the wives of my other sons jealous, boasting about my attention to her in front of them, and then treating me poorly when the two of us were alone.[54]

She adds:

> I soon realised I was not in charge of my life, and felt like I was in a cage. Every time I left the farmstead I had to be accompanied, and the only times I could do so were to go to the jail to visit or go shopping at the market.[55]

In 1998 she found the strength to turn state's witness and testified against her brothers-in-law that she accused of being the killers of her natural brother.[56]

Moving from the 'Ndrangheta to Cosa Nostra, the fiancé of fugitive Matteo Messina Denaro, when she became pregnant in the 1990s, also started to live in her mother-in-law's house, controlled by Matteo's sisters. They took care of the woman and insisted on their role in the letters sent to their brother. Matteo's elder sister wrote: 'Franca is fine, she is very well. The thing that makes me sad is the fact that you cannot be close to her in a moment so special'.[57] They wrote that they had prepared a suitcase for the hospital, which was ready in case her contractions started. In this case physical abuse did not emerge, but nevertheless, women relatives of male mafiosi controlled the life of their daughter and sister-in-law. This power continued until Matteo Messina Denaro's daughter became an adolescent and showed her desire to live freely, like her friends: going out, having boyfriends, wearing miniskirts. Yet this lifestyle did not go down well with her aunt, who complained to her mother. After conflicts among the women, in 2013 they moved in with Franca's parents.[58] This story shows that not all mafia families are static, but can adapt to changes in society. In mafia contexts, female control seems to be exercised in particular by women belonging to a mafia family towards wives of male members that do not share the same origins. As they have not internalized the same mafia rules since childhood, they are perceived as riskier for the survival of the organization. At the same time, to avoid these constrictions leading to rebellion, there is room for negotiation. It is considered more convenient to grant women a bit of freedom in exchange for silence and conformity to the organization. Mafiosi seem to be aware that keeping traditional rules alive allows the mafia to show that it is a solid entity from a moral perspective – thus underling its difference with the liquid and unrestricted contemporary wider society – yet at the same time it might be dangerous, since their ancient norms inevitably clash with contemporary habits and customs. This awareness has led the mafia system to find a balance between the organization's traditional rules and modern individual needs.

Generally speaking, the current model of gender relations in the mafia seems to be the result of a balanced interplay between the application of its strict norms and the concession of free movement and behaviour. However, in some circumstances – when friction among mafia groups or female defections occur – there is a need to reposition gender relations within traditional mechanisms based on control and violence, driven by honour codes, in order to avoid rebellion and discontinuity in the cultural transmission underpinning the mafia system. Especially in the 'Ndrangheta, mafiosi bring strong and extreme forms of honour-related violent practices, such as honour killings, into the present day. This shows us that the mafia is not, indeed, merely organized crime, but an organization that aims to obtain power in all its forms, both through violence and corruption and by using and displaying a certain cultural ideology. The fundamentalist belief in honour, expressed by murders of females and males in the name of honour, serves the latter purpose.

Honour killings

Honour killing, the most extreme form of honour-related violence, provides evidence of the total possession of a woman's body by men, families and clans.

Scholarly research has shown increasing interest towards honour killings in the last twenty years, as a result of the growth of Western countries' concern over cases of female deaths related to honour within communities of migrants coming from South Asia or the Middle East. This phenomenon has given rise to a debate among those who see specific cultures, ethnicities and nations behind honour-related violence, and those who read honour killing as a form of violence against women and, as such, the result of male dominance embedded in the wider society.[59] The latter position sustains that honour killing:

> is often viewed as an expression of minority cultures, while little attention is paid to perpetrators as individuals or to the patriarchal values and norms that underpin all forms of violence against women (VAW).[60]

The literature on the persistence of the honour code in modern society observes that honour-based violence is characterized by ubiquity and similarity.[61] Indeed, violent sanctions for transgressing honour-related norms are found across many historical periods, cultures and places. Acknowledging that honour killing is a subspecies or type of domestic violence[62] allows observers to avoid 'designating honour-related violence as separate species on the basis of the presence of allegedly unique "cultural" factors, such as stigmatisation and stereotyping of ethnic communities'.[63]

Violent reactions against women who have not behaved according to expectations involving honour inform for example, in many instances, homicides of women in Italy, bringing the question beyond solely mafia-related contexts. This suggests that violence against women and honour killings are the results of the 'same rules of patriarchal order and symbolic masculine domination'.[64] Hence, honour killings must be seen as 'the ultimate end of a continuum of violence against women'.[65] However, as rightly underlined by Gill, Strange and Roberts, 'even though honour crimes are found in many different societies, each unique cultural context should be individually evaluated to determine how and why these practices have arisen'.[66] Indeed, as regards honour killings in a mafia context, it is crucial to understand the peculiar meaning that mafiosi attribute to this crime.[67]

We have seen that honour-related rules in the mafia have to do not only with 'respect' for individual men or single families, but also with the power of the entire criminal group. In other terms, dishonourable acts might affect the credibility of the clan and thus its governance over the territory. Family-group power depends upon its capacity to deal with female 'misconduct' and regain a positive reputation. The act of killing a female relative is so costly that it allows the dishonoured men/family/clan not only to recuperate respect, but also to reinforce its power. 'Killing a daughter who has transgressed is a horrific cost, but precisely because of its cost, it is a far more credible signal.'[68]

The code of honour is a source of symbolic capital for the organization, insofar as it contributes to reinforcing the members' feeling of belonging and to justifying the norms proposed by the organization. As with the state, the system of norms guides members by defining what is allowed and what is prohibited.

The family, by exploiting the traditional functions of honour, including reputation and deterrence, becomes one of the criminal organization's mechanisms of control. The persistence of honour killings in the mafia, a punishment that has to do with 'wrong' sexual behaviour, is a key element for understanding how traditional symbolic representations and order, in current 'Ndrangheta family configurations, can acquire renewed validity for criminal-organizational purposes.

Behind homicides of women and men for honour, often there are not only symbolic motives, but also practical ones, including avoiding feuds or preventing collaboration with justice. Interestingly, when only ideological factors are at stake, there might be space for negotiation, as shown by a case of a thirty-year extra-marital relationship involving the wife of an important 'Ndrangheta boss in Milan, which police discovered by intercepting her conversations.[69]

Most of the cases of honour killings that occurred in mafia contexts, as identified by law enforcement agencies, regard the 'Ndrangheta. In the history of Cosa Nostra, however, there have been cases of capital punishment against women for questions of honour. Evidence provided by state witnesses was crucial in order to identify them. According to Francesco Mannoia's testimony, given to magistrate Giovanni Falcone, the sister of Giuseppe Lucchese, belonging to the Ciaculli family, was killed because she was in love with singer Pino Marchese, who was murdered as well. As a symbolic sign, his testicles were inserted in his mouth. Even Lucchese's sister-in-law was punished, because her behaviour was deemed too libertine while her husband was in prison.[70] According to state witness Francesco Onorato, the daughter of Antonio Pipitone was killed in 1983, because she refused to get married to a man imposed by the family.[71]

Maria Concetta Cacciola, Lea Garofalo, and Francesca Bellocco are three quite recent and well-known cases of women that died for reasons involving honour. The following reconstruction of their stories is aimed not at entering their intimate sphere, which is unfathomable and would be overwhelming, but rather at grasping the entwined dimensions behind their homicides, including ideological and organizational.[72]

Maria Concetta Cacciola

Maria Concetta Cacciola, born in 1980, paid a heavy price for offending her husband and her family, who belonged to the 'Ndrangheta. She had an extra-marital affair and, in order to escape the honour system's sanctions for this 'misbehaviour', she became a state witness.[73] While she was protected by the State, she confided to her best friend, as appears in a call intercepted by the police: 'Like they say ... the family does not forgive these things ... They don't forgive honour.' And she sent by phone the following text message to her lover: 'My family does not forgive honour and dignity, and I offended them in both of these areas.'[74]

This double branding as a 'traitor' made her ashamed, as she confessed during another phone call with her friend. From the place where she was hidden by the authorities, as state witness, she told her friend she did not want to come back home, because she was afraid not only of retaliation, but also for her reputation.

> **Cacciola Maria Concetta** ... I'm even ashamed of all this.
>
> **Friend** What do you have to be ashamed of? What do you have to be ashamed of?
>
> **Cacciola Maria Concetta** My mother says I shouldn't care what people say.
>
> **Friend** What do you have to be ashamed of? What the hell did you do that you should be ashamed of? Ah ... what did you do?
>
> **Cacciola Maria Concetta** Okay, alright.
>
> **Friend** Were you with someone?
>
> **Cacciola Maria Concetta** ... I'm here now, and it's even worse ... can you realize that?

Shame is the typical female feeling in honour-based societies and, in the case of Maria Concetta, it was a clear product of the deep internalization of the 'Ndrangheta's rules regarding honour that she assimilated in her family. Maria Concetta's life was marked by constant family monitoring, from childhood to death. When she was an adolescent, she ran away with a man (*fuitina*) to escape from her family's oppression. Still very young, she had three children in less than ten years (the first at sixteen, the second at nineteen and the third at twenty-four years old). Her husband, who married her because he wanted to begin a career in the mafia, turned out to be violent with her. Although she asked her family for protection, they refused to help her because of the rule of honour that forces wives to be subjugated to their husband. Her father said to her: 'This is your marriage and you keep it.'

When her husband went to prison, condemned for a mafia crime, she was strictly controlled by her family and the organization. In a letter she sent to her husband, she complained about these controls and the lack of freedom. She could only go out to drop off her children at school, but even in that circumstance she had to go with a trusted person:

> How can I live this way if I cannot even breathe . . . ? I go out in the morning to drop off my children at school . . . I cannot have any contact with anybody . . . What good is my life when I cannot have contact with anyone?[75]

In this 'domestic prison', as one magistrate defined her family environment, it was, however, possible for her to use the internet. Registered with a nickname in a social network, she met a man from Reggio Calabria, who lived in Germany and with whom she started a virtual relationship. In the summer of 2010, anonymous letters arrived at her house revealing that Maria Concetta had a lover. Her father and brother beat her badly enough to break a rib, and her brother and cousins started to tail her. She was particularly scared by her brother. To the police, in fact, she said: 'my brother has a bad temper and there's nothing he wouldn't do. He'd even make me disappear'.

In this oppressive system of male control, there were traces of female solidarity. Maria Concetta's sister-in-law, for example, 'several times warned her that when she was inside the apartment where she lived she must not speak, not even on the phone, insinuating that her brother had installed something at home that allowed him to listen to her'. Moreover, she told her sister-in-law each time her husband went outside Rosarno, to give some relief to Maria Concetta.

When Maria Concetta went to *Carabinieri* for a notification of her son's fine, she met a policewoman and started to talk about her oppressive life and domestic violence. This first contact with the state developed so much that she turned state witness. The process was not smooth, as she went back to her family after a few months. Back at home, she experienced once again total control and deep psychological violence until she was murdered, though it was made to look like a suicide. Her relatives were sentenced for abuse. Magistrates are still searching to identify exactly her killer.

In the sentence, the magistrate stressed that the family practiced a 'cult of honour'. The Cacciola is not a traditional 'Ndrangheta family, although in recent decades it was able to make alliances with the 'Ndrangheta's élite families, such as Bellocco and Pesce. The cult of honour might be read as a sign communicating it is able to be a real 'Ndrangheta family. Following strictly the mafia's rules proved the family's adhesion to the organization's ideological system. Sharing this culture is an instrument of homogenization within a process of isomorphism that the groups composing the 'Ndrangheta tend to activate. Maria Concetta Cacciola's case shows this strategic function of honour practices and thus the way ideological and organizational traits of the mafia system merge together.

Lea Garofalo

Lea Garofalo was killed in 2009 at the age of thirty-five by her husband, Carlo Cosco, who was an 'Ndrangheta boss living in Milan, where he managed drug trafficking.[76] While growing up in a small town in Northern Calabria, Petilia Policastro, she came to know the 'Ndrangheta system during her childhood. Her father, who was the boss of a town's faction, died during a feud when she was quite young. Her older brother substituted their father and organized revenge. As an adolescent, Lea fell in love with Carlo Cosco and followed him to Milan. They had a baby, who was compelled to live in a criminal environment. Lea was not pleased with this situation and thus, in 1996 when the police arrested her husband for drug trafficking, she decided to leave him and move away, along with her daughter. She communicated this decision to her husband, while he was in prison. The man's reaction was extremely negative, because he could not bear to abide by a choice made by a woman. Lea's action stimulated not only his husband's anger, but also her brother's, who was worried about his honour just like his brother-in-law. According to the rules of honour, Lea's behaviour had brought shame to both men and her brother was bound to kill her. However, the latter could not find the courage and therefore tried to convince her to go back to her husband by beating her. Yet, she was unmovable. As soon as her husband left prison, he started to organize Lea's murder. Aware that she was seriously in danger, she decided to ask help from the authorities and became a state witness. This increased Cosco's need to kill her. Cosco tried to murder her first in a town where she had moved after escaping from Calabria, in search of a safe place. He sent a killer to her house, yet Lea was saved by the intervention of her daughter. Later Cosco, with some companions, successfully carried out his homicidal plan in Milan, where Lea had gone to meet him after accepting his proposal to take care of their daughter economically. Her precarious economic conditions made her so vulnerable that she took this high risk, which proved fatal to her. Lea Garofalo was killed on 24 November 2009 and her body was dissolved in acid.

From Lea Garofalo experience it emerged clearly that a double label of 'infamy' is attributed to those women who 'dare' to abandon their husbands and at the same time follow the path of collaboration with justice. The punishment is motivated by reasons involving both revenge and purification,[77] bringing together the two pillars of mafia organizations, ideology and organization. By killing her, the man satisfied his individual desire and the organization's, which in a totalitarian mafia structure overlap. He eliminated not only the female body, guilty of dishonouring him, but also the risk that she would talk with the police again.

Francesca Bellocco

Francesca Bellocco was the victim of an honour killing, because she had an extra-marital affair with an 'Ndrangheta member, Domenico Cacciola.[78] Her son murdered her in August 2013, following a family tradition.[79] In 1977 Francesca's aunt, Maria Rosa Bellocco, her husband and her little child were brutally killed in their house: the wife because she had a love affair outside her marriage, the husband because he did not punish his wife for her dishonourable behaviour, and the child because it would have been a witness. For these three assassinations the Court condemned, after an appeal, Antonio Bellocco, Maria Rosa's brother. However, it stated that the murders took place in a family context (in the previous hearing of the trial, the father and other brothers of the sister were also condemned). The three killings had a positive impact on the 'Ndrangheta family's reputation, as the magistrate underlined: 'This serious and atrocious crime contributed to the Bellocco family's prestige as local criminals, restoring the family's honour in an extremely clear and exemplary way, after it was tarnished by the woman's betrayal of her husband'. The extramarital relationship was well known in the town. However, the relatives did not react immediately, since they were waiting for the husband to react and restore his honour. Yet, when the woman's father discovered them together in her house and the community knew that the head of the family was aware of it, the family had to take, in front of the people, the disciplinary provision called for by this circumstance, i.e. the death penalty. If not, the family would have sullied its reputation.

As in the 1970s tragic act of revenge, many in the family knew or had suspicions about the relationship between Francesca Bellocco and Domenico Cacciola. However, no one intervened until the love affair risked bringing about a feud, since the relationship between the two criminal groups was worsening. The two families preferred to resolve the issue through honour killings that would re-establish order.[80] In mafia contexts, a private dispute might become relevant to the association from a business perspective.

The family tradition of violently solving issues of honour was well known. In the 1990s, one of the sons-in-law of the mafia group's leader and a member of the criminal organization decided to collaborate with the magistrates, because he was worried about his safety, since his father-in-law had discovered he was betraying his daughter. He explained to the magistrates:

> When I talk about codes, there are two that cannot ever be violated, so to speak, and they are infamy and betrayal, disgrace and dishonour. Not respecting these two codes leads to a sure death. . . . For them, it's like a loss of prestige, let's say, it's an offence. . . . They have no pity over things like this, there can be no pity, not for sons, nor for fathers, nor for mothers, not for anyone. These two codes must never be violated.

He also declared that he was compelled to send his sister away from the town, because his criminal group expected that he would have killed her, since she had an extramarital relationship.

The other group belonging to the elite of the 'Ndrangheta controlling the Rosarno area – the Pesce family – also dealt with the violation of honour codes by a female member by killing her. Giusy Pesce told magistrates that her aunt was killed by the woman's relativez. With help secretly lent by a cemetery guardian, her body was interred in a burial recess at the family's grave site.

Moreover, there is evidence that the practice of honour killings was present not only in the 'Ndrangheta clans found on the Tirrenic side of Calabria, but also in those established near the Ionian Sea. In the late 1990s, at Bovalino in the province of Reggio Calabria, a woman was murdered in front of her son. She was condemned because, during the detention of her husband, who belonged to the Nirta-Romeo clan in San Luca and was imprisoned for kidnapping, she betrayed him. This behaviour went against the expectations of the honour-based criminal community.[81] When state witness Maria Stefanelli heard the news of this killing on television, she was extremely frightened, as she narrated in her memoir, *Loro mi cercano ancora*: 'I felt like I was dying. What happened to her could have happened to me. It's a risk I was still facing'. This reaction gives evidence about the fear that violence against women gives rise to in other women.

Honour killings have a powerful function as deterrence. Their aim is not only to perpetuate women's subordinate roles, as is stressed in international human rights documents,[82] but also to send a clear message to other women that might want to engage in a process of collaborating with justice. Prosecutor Alessandra Cerreti has underlined the deterrence ensuing from the violence used on Maria Concetta Cacciola: 'since Maria Concetta Cacciola no more collaborators have appeared'.[83] In other words, since her collaboration with justice no more significant testimonies of women belonging to the 'Ndrangheta have been seen. Rather than risk being killed or negatively stigmatized, women prefer to express their agency in conformity with the organization's need to gain symbolic and material advantages; that is why they contribute to transmitting mafia principles in encouraging vendetta, or participate in mafia activities such as drug trafficking, economic crime, carrying messages from prison and leading mafia clans on behalf of their men, when the latter are in prison or underground. Eventually, in many instances, they prefer to assume male roles, searching for a criminal equality, and keep suffering honour-related gender discrimination and male domination.

Honour-related violence can also be directed against men, as the case of Francesca Bellocco has clearly shown. The 'Ndrangheta is ready to punish men who defy the 'Ndrangheta group by falling in love with female relatives of mafia members, thus putting at risk the family's honour.[84] This was the case with Pino Russo Luzza, who had a love affair with an 'Ndrangheta boss' sister-in-law. In the early 1990s, both very young, they started to spend time together. This did not please her family and therefore the young man was murdered and then burned, as a state witness told magistrates. At the resulting trial, Antonio Gallace was condemned for Pino's murder who, according to the court, was motivated by honour issues, as is written in the judge's notes: 'Protecting the family's honour and their personal prestige, understood according to the rules of 'Ndrangheta subculture'.[85]

The brutal modalities of these killings were a symbolic means intended to demonstrate their ability to protect their women and thus their territory. Following this same reasoning, a boss of the Cammarata group that controlled the Riesi area in the Sicilian province of Caltanissetta, in the 2000s killed a man simply because he dared to give a lift to his wife who was coming home with heavy shopping bags.[86]

These examples give further evidence of male control over women's lives. Women are precious resources because they guarantee men's honourable reputation, and when their honour is preserved they are a family resource to be spent when necessary.

Blood alliances through marriages

In some mafia families, women are not free to develop a relationship with those with whom they fall in love. This is because women represent a precious family commodity to spend in the marriage market, which in an honour-based community 'are a very significant social and economic transaction between families'.[87]

Studies of the history of marriage agree that arranged marriage was a common practice in the past.[88] Gradually, matrimonial union has increasingly become a matter of companionship and romance rather than business. Nowadays, in some contexts and cultures, utilitarian unions are still grounded more on relatives' calculations than on sincere love.

In Mediterranean societies, marriages were prescribed by kinship groups and conceived in terms of honour and shame, hence the importance of virginity. As Jack Goody put it:

> the Mediterranean stress on virginity has also to be seen in the context of the control of marriages by kin, who are more concerned with contracting a union which is 'honourable' than one based on the agreement, choice or love of the partners.[89]

The Arab world has influenced Mediterranean societies' conception of the union between the sexes as a matrimonial alliance, as Guichard explains in his study of Eastern versus Western structures in Medieval Spain.

Generally speaking, in southern Italy, great importance has been given to kinship, including not only blood relationships, but also bonds between in-laws and *comparatico* (god-parenthood). The latter were sealed by marriage, which was intended to build bonds through blood. Studies on Calabrian and Sicilian villages illustrate that marriages between cousins, typical of the oriental structure observed by Goody, were traditionally meant to strengthen the family.[90] In traditional

Sicilian families, the high percentage of weddings between cousins permitted family groups to be stabilized, with patrimonial family relations, because the wives were recruited from within the same family group.[91]

It is self-evident that blood alliances are fundamental in a risky context, such as the mafia, where untrustworthiness and uncertainty dominate everyday life. Widened by marriage, trusted kinship between mafia families sharing the same 'values' acted as a sort of defence against external attacks.[92] In this sense, prescribed marriages (in Sicilian *'matrimonio portato'*)[93] in mafia organizations aim at making an alliance between two clans, in order to expand their control over a given territory and thus increase their power. The practice of arranged marriages within mafia families has been defined as a form of *endogamia di ceto*, meaning 'the use of the female branch of the mafia family for the purpose of expanding the dimensions of the *cosca* (Family) via the activation of matrimonial alliances with territorially closer mafia groups'.[94] There are many examples of this exploitive use of marriage.[95] One significant case involved the important 'Ndrangheta families Condello and Imerti, who built alliances through cross-marriages in order to confront the powerful De Stefano family during the war in the area surrounding Reggio Calabria from 1985 to 1991. Arranged marriage also reduced the probabilities of feuds, as *pentito* Saverio Morabito maintained, talking about his Calabrian village, Platì:

> often families crossed through marriages ... intermarriages were useful in maintaining the peace in Platì, which in fact is the only town where no feud has ever broken out. It is a bit like what used to happen between royal families. The families from Platì – Seri, Papalia, Barbaro, Perri – are all related to each other now; daughters and sons get married, they become *compari*; they become relatives through cousins, second and third cousins. So everybody knows that if a feud breaks out, it would immediately involve all of them, and so before avenging anybody they think about it three times.[96]

In some small villages on the Ionian coast, these kinship combinations have made criminal investigations difficult since relatives often have the same names and surnames, as well as many physical similarities.[97] Magistrate Michele Prestipino explains: 'In some places it is true that a Mafia family has a well-known name, but behind that name it is possible to identify a number of family units with the same last name.'[98] He added: 'To untangle people that not only have the same last name, but also the same first name, a specialized study on genealogical tree is necessary to understand the dynamics, alliances, and contacts that often conflict with each other.'[99]

'Ndrangheta members living in the north have to face the same difficulties as investigators in terms of identifying people belonging to a single family. Two bosses living in Lombardy underlined this difficulty during a conversation, intercepted by police.[100]

According to magistrates, arranged engagements involve underage girls are widespread even nowadays. Priests committed to fighting the 'Ndrangheta underline that using women as object of exchange is more widespread in the lower level of the 'Ndrangheta.[101] A good marriage might in fact help to improve one's own position in the layers of the mafia system.

Moving from 'Ndrangheta to Cosa Nostra, two examples of arranged marriage are quite significant. The first regards the Grecos, one of the families in the Conca d'Oro, whose progress from trafficking citrus fruits to narcotics was helped in part by reinforcement through strategic intermarriages between the Greco family from Croceverdi Giardini and the Greco family from Ciaculli. Through these alliances, they became one of the leading mafia families in the 1950s and 1960s.

The second example involves the saga of the Riina and Bagarella families, which formed the heart of the Corleonese faction.[102] Totò Riina, the so-called 'boss of bosses', wanted to marry Ninetta Bagarella, so he offered Ninetta's brother, Calogero Bagarella, his own sister Arcangela in exchange. Before Arcangela and Calogero's marriage was celebrated, in 1969 Calogero was shot dead in the so-called *strage di viale Lazio*, mentioned above. There is no doubt that the Corleonesi's rise to power was due to their ruthlessness, but their criminal-business unity was also enhanced by the cohesion gained from constructed kinship.[103] This shows that cultural practices circulating in the mafias were strictly interwoven with their criminal functionality. Ninetta's union with Totò was not only strategic, but was apparently characterized by sincere affection. As observed by Goody, 'love is not incompatible with arranged union'.[104] Speculations about the Riina-Bagarella union, like their supposed honeymoon in Venice while Totò was on the run, fed curiosity in Italy for a long time. This case shows that in Cosa Nostra even matrilineal relations are meant to build alliances: Giuseppe Marchese became a close lieutenant of Riina because he was the brother of Vincenzina, wife of Leoluca Bagarella, brother of Ninetta, Riina's wife.

Cases in which mafia power is inherited through the female side of the family are also interesting, showing that 'the position of leadership may also be transferred matrilineally'.[105] For example, Salvatore Inzerillo took over a powerful clan at the end of the career of Rosario Di Maggio, who was his maternal uncle.

This family, moreover, was characterized by unions between cousins, aimed at strengthening kinship and criminal bonds as much as possible. This was noted by Giovanni Falcone, who wrote as follows in the report that set off the inquiry leading to the 'maxi-trial': 'the incredible interlacing of kinship ties ... with each new generation, the links become more binding as a consequence of marriages between cousins ... render the group more cohesive and homogeneous'.[106]

Arranged marriage, including the sacrifice of individual feelings for the sake of the family, clearly shows the instrumental use of kinship in mafia organizations.[107] The practice seems to constitute a constriction for both sexes. Upon closer analysis, it is clear that undesired yet strategic unions have advantages for men, but not for women. Indeed, sacrifice helps improve a man's mafia career, whereas for women it helps the career of the men in their families. Mafia boss Leonardo Messina affirmed he was a man of honour not only because of heritage, but also because he married 'a woman from my environment, niece of the *sottocapo* of the San Cataldo Family, so I was destined to become an important person in this town and in some ways I became one'.[108] One good example of an alliance between clans through a woman's sacrifice involves Grazia Ribisi. Grazia's marriage to boss Allegro was meant to create a useful alliance for her brothers' clan. Indeed, Grazia 'constituted the element of connection between her family and that of Allegro'.[109] This discrimination against women in arranged marriages becomes clear when considering that in many cases men keep seeing their true loves after their investment in a 'good' marriage. As already mentioned, having a mistress is often tolerated, despite the fact that it goes against mafia norms.[110] For example, Francesco Marino Mannoia married the daughter of important mafia boss Vernengo in order to improve his position. However, he did not give up seeing his first love with whom he would finally reunite in 1989 when he began collaborating with magistrates.

The gender-discrimination side of arranged marriages is even more evident when they are used to make peace between clans after a feud. In this case, symbolically, the virginal blood yielded by the bride to her husband during the wedding night balances metaphorically with the bloodshed seen in warfare. Moreover, this 'seals the pact of not provoking new deaths between families already related and linked by a blood tie'.[111] This purpose of arranged marriages is true even in other cultures: among the Bedouins, for instance, the shedding of the blood of a virgin, intended to settle a feud, was seen as a kind of symbolic vengeance, blood for blood.[112] Or again, in Barbagia, Sardinia, 'the most typical form of reconciliation is marriage of a man from the clan of the victim with a woman from the clan of the killer. The virginal blood that is spilled in fact presents a symbolic compensation for the blood spilled in the homicide that preceded it.'[113]

Another function of prescribed marriages organized by mafia families has to do with their aim to enter the legitimate world by offering their daughter, along with her sizeable dowry, to a family (often noble) with a clear name but having financial difficulties.

Finally, family alliances have been fundamental in transforming the mafia into a trans-national organization. The Italian mafia is competitive in the global criminal market partially because of its strong kinship bonds that go beyond the local level.

In addition, wedding ceremonies are good opportunities for meetings, in which mafia members make important decisions. During the wedding between Elisa Pelle, daughter of Giuseppe Pelle (better known as Gambazza), and Giuseppe Barbaro, son of Pasquale Barbaro of the 'u Castanu' family, celebrated in August 2009, an 'Ndrangheta summit occurred in which the new head of Crimine was appointed. This was the result of a complex 'negotiation' that saw the opposition of Tyrrhenian, Ionic, and Reggio Calabria clans, which was solved with a painstaking agreement.[114]

The details of this wedding show the customs followed by important 'Ndrangheta families in the field of matrimonial ceremonies. Intercepted conversations revealed that the families sent invitations both to the *locale*, i.e. the criminal group, and to individual persons.[115] In the first case, the head of the *locale* decided what members would participate. This custom, related to a wedding's invitations, shows that a family event becomes an entire organization's affair, as results from the family-based structure of the 'Ndrangheta.

Wedding parties are also good places to carry out attacks on enemies, as they bring many people together. Rosa N., the collaborator with justice I interviewed in 1998, who belonged to a 'Ndrangheta family once explained to me: 'Usually when they want to kill someone they do so at weddings, funerals, or baptisms.'[116] She referred specifically to the attack that was organized in vain against Emilio Di Giovine, during his daughter's wedding.[117]

To conclude, the most important result of matrimonial strategy is the perpetuation and enhancement of mafia ideology. In this regard, exogamy would be risky, because it would bring a destabilizing foreign element into an otherwise compact mafia organization. A woman's involvement in the role of transmitting mafia values might in fact change according to her origins. Those with mafia pedigree are more likely to pass on her husband's mafia family values. On the contrary, a conflict between the woman's values and those of her husband might arise in the case of a mother who was not brought up in a mafia family. Arranged marriages aim to avoid the latter possibility.

Marriage is thus pivotal in nourishing the cultural homogeneity and cohesion of the organization. Following the centuries-old example of the aristocracy, mafia clans, especially in the 'Ndrangheta, have made the biological family correspond broadly with the social family through marriages within the organization, thereby facilitating the transmission of mafia members' fundamentalist belief and behaviours.[118]

4

Conformist Agency: Performing Soft Power

Education

For the mafia system, the process of education is crucial in order to reproduce its basic principles. Women contribute to *instilling* in children the fundamentals of the mafia ideology, including vendetta, honour and the law of silence. Female participation in this training is quite evident when the basic nucleus of the organization and the blood family overlap: always in the 'Ndrangheta and most of the time in Cosa Nostra.

One must, however, consider that, even in the case there is no overlap, when a man enters the criminal group formally through an initiation rite, the criminal clan becomes as natural as his own family. What is more, theoretically he devotes himself to the mafia family, and as a consequence neglects his blood relationships.[1]

Interestingly, in Cosa Nostra there are linguistic associations between the family and the criminal organization. The terminology identifying a mafia structure and its members resembles that of a blood family. Not only, as we have already seen, is the *cosca* called a 'family', but also the mafia members are called 'brothers', powerful mafia leaders are known as *padrini*, 'godfathers', the mafia boss is *mammasantissima*, 'holy mother', and a politician who helps the clan is called *zio*, 'uncle'. This use of family terms might be intended to create a hierarchical system, as in traditional family relationships. Like in other organizations, such as factories, the allegory of the family is used to create a condition of subordination, as it involves the idea of belonging. Using family terminology may also serve to create a positive model by associating the criminal group with an institution that in Italian culture has been highly important.

The reasons explaining the relevance of the family in Italian society as a social group can be attributed to various factors, including the historical formation of the Italian state and the weakness of the welfare state.[2] Family and kinship networks were indispensable both in the past, when a centralized state was absent, and later when it did not develop socioeconomic instruments capable of supporting individuals. These conditions were even more marked in southern regions that, before the Unification of Italy, had lived under several foreign administrations with distant and consequently negligent central governments. The situation in the south did not improve either with the Piedmont administration or with the formation of the Republic (since the post-Second World War period), because the historical gap between the north and the south had not been eliminated. Kinship relationships have played a key role in many fields and at many levels of society in southern Italy.[3]

To some observers, the closeness of the family in the south brought about a lack of civic sensibility that thus led to the patronage system and finally the mafia.[4] Sociologist Edward Banfield employed the term 'amoral familism' to describe this process, on the grounds of the findings of his fieldwork carried out in a little town in Lucania in 1958.[5] According to Banfield's followers, who apply his monolithic category of analysis to different realities, 'the southern family would show no public ethos, no form of solidarity outside itself and within a larger social context, no interest in taking part in realities which do not directly concern the domestic nucleus of belonging'.[6] More recent studies on the south contested the generalization of the 'amoral familism' category by maintaining that defining the Southern family through it reduced the family to a single, stereotyped model.[7] Moreover, this monolithic category of analysis was applied to different realities, resulting in blaming the family for a societal fabric characterized by nepotism and clientelism, instead of attributing the causes of these negative features of society to the area's historical marginality.[8]

The concept of 'familism', however, without the 'amoral' attribute, is appropriate for describing the traditional family in rural areas of Sicily and Calabria, which was defensive, with strongly inclusive bonds, perceiving the world outside itself as an enemy.[9] In the sexual division of labour and social roles within this household, the father was expected to show power as well as intimidate the other members of the family through his authority. This increased when the father emigrated because he then became a mythical figure.[10] In this traditional southern family, even the role of the mother was highly important, since she guaranteed the internal cohesion of the group.[11] Moreover, the nuclear group and the kinship web was essential. This included not only uncles, cousins and brothers-in-law, but also *compari* and *comari*, godfathers and godmothers, in order to institutionalize external relationships through kinship. The extended family showed a defensive inclusiveness, in order to protect individuals within a difficult socioeconomic context.

Such familiar inclusiveness, which characterized the traditional family in the south, became particularly accentuated in violent contexts, such as those in the mafia. Mafia families, indeed, show defensive and offensive attitudes at the same time. The cohesion in mafia families exists only in order to carry out mafia activities for which the family is ready to sacrifice its members. Family relationships tend to be exploited. The mafia family has been defined as a 'greedy institution', that is an institution expecting total adhesion from its members and attempting to incorporate their whole personality and identity.[12]

A mafia family achieves the total assimilation of its components through the intensification and extension of primary socialization. Generally speaking, primary socialization is fundamental in the construction of personality.[13] The first stage of socialization, taking place in the household, is 'crucial to the process of identity building' in that it 'allows children to become members of society'. In this process, 'the members of the family are fundamental and are imposed on the subject'.[14] The child identifies himself/herself with the people who take care of him/her at the beginning of his/her life, on whose model of values and principles the child builds his/her reference framework. Later, during their development, boys and girls should have the opportunity to draw away from their parents and enter the world of secondary socialization. In mafia families, this passage from primary to secondary socialization is lacking.[15] A mafioso's first formation occurs within the family by adopting those sets of beliefs, values and concepts on which the criminal organization is grounded. The parents indicate them as 'worthy' and are suspicious of all educational programmes, promoting lawfulness, carried out in schools or in parish recreation centres. The mafia considers these initiatives more threatening than police investigations. The case of Padre Pino Puglisi was emblematic, a priest who worked in the slum area of Palermo known as Brancaccio and was murdered in 1993. The mafia death sentence came because he was trying to propose other values, such as gender equality, within a context sustained by mafia culture.[16]

Not surprisingly, mafia families tend to maintain the nurturing process as long as possible within the household, presenting the values proposed outside the kinship group as wrong and unworthy.

The transmission of a cultural system leads either to a simple acquisition or total internalization.[17] Both these forms of learning occur in the mafia. In the beginning, there is mere acquisition through observation and participation. A Cosa Nostra collaborator with justice described how his wife and he taught their children mafia values. He told me:

It is the ideology, the doctrine that I have inculcated in them ... We talk, and they ... it is a spontaneous thing, it is a spontaneous thing because they see a policeman, 'Who is that?' 'That is an asshole.' So you teach them to hate as of when they're little. When they come to search your house you say, 'Keep hidden from this guy.'[18]

The mafia educational process leads boys and girls from mafia families to internalize the mafia's principles. A mere transmission of cultural systems is not enough, as it may be 'sufficient for the reproduction of cultural systems as clichés, but not sufficient for their reproduction as cognitively salient beliefs'.[19] For the latter, the cultural system must be internalized.[20]

The mother has a fundamental role in the intra-domestic process of socialization, the reproduction of cultural systems and the acquisition of one's own gender identity. The early psychic life of the child is based on the relationship with the mother and the later development of the child's personality and identity is influenced by her maternal work. This is oriented to satisfy three of the demands made by children, including preservation, growth and acceptability.[21] What is interesting for understanding training in mafia families is how mothers respond to the last request. Generally speaking, mothers are committed to shaping acceptable children by training them according to their social and cultural group's values, which she has already internalized.[22] What Sara Ruddick observed in relation to patriarchal society occurs in the mafia system: 'Maternal work is done according to the Law of the Symbolic Father and under His Watchful Eye, as well as, typically, according to the desires, even whims, of the father's house'.[23]

Teaching the law of the father means transmitting female subordination,[24] thereby contributing to the persistence of patriarchy. Both boys and girls learn to respect their parents, their fathers as representatives of manhood, endowed with the high value given to virility, but women only as mothers, not as representatives of womanhood. The two are in fact distinguished in the mafia concept of gender. In the male-centred mafia system, women count because of their role as mothers, insofar as they give birth to male babies.[25]

In the mafia system, women themselves tend to overemphasize their role as mothers because they know that womanhood separate from motherhood deserves mostly contempt.[26] Rosa N. told me about the generational transmission both of contempt toward woman and the exaltation of men by women themselves, to whom 'all women are whores since their birth',[27] apart from those who are mothers.

The mother teaches both boys and girls the belief in women's inferiority and thus the hierarchy of the sexes; she teaches her son to distrust women and encourages him to disdain them, unless they are their future wives and as such, mothers of their sons. In essence, the mother occupies a vital role in patriarchal transmission within the family, because she transmits the concepts of male superiority and female inferiority. The relationship between mother and daughter is key to the perpetuation of this model. It might be read as a 'masochistic' educational pattern, since by perpetuating female subordination to patriarchal authority women go against their long-term interests as women.[28] Or it can be seen as a 'self-defensive' mechanism, since mothers transmit their daughters a modus whereby they can achieve recognition in a male-centred context.[29]

The fact that women are more highly regarded by the community because they give birth to male babies explains the strong relationship between mother and son that exists in mafia culture.[30] Renate Siebert clearly explains this:

> The birth of the male allows the woman, if only at second hand, to participate in the splendour of the male principle – the dominant principle in the public sphere – and, simultaneously, it gives her the opportunity to form it and bind it, to make it dependent and make it hers by proxy – in private.[31]

This mirror effect renders clearer why women who cannot have babies might experience this as a failure. Annamaria, from a town in Calabria, due to a series of abortions felt not suited to the role of a woman demanded by her relatives.[32]

In their role as mothers, women tend to emphasize the male status and to devalue the female.[33] Eventually, they tend to transmit gender discrimination, the superiority of male compared to female. Rosa N. describes to me her mother's attitude towards sons and daughters:

> They [the brothers] were gods; I was the whore and they were kings. I, to do a favour for my brother, had to sell everything: my dowry, my gold, everything. Do everything for them ... If her son told her: 'Give me a million!' his mother would go around to find the million and she would end up finding it. I asked her: 'Mom, I need a pair of shoes.' 'Never mind, you can do without them,' she responded. This is the type of mentality that you carry with you for generations.[34]

Moreover, the mother plays a fundamental role in the relationship between father and son. Supporting the figure of the father, and facilitating the assimilation of his message, she encourages the son to accept his father's authority and adopt him as an upright model of maleness.[35] As in the patriarchal family, the 'ultimate authority belongs to Fathers; whenever they conflict, maternal power is meant to submit to paternal authority'.[36]

Bringing up children according to the law of the father becomes more important in cases where the father is away, in prison or in hiding. Hence, the endurance of patriarchal authority in the household depends on the nurturing work that the women dedicate to their children. The mother passes on an ultra-positive image of the absent father, thus contributing to a myth-making process.[37] Public Prosecutor Alessandra Camassa stated that some women from mafia families in Valle del Belice, near the town of Trapani in Sicily, involved in a mafia trial, told her in the 1990s that 'their fathers were absent from the household, yet always present through the mythologizing accounts of their mothers'.[38]

Testimonies of imprisoned women, charged with mafia association, point in the same direction.[39] When discussing their childhood, they underline that their father's absence marked their everyday life.

Women's social recognition through their role of mothers implies female endorsement of values that go against women's interests. This is similar to what Ruddick observed years ago, addressing universal mothering: 'A "good" mother may well be praised for colluding in her own subordination, with destructive consequences to herself and her children.'[40] Mothers, once they have internalized the values of their social and cultural group, transmit them to their children, even if these values are clearly inimical to them. In 'Ndrangheta families, mother contribute to teaching girls to become 'good' women who will get married to a member of the mafia, and boys to conform with mafia version of masculinity,[41] in order to enter the criminal association as a man of honour.

According to Gilmore's cross-cultural anthropological study, masculine ideology has the social and economic function of motivating men to work.[42] This ideology fits mafia organizations, given that they are machines based on illegal and violent work. Indeed, masculinity is the primary feature of the mafia system: the official members of the organization are male, great importance is given to the birth of male babies, only men are worthy of initiation rites, and every man has to adapt to the mafia's hegemonic model of masculinity. The latter is made up of behaviour, attitudes and skills that are violent and male chauvinist, pushed by an exacerbated and aggressive conception of virility.[43] Boys have to interiorize and comply with this model, otherwise they do not gain a positive reputation and are condemned to isolation. To acquire this strict masculinity, the son's identification with the father is crucial. In this process, the son has the perception that the masculine model passed on by his father is completely realized.

Male children learn how to become men of honour from childhood. Boys are exposed to 'virility tests', from eating hot peppers directly from the plant to killing animals (i.e. horses). Emilio Di Giovine was compelled to undergo this kind of ordeal. His testimony offers a clear understanding of 'performing masculinity' in an 'Ndrangheta family:

> I was a little boy when my grandfather, to make us more masculine, forced me and my cousins to eat chilli peppers directly from the plant. My eyes were crying, but I had to resist and prove that I was a man. I was crying like a crocodile. They also made me turn pig's blood at Christmas. I was about four years old, at most five. The pig was put on a table, and many people kept it tied up. In *Gambarie* it was done in the country. Grandfather slid the knife along the pig's throat, the blood came out, it screamed like a damned soul, and I had to turn the hot blood, so that it would not coagulate, to make black pudding. If you do not turn it, the blood coagulates. So as a child, to make me feel courage, they made me do this job. And, as a child, I acted like I was able to do it, and I also figured out how stupid I was, with that mentality, the mentality that you had to be a tough guy.[44]

Patriarchal heteronormativity, which compels men to perform a highly demanding masculinity, can lead them to suffer, as underlined by scholars who have investigated honour.[45]

Giuseppina Pesce wanted to change the destiny of her children so that they would not feel compelled to respond to expectations of extreme femininity and masculinity. This is evident from what she confessed to Prosecutor Alessandra Cerreti, when she became a collaborator with justice:

> If I don't change my ways now and take my children with me when I get out of jail, my son could already be in a juvenile detention centre, and they will put a gun in his hands anyway. My two daughters, on the contrary, will have to marry two 'Ndrangheta men and they will be forced to follow them around. I want to try to create a different future for them.[46]

She wanted to act on a maternal thought oriented towards the real interests of her children, rather than the mafia group's aims of indoctrination. She ceased adapting to a version of 'maternal thought – that – embodies inauthenticity by taking on the values of the dominant culture', which was the mafia.[47]

Gaining female recognition through their role as biological mothers might be the reason why women tend to promote the superiority of their sons. This ends up creating a strong and, above all, ambivalent relationship between mother and son that endures even when the boys become adults, seeing in her the mother to be loved and the woman to be hated.

On the one hand, mothers remain an essential and indispensable point of reference for their sons. At the risk of being heard by the police through intercepted conversations, a man belonging to one of the most important 'Ndrangheta families updated his mother about himself, giving her details on his movements and actions while he was working in the drug trade. In January 2017, for example, he provided her with indications about his own movements on his way back from Brazil, before reaching Calabria. He narrated meticulously his stop in Milan and his meeting with some fellow 'Ndrangheta members in a bar. Then he discussed the possible release from prison of his uncle, his mother's brother. He argued that when his uncle left prison, the man should take over a portion of the territory of the municipality of Bovalino (a small town close to Reggio Calabria). This latter topic showed that talking with his mum also involved important strategic organizational dynamics. The matters dealt with in these conversations were so significant that through their analysis investigators were able to identify the 'existence of a hierarchical structure of the group' and the fact that the man was the representative of the 'Ndrangheta group, composed by his family and another powerful 'Ndrangheta family, in the drug organization.[48] When he was a minor, he was followed by the Youth Court, which in the end did not sentence him for mafia crimes. The magistrates did, however, define his conduct as 'adhering to and serving the interests of the criminal group'.[49] Given his career, it seems evident that his mother had not eradicated the germ of the process of indoctrination planted at that time.

On the other side, the aggressive and misogynous masculinity that mothers have helped forge in their children might pour out against women themselves. There are cases of women who prove to be dependent and subordinate to their adult sons. A lawyer supporting mafia victims told me that some women who decided to remain in their 'Ndrangheta families were scared about the reaction of their sons. In the previous section we analysed the case of Francesca Bellocco, who was killed by her son, because she betrayed her husband.

The maternal biopolitical power exercised over daughters and sons finds its instrument in the family, which is the means for completing maternal work.

As seen in Emilio's testimony above, not only parents are involved in the educational process, but also other actors belonging to the extended family, including grandparents and uncles. Rosa N. told me about the influence of her mother on her son:

> She is [last name of the woman] my mother. Are you kidding? Not at all ... It is deeply rooted in her; she was born and raised, and even raised my son, that way. She instilled in his mind what she was unable to do with me; in fact, if my son sees me, he will kill me.[50]

Giusy Pesce's brother cared about his nephew's criminal training, as she explained: 'When my son once said that when he grew up he wanted to be a policeman, his uncle beat him, and then he promised to give him a gun as a gift.'[51]

Emilio Di Giovine learned the law of silence from his uncle, as depicted in this childhood memory he recounted during our interview:

> *Omertà* was normal. It was one of the first things they taught me. One day a brother of my mother, knowing that I had witnessed an argument between two cousins, asked me who it was that had started it: 'Tell me, I will not do anything to you'. I was silent but he continued, insisting: 'Tell me, I will not do anything to you'. And I kept quiet. But he insisted: 'Tell me, I will not do anything to you'. At a certain point, he gave up and I gave in. But it was nothing but a trap, to test me. As soon as I told him, he punished me with a bad backhand, so strong it made me dizzy for half an hour. I still remember it ... These are things you cannot easily forget. The violence was followed by an explanation: 'You see Emilio, it's not that I slapped you because I don't like you, but to make you always remember in life that before you say anything to anyone, especially the police, think about it a lot. Don't say a thing, even if they tell you it's like that, it never is'. This rule was useful to me in the criminal environment, I never forgot it. My uncle was a good trainer. As a kid they teach you what you must do and what you must not do, policemen must be kept away, you do not have to say anything ... you remember these things forever.[52]

The family, through all its members, acts as a powerful device for the criminal organization. From childhood, the subject is trained directly, a seen in the case of Emilio, or by involving him/her in everyday practices of the organization. In 2010, the sister of the most powerful boss of Cosa Nostra, who was at large, brought her children to visit in prison their father who had been sentenced for mafia association. During these visits the children were used to facilitate the communication between their parents, who were talking about important issues that the woman would have communicated to her brother during the following days. A prosecutor describing the scene to me underlined that 'It was like a theatre play'.[53] The video shows the conventional mimic language used by the two adults to cover the content of their dialogue. For example, they 'looked up and sometimes raised the index finger at the same time to refer to'[54] the boss in hiding. Also the video clearly shows the gestures of the children that served to disguise an apparently loving exchange of words among family members. The children had been trained to perform a specific role, useful to the strategy of their parents and uncle. Similarly, the Vitale family in the mid-1990s used children to transfer messages from the detained boss. Being minors, they were allowed to hug their father during prison visits, thereby receiving from him information to bring outside. In the judicial files it is written that Vito Vitale 'did not hesitate to take full advantage of this possibility, passing, orally, to his ten-year-old son, messages of fundamental importance for the mafia association'.[55]

Understanding the family as a device means reading its power strategies not only as regards repression, but also, along with Michel Foucault, in its productive aspects.[56] Indeed, this institution is able to generate new forms of life serving the criminal organization thanks to the integration between old and new symbolic representations that are passed down through a gender-differentiated education. Men and women learn how to embody manliness and femininity both in relation to the domestic and intimate sphere and in relation to their criminal work. In this learning process, individuals show an agentic capacity that is forged by the institution of the family. The mafia family's biopolitical influence over its members produces men and women who perceive themselves as having agentic capacity, not as being pawns of the system. The mafia's structure lays on this internal and domestic environment, able to shape the minds of the individuals who became available and active in the criminal sphere: men through official positions, and women through informal and substitutive roles.

Vendetta

Vendetta is an action of revenge aimed at extinguishing the shame caused by an offence that has brought dishonour. Basically, it is an instrument of restitution for the damage done to a person's honour. Broadly speaking, vendetta was traditionally a popular institution endemic in areas of Italy (such as Calabria, Sardinia and Sicily)[57] where state control over violence was absent. It was used to regulate relationships between people and satisfy their desire for justice. The use of vendetta settled disputes of various origins. A typical example of an offence that traditionally required revenge was the breaking of a marriage promise, which affected publicly the honour of the promised bride, along with the dignity and honour of her family.[58]

With the growth of centralized control, vendetta was no longer an institution of judicial order and an alternative to the absentee state, and yet remained, in some contexts, as a custom.[59] In other words, although the development of a state justice system made the institution of vendetta unnecessary, this practice has endured. For example, it persisted in the mafia code, in which it has become a justification for violent deeds aimed at exercising control over a given territory. The mafia has used this deeply rooted social custom instrumentally in order to maintain a sort of consensus in the social context in which it is embedded.

According to the traditional code, an act of revenge constitutes in turn a new reason for revenge. However, vendetta is also driven by power and economic factors. In many circumstances, it is an alibi for carrying out violent actions. The final aim of its instrumental use is to avoid social condemnation. Mafia feuds in Calabria, for example,[60] were apparently caused by matters of honour. In reality, they occurred for governance reasons, as Salvatore Boemi, former Prosecutor of Reggio Calabria, pointed out in relation to a conflict that occurred between 'Ndrangheta families: 'above and beyond the blood feud, there was a series of criminal economic interests that led some families, previously accustomed to sharing profits and territorial control, to dominate an entire town'.[61]

Often, the origins of vendetta are both ideological and practical. One paradigmatic example is the 'Ndrangheta war, which occurred from 1985 to 1991 in the area surrounding Reggio Calabria. This conflict broke out with the murder of Ciccio Serraino, followed by several other murders according to the reasoning that 'blood washes away blood'. However, behind this feud lay economic factors linked to the potential construction of a bridge between Calabria and Sicily.[62]

Women play an active role both by transmitting the ideology and practice of vendetta and encouraging their men to commit revenge.[63] The media, including cinema and television, has transmitted the image of mafia women dressed in black, demanding vendetta while crying over the bodies of their dead relatives. Often this is yet another stereotype that leads observers to neglect the more complex involvement of women in the mafia. However, reductive as it is, this image gives us a piece of reality: asking for revenge for a murdered relative has always been a female task.

Documentary evidence of women calling for vendetta dates back to the beginning of the twentieth century. In 1911, a journalist from *L'Ora*, in recounting the funeral of the Sicilian socialist leader Lorenzo Panepinto, wrote: 'female figures showed their grief: the daughter of the mafia boss was surrounded by women from Saint Stefano, all dressed in their black shawls. They seemed possessed by some mysterious passion and screamed terrifically ... Vendetta was the word that came from all their mouths ... the widow repeated "Revenge him, revenge him" like a singsong'.[64]

In Calabrian tradition, women called '*periferiche*' had the task of mourning during the funeral.[65] Crying at the funeral where revenge was called for is central to the custom of vendetta.[66]

Based on his experience as Public Prosecutor in Calabria, Boemi maintains that women perform strong agency in the sector of vendetta. According to him: 'the woman is not a passive subject in the feud; she is an active subject. She is a subject who strongly calls for vendetta and she will be heard, because she is respected even though not part of the organisation'.[67]

Rosa N. told me about her female cousins in Calabria who, after a man in their family was shot dead by a rival clan, did not shed a single tear and stated: 'So they murdered him? Well, tomorrow they'll die.'[68] And, indeed, the suspected culprits duly disappeared a short time later.

In mafia contexts, the murder of a relative provokes not only sorrow but also shame. This is what Grazia felt when her brothers were murdered. In the early 1980s, Laura's brothers established control over a small town near Agrigento, in Sicily. Married to the boss of a clan allied with her brothers, Grazia was in touch with them while they were on the run. Her husband's clan first decided to abandon the brothers; but when they became an obstacle to the organization, it decided to kill them. By reorganizing her brother's clan and double-crossing her husband's family, she became one of the protagonists of the feud that took place in the town. Eventually she was arrested, yet she was never convicted since her involvement could not be proven.[69]

One of the greatest disgraces that must be redeemed through vendetta is betrayal by mafiosi who turn state's evidence. Mafia rules prescribe their assassination. The purpose of punishing the turncoat is both ideological and practical. The collaborator with justice, called derogatively *infame*, must be punished because he/she betrayed his/her mafia family as well as, quite often, his/her natural one, when the two coincide. Vendetta eliminates the shame of having an *infame* in the family, thereby regaining lost respectability. In practical terms, vendetta has a powerful deterrent effect in preventing others from collaborating with the state. The same reasons, retaliation and deterrence, might engender a so-called *vendetta trasversale* ('adjacent vendetta' or vendetta against the next of kin) entailing the murder of the relatives of the collaborators with justice. One of the cruellest cases in the history of Cosa Nostra was that of collaborator with justice Santino Di Matteo's son, Giuseppe, who in 1996 was strangled and dissolved in a vat of acid. Another tragic case involved the wife, mother-in law and sister-in-law of supergrass Francesco Mannoia, brutally executed in the mid-1990s.

According to the principle of *vendetta trasversale*, revenge will be carried out until the seventh generation of kinship of the person the vendetta is directed toward. Tommaso Buscetta lost a great number of relatives even a long time after his *pentimento*.

Through cross-cultural investigation, Blok registered the persistent use of vendetta in various regions of the Mediterranean, including Sardinia, Corsica, Montenegro, Albania, the Moroccan Rif, and among the Bedouin.[70] He observed that traditionally, people who have lost their honour occupy a difficult position in the community because they have to take revenge, in line with social expectations. As he explained:

> Plunged into mourning, these victims have all the features of people 'out of place'. They are avoided, excluded, ostracized – until they have taken revenge. Only after they have 'taken blood' (and thus removed their defilement) is their mourning over and can they be reincorporated into everyday social life. This often happened in a festive way and they feel, as they say, reborn and sanctified, having moved from shame to honour.[71]

This feeling is still widespread in mafia areas, where the shame of being betrayed by a relative is unbearable. From the testimonies of Rosa N.'s brother-in-law, the fact emerged that her Calabrian aunt was planning to kill her in order to wipe away with blood the shame of having a *pentita* in her family. Her aunt will keep mourning as long as Rita is alive. 'The period of vendetta is as long as the period of mourning.'[72] And the vendetta's execution follows a timetable in that it is carried out on the anniversary of the offence. This practice, called *calendarizzazione* (calendarization), is meant to remember the day of the event that caused dishonour. In symbolic terms, vendetta is a sort of ritual in memory of the dead, and thus it is executed on the anniversary or else a day symbolically linked to the original event.[73]

The task of remembering when revenge must be taken is a female one. Women are the guardians of family memory. The practical purpose of the custom of *calendarizzazione* is to display the ability to maintain one's commitment to the threat, thereby proving the family's power even after long periods of time.[74] According to a coroner from Messina, in charge of autopsies in the region of Reggio Calabria in the 1980s, the female relatives of mafia victims fought to gain access to the dead body of one of their relatives in order to count the number of gunshot wounds. They would then plan to inflict one wound more when the vendetta was carried out.

Women stimulate their men to commit revenge due to the necessity to eradicate the offence both in the past and the present. Magistrate Camassa reported that 'in the 1950s the mother of one of the Partanna family bosses, who was murdered in front of his house, ordered her son to commit revenge while his father's body was still warm'.[75] There have been cases of men committing revenge against their will only because women compelled them to do so. One of the most famous examples involves Serafina Battaglia, who in 1960 sent her son, in vain, to avenge the murder of his stepfather, shot dead in a mafia feud in the late 1950s. Serafina had entrusted the vendetta to her son, for whom she had procured a weapon and a bodyguard.[76] Every morning Serafina said to him, 'Get up, they killed your father! Get up and go kill them!'[77] He was not involved in criminal activities, but had to obey his mother's orders and was shot dead in 1962 before completing the mission that Serafina had given to him.[78]

Another instance of women putting pressure on men to extract revenge concerned the female relatives of a Cosa Nostra collaborator with justice, who told the Public Prosecutor that heard his testimony that his grandmother and aunts called him *infame* because he refused to avenge his father's murder. Eventually, he decided to please them.[79]

Female roles in the practice of vendetta show women's complicity in reinforcing hegemonic masculinity, to which all men belonging to mafia families are compelled to conform. By insisting on the male duty of taking revenge through violent deeds, women stress the expectations for men's virility, according to the type of gender behaviour established by the code of honour.

Recent evidence of women's active involvement in vendetta practices emerged from an investigative operation called '*Artemisia*', which in 2009 ended a bloody feud in Calabria. The conflict between two 'ndrine had started in 2006 in Seminara, a small village of 3,500 inhabitants on the plain of Gioia Tauro, in the province of Reggio Calabria.[80] Court records illustrate the significant role that women on both sides of the war played, in order to carry on the chain of revenge. These women belonged to different generations, confirming that vendetta is a long-lasting way of resolving problems between mafia groups. Phone conversations revealed everyday talks between women, focussing on deaths and vendetta actions, that the men of the family were to carry out, as much as on cooking recipes and doctor's appointments. These women do not seem intimidated. On the contrary, they showed an aggressive attitude and a desire to eliminate their adversaries, and they 'call to arms' all members of the family. For example, the Seminara 'ndrina *capobastone*'s wife, in the aftermath of the attack on her husband, called her daughter living in northern Italy and, with a threatening tone of voice, demanded she come back to Calabria, otherwise she would be disowned by the family:

> This is the last thing I will tell you... this morning we left for work and they shot at... your dad, but thank God they didn't get [him]; now your brothers are around. If you want to come, come; otherwise be aware that you will not have anybody else... without eating or drinking.[81]

When discussing the numerous recordings that show this familiarity and cultural acceptance of violent death advanced by conflict between 'ndrine, in his report the judge wrote: 'More than fear or sorrow for what has happened, those speaking, who are often women, only think about the next move: To avenge what happened'.[82] One of the women, after the attempted murder of her brother, protested against her relatives who were hypothesizing a possible reconciliation, stating that the bloody feud should not end and last until the seventh generation. The female relatives of the feud's victims not only did not report the killings or injuries to the police, but even offered conflicting and unreliable statements in order to set investigations on the wrong track. Justice for them was a private matter, which could compensated only by an act of revenge showing the will – as written in the order for custody – 'to exclude the state and its institutions from the dispute that they intend to solve with their barbaric methods'.[83]

Another town in Calabria that was quite recently characterized by mafia wars is Lamezia Terme. Until the 1990s, various 'Ndrangheta groups governed the territory peacefully. After the police intervened and some members of the families turned state witness, a war between two groups erupted. The first one became increasingly weak due to the criminal investigation called '*Medusa*' carried out in 2012. The second group exploited their adversary's difficulties and expanded its power until a series of police investigations – '*Chimera*' and '*Crisalide*' – confronted it.

One of the heads of the historical clan, composed of more families, was Lavinia, born in 1933.[84] According to the Prosecutor dealing with the judicial case, she was the 'instigator of vendetta practices'.[85] According to various collaborators with justice, she was driven by feelings of vendetta due to the death of three sons during the warfare. One of the members who used to belong to her group during the trial against the 'ndrina stated: 'This woman has always sworn a vendetta against the adversary family.'[86] In the prosecutor's statement, various collaborators with justice refer to episodes in which this woman sustained the decision to kill people in the enemy clan or supported relatives who committed acts of revenge. A collaborator with justice maintained that in the early 1990s he saw this woman burning the clothes of her relatives in the oven in order to conceal the proof of the assassination they had committed of a man, who had murdered her brother's son-in-law in a car accident. Another collaborator spoke of an episode in which she told him that they were waiting for a killer who was charged with committing a murder, and that this killer would have been supported by other women who had the task of monitoring the movements of the pre-designated victim. Despite the collaborators with justice's testimonies about her involvement in presiding over the homicides committed, the evidence was not sufficient to charge her with homicide.[87] However, as seems to be clear from the picture that emerges in the prosecutor's file, she did not stop the men of the family from committing revenge, yet actually she 'was animated by feelings of vendetta'.[88]

The will to strike their enemies for reasons involving revenge has driven women even to collaborate with justice. Serafina Battaglia, for example, given that her son failed to avenge his step-father and was murdered, took it upon herself to exact revenge by testifying against the people from her husband's rival clan, guilty of murdering her men. Called by the media 'the mafia widow', she attempted to commit vendetta by law.[89] She told everything she knew about the mafia from Alcamo, a Sicilian village, to judge Cesare Terranova. She testified at many trial hearings. However, in the end, after nine years of wandering among Italian courts, she never obtained justice. Indeed, many of the convicted mafiosi were acquitted for lack of evidence.[90] As Renate Siebert rightly commented, for this woman, 'unfortunately, justice did not show itself a valid alternative to a private vendetta'.[91] It must be added that Serafina showed great courage, because she conducted her battle before any witness programme existed.

Again, vendetta was at the core of Giacoma Filippello's testimony after her partner, Natale L'Ala, boss of Campobello di Mazara, a little town in Sicily, was murdered in 1990. His rivals had already attempted to murder him several times.[92] Giacoma described her feelings to journalist Francesco La Licata after her lover was killed:

> When they came and told me they had killed Natale, my eyes clouded over and my legs started to shake. I ran like a crazy woman: I found him in the supermarket in Campobello. They had made a mess of him. Twenty-five shots from a machine gun, every one a bullseye. They used Kalashnikovs because he'd had his car armoured and so they needed a gun that could shoot through the bullet-proof body. Excessive prudence. They'd surprised him, defenceless as a bird. He didn't even realise he was about to die. He was standing; he fell like a ripe fruit. I had expected it after the two earlier attempts. I knew that sooner or later the bad news would come. But I couldn't imagine the pain would be that strong. I hugged him; I kissed his forehead. I didn't cry; I didn't scream. I was made of stone. I felt there was a crowd behind me, but I didn't see anyone; I heard no voices. I saw his pistol, touched it; I took it and hid it under my jacket, right in front of everybody. And I left, with my head held high. I thought of avenging him right away. I said to myself then, 'If I see Don Alfonso, I'll shoot him in the mouth.' I saw neither Don Alfonso, nor the others that I was sure had done that massacre. I said, 'Those who must pay, will pay.'[93]

Significantly, Giacoma stated: 'Collaborating with the law was my vendetta.' These words showed that her testimony was in line with mafia principles. Thus, Giacoma

Filippello's agentic capacity of speaking out, as much as Serafina Battaglia's, revealed conservative features, since it was moved by one of the pillars of the mafia value system, that is, vendetta. Even the verbal expressions used by both women demonstrated their strong attachment to the vendetta culture. During one of the hearings of the trial concerning the people she accused, Serafina Battaglia said to the Alcamo boss: 'You drank Totuccio's blood and therefore I spit on you in front of God.'[94] In an interview with journalist Francesco La Licata, witness Giacoma Filippello told him that during the period before her partner, Natale L'Ala, a mafioso from Alcamo, was murdered, she stopped a man who was following them and said to him: 'If you touch a hair of my man's head I will come after that bastard your leader and rip out his heart out with my teeth.'[95]

A similar expression was used by the fiancée of Placido Rizzotto, the trade unionist murdered by mafioso Luciano Liggio, who stated after his murder: 'I will rip open the chest with my hands of the one who killed you and eat out his heart.'[96]

Anthropologists, examining the language of expressions referring to blood revenge, found sayings for threats and describing blood revenge similar to those used in mafia contexts, such as 'blood washes away blood', 'offences must be washed with blood' and 'vendetta is the best forgiveness'. Campbell, in his well-known work on a Greek community, reported they 'believe that in some way a killer absorbs the strength from the blood of the men he slays. "I shall drink your blood", is a phrase that threatens murder.' He also reported that 'one avenger bathed his hands in the blood of the original killer and returned to show his mother "the blood of her son"'. Blok observed that 'similar customs prevailed in Montenegro'.[97]

Finally, it is interesting to recall that some ritual practices exist in Calabria in relation to vendetta. For example, in Aspromonte women keep the clothes or tools of the murder victim in order to remind their sons they have to carry out revenge. Lombardi Satriani reported the case of a woman from Drapia (in the province of Catanzaro) who kept the jacket of her dead husband and gave it to her son, who was only a baby at the time. After many years, when the guilty person was out of prison and the son had grown up, the latter put on the jacket and took revenge. This shows that women teach men how to wait.

Through performing roles in vendetta practices, as much as in the process of indoctrination through education, women exercise what can be called 'soft power'. This notion is borrowed from international relations,[98] where it indicates the ability to get the outcomes you desire because of your cultural or ideological appeal, as opposed to hard power. Interestingly, 'Soft power uses a different type of currency (not force, not money) to engender cooperation – an attraction to shared values and the justness and duty of contributing to the achievement of those values.'[99] Here the concept serves for reading the female use of cultural tenets as arms for consolidating the ideology underpinning the mafia system. Thus, it refers to a power that is not exercised externally, as in Joseph Nye's model, but internally, within the basic nucleus of the organization, i.e. the family. Through their positive reputation, grounded on being the custodians of a family's honour, women exercise power as long as they are entrusted with transmitting mafia ideology and with the 'pedagogy of vendetta'.[100] Thereby they hold a significant control over their sons, daughters and nephews.

5

Compliant Agency: From Margins to Delegated Power

The drug trade

Since the 1970s, increasing drug consumption has modified criminal businesses in most European countries.[1] Criminal organizations have adapted their structures and modus operandi in order to respond to this increasing demand for drugs. In Italy, as seen in Chapter One, mafia organizations found it profitable to penetrate this market, which eventually contributed to their financial growth.

The expansion of this activity also led mafia groups to involve women in their criminal sphere. They considered it very useful to employ women for jobs related to drugs, since their female sex rendered them inconspicuous and less likely to be discovered by the police during transportation. Furthermore, drug trafficking entails activities that can be practiced at home, including packaging and hiding bags of drugs or receiving stolen goods.[2]

The international literature on female involvement in drugs underlines both victimization and empowerment, depending on the level at which women are inserted into the drug trafficking chain.[3] However, this different type of involvement depends on the context and the characteristics of the drug organization. In Italian mafia organizations it is common to find women involved in drug trafficking at various levels, namely as couriers, dealers and managers. In Cosa Nostra and the 'Ndrangheta, the top ranks of drug trafficking are still dominated by male figures, although there are cases of women leading drug distribution.[4]

Cosa Nostra

The Sicilian mafia's increasing interest in the drug business forced 'men of honour' to form new alliances and set up partnerships with 'ordinary' men, sometimes even neophytes. As part of this general increase in recruiting workers, mafia families started to employ even women. It was immediately evident that they were useful because of their inconspicuousness. Carrying bags of drugs was a particularly suitable job for women since they could conceal them by pretending to be pregnant or by rounding out their figures.[5] As early as the beginning of the twentieth century, women were used as couriers of illegal goods; certain women, called *femminote*, transported smuggled salt from Sicily to Calabria by concealing it beneath their wide black skirts.[6]

As mentioned above, other jobs related to small-scale distribution of drugs and those practicable in the household, such as repackaging drugs or receiving stolen goods, were particularly suitable for women.[7]

Evidence of the use of women in Cosa Nostra's drug trade dated back to the early 1980s. Journalist Marina Pino, in her pioneering book '*Le signore della droga*' (Drug ladies), narrated stories of women who were not initially part of the mafia but entered it by occupying the lower ranks of the drug chain.[8] Among these women there was a group of housewives from Torretta, a poor area near Palermo, who in 1982 were employed by the mafia organization to run drugs from Palermo to New York. Throughout their journey, the transported drugs were taped to their bodies and doused with perfume in order to deceive sniffer dogs.[9] These women were employed because police did not check them. The use of women due to their potential for hiding drugs was confirmed to me by one collaborator with justice, belonging to Cosa Nostra, whom I interviewed.[10] In the beginning he tended to avoid discussing this female involvement, because the use of women in these activities brought shame to the clan. Later, when I formulated these questions more indirectly, he ended up telling me stories of women carrying drugs or money. Moreover, he pointed out that they used women because they were unlikely to be body-searched by police.[11]

The women from Torretta wore bags containing heroin, tailor-made by a female dressmaker to be attached to the body. They were made 'of a thin plastic membrane inside, and outside a piece of cloth to soak up the body's sweat'.[12] After being loaded with drugs in a residence close to the airport, the housewife-couriers flew to New York where they delivered the heroin to a member of the organization who then, fifteen days later, gave them money to be transported via the same method as their outbound journey. For their part in the operation, the women were paid £12,500 (a high amount for the time).[13]

These methods of carrying drugs and money were inhumane; both wearing the bags and removing them were quite painful. More than once it was almost impossible to undress the couriers. One of them, on her return from the US, was put under boiling water because the bags had become so badly stuck to her body.

She was eventually freed but the boiling water caused serious burns.[14] Furthermore, these women were sexually abused by the men who prepared them for travel. As one of these men confessed to the Public Prosecutor: 'Before dressing them, I had sex with them.'[15] The same 'sexual procedure' occurred upon arrival in New York.[16] Investigations started with a tip-off, revealing the 'clever' way drugs and money were being transported. Then police arrested a male courier who told them most of the couriers came from Torretta and revealed who was the man in charge of loading the women with drugs.[17] The latter soon confessed his involvement, observing that the organization chose to employ women because 'the transport runs less risk if carried out by women.'[18] His words confirmed the suspicions aroused from an intercepted telephone call by the son of one of the housewives involved, saying: 'Mamma's going to America and she is going to bring back dollars.'[19] On 24 May 1986, she was arrested at the airport and, in 1988, charged with drug smuggling. In September 1992, journalist Clare Longrigg met her daughter, who justified her mother's actions by saying: 'We were in real financial trouble before my mother went to America. She did it for us, to give us a chance to study, and give us a better life.'[20]

Dwelling upon the details of these stories is intended to stress the victimization of women at the bottom of the criminal organization. All the women involved in the drug trafficking discussed above shared the common ground of being women from poor areas of Palermo and having many children, struggling to *'tirare fino alla fine del mese'* ('make it to the end of the month'). It is not surprising they took this chance to make money very quickly by accepting the work offered by the mafia. The analysis suggests we should see their experiences in the light of some of the theories elaborated by the Chicago School of Sociology (1920s–1960s), namely the 'anomie' and the 'different opportunity' theories. Robert Merton, father of 'anomie theory', also known as 'strain theory', borrowed the notion of anomie from sociologist Emile Durkheim. Merton used the term, meaning 'without norms', to explain a lawless social condition in which rules were relaxed. He felt American society during his period was in a state of anomie, as socio-economic changes occurred, leading to a new ideology grounded in money. As a result of this ideology, people desired to reach a high economic level and yet were unable to obtain it. This occurred because of a gap between the goals stimulated by society and means supplied by it. This situation was particularly true for the lower classes, which were disadvantaged in terms of educational and employment opportunities and forced to overcome great barriers in order to obtain social and economic success. Merton maintained that one of the responses to strain was employing 'deviant behaviour' whereby 'strained' people balanced their frustration. In other words, 'deviant behaviour results when people want to attain the socially accepted goals (financial success) but do not have the legitimate means to do so (a lucrative job)'.

Later, sociologist Albert Cohen applied the strain theory to the behaviour of lower-class adolescent males through observation. He noticed they dealt with the impossibility of meeting middle-class standards by creating an alternative culture (subculture) wherein they could reach a status and be accepted. Since they were excluded from the race to achieve the goals dictated by middle-class criteria of responsibility and acceptance, they used illegitimate means advocated by their subculture. Richard Cloward and Lloyd Ohlin's differential opportunity theory stemmed not only from Merton's work, but also from Sutherland's theory seen in the analysis of educational process in mafia families. Indeed, Cloward and Lloyd referred to the gap between goals and means and believed criminal behaviour was learned. Once lower-class boys encountered frustration due to experiencing the gap, they adopted behaviour that was influenced by the sort of illegitimate opportunities available in their community. Though Merton almost wholly overlooked the question, Cohen and Ohlin investigated female criminals in contrast with juvenile male criminals. They identified desires pertaining to women and men and regarded male criminality as the result of tension provoked by the frustration coming from the impossibility of gaining power, money and success. Society proposed male values and goals that did not concern women.

Later these theories were applied to female crime through a critical approach. As Ngaire Naffine pointed out referring to Cohen's observations: 'His characterisation of what is valued in American culture, he says, is the modus vivendi of the successful male, not the female. Autonomy, rationality, ambition and restraint with one's emotions are the attributes of the person who makes it in America, but the person is male.' As women were only devoted to the private sphere, they did not participate in the race for society's public goals. Consequently, they did not use illegal opportunities to reach them. Although the attention given to women by anomie/strain theorists might seem reductive, as underlined by feminist scholarship, since the few passing references to them were always in relation to male analyses, and women were studied only as the antithesis of men, these theories are useful in explaining why marginalized women are attracted by mafias and accept jobs in the lower level of these organizations. Theories that emphasize marginalization in understanding female crime are also extremely useful. The motivation behind the illegal actions carried out by the women mentioned above stemmed both from extreme financial needs and from experiencing a gap between the goals proposed by society and the means available to achieve them. Earning money through carrying drugs, a crime easy to commit because the victim is not visible and thus is perceived as less morally regrettable, was aimed at reducing the frustration coming from that gap. This was clearly demonstrated by the way they spent the money, which was not invested but rather used to buy superficial consumer goods advertised on television. One woman's statements expressing her need for money to pay bills and her wish for money to beautify the house is quite indicative of the intertwining between marginalization and anomie conditions. At the beginning of the interview with Marina Pino, she cried: 'I did what I did for my children and out of great financial need . . . When I was asked to do this service, I had just received an electricity bill for one million lire.'[21] Later she proudly said about her council house:

> When they gave it to us it was awful, walls, doors, windows, bathroom, kitchen, everything was bad quality, just like in all the council houses in this neighbourhood. We transformed it, because I always dreamt of a beautiful house, like the aristocrats have.[22]

Significantly, she concluded: 'God, what satisfaction and breath of fresh air, that money in the house,'[23] suggesting that the money earned, even if illegally, alleviated both frustration and necessity. There is no doubt that when a concomitance of poverty and societal exaltation of consumer goods exists, the dichotomy between means and goals become wider. Within such a state of anomie, it is not surprising that the mafia easily recruited workers, particularly in poor areas.

The experience of another woman, narrated by Pino, reflects at micro level this anomie condition produced from the macro context. She was a young Sicilian woman who wished to become a rock star, and in the late 1970s and the 1980s, performed in places such as night clubs, public dance-halls, piazzas, etc.[24] During one of these performances, she met a Sicilian-American drug trafficker who organized musical events in the US. He told her stories of glamorous people involved in the music industry. This attracted the woman, who believed that her long-awaited chance had finally arrived. Thanks to him, she produced a record and went on tour. Yet, the music production concealed a substantial narcotics-trafficking operation going from Palermo to Milan, and from Milan to New York. Drugs were transported hidden in boxes of vegetables during the first leg and in the woman's records on the last leg. When the smuggling ring was discovered, she was arrested and gave birth to a baby in prison. Eventually she was acquitted since there was insufficient evidence to convict her.

So far, we have seen women involved in carrying drugs. Now we turn to stories of drug dealers. Once again, the setting is a slum area of Palermo called the ZEN (*Zona di Espansione Nord* – Northern Expansion Zone), built in the 1960s during the so-called 'Palermo sack' and immediately occupied by people who had been made homeless by the 1968 earthquake. Composed of huge, dingy buildings with no services, it was used simply as a dormitory. In the 1980s, the ZEN was expanded; yet the project of renewing the area failed.[25] Female life in the ZEN was tough, as Marina Pino described in relation to the early 1980s. There were many cases of girls of thirteen or fourteen years of age who were compelled to stay at home and help their mothers mind the house, thereby experiencing a form of segregation they managed to interrupt only by running away with young men they eventually married and with whom they started having children.[26] In the 1980s, 80% of the Palermo drug market was located in the ZEN. Hence, it is not surprising that most of the families living there worked for the drug industry. Often the system of drug dealing was organized by mothers who got their numerous children involved.[27] The younger sons were in charge of acting as 'look-outs' and warning if *Beppe* ('police' in the family code) was arriving; the elder sons acted as a link between drug addicts and drug suppliers, by bringing the drugs to the customers from whom they collected the money; as a supplier, the mother held and prepared the drugs in her home. From the balcony, she lowered a basket containing the drugs and then pulled it back up to collect the money.[28] The entire drug business was organized by women, because the men were in prison or in some cases had been killed.[29]

These 'queens of ZEN', as the media called them, were captured in 1987 after much difficulty, since a wide network of neighbours and relatives protected their system of drug dealing.[30] As with the couriers discussed above, drug dealers living and working in the ZEN spent the money quickly 'for buying the kitchens advertised on television, tiling the bathroom like they had seen in television series, for achieving the appearance of a normal life'.[31] Again anomie and marginalization were at the root of their illicit action.[32] At the same time it is important to stress that women were actively part of the drug economy, showing that their involvement in the drug trade was the result of agentic abilities that were compliant with the organization.

Even women who led criminal groups working in the drug trade have shown compliant agentic aspects. The story of Angela Russo, gathered by Pino in the early 1980s, is emblematic. She was arrested in February 1982, along with her sons and daughters-in-law, at the age of seventy-four. She initially appeared to be a simple drug courier, exploiting her age and gender.[33] Afterwards, it became clear she was one of the leaders of a drug trade that involved members of important mafia families who were later sentenced in the 'maxi-trial'.[34] In the neighbourhood she was called '*nonna eroina*' ('grandma heroin'), and the press during the trial took up this nickname. The investigative evidence against her consisted of intercepted phone calls and the testimony of the youngest of Angela's sons, who denounced his companions as well as his mother, sisters, brothers and sisters-in-law. His collaboration with justice was punished with the murder of his brother Mario (*vendetta trasversale*), who was not involved in the criminal organization, unlike his wife, son and daughter.[35] Afraid of being murdered himself, he eventually withdrew his confession.

Coming from a mafia family, Angela Russo managed the drug trade by involving members of her family. Although the evidence put forward in the trial showed Angela was not a simple courier, and that she instead ran the operation, she denied the accusation, contending:

> So, according to them, I went up and down Italy carrying packages for other people. So, why would I, who in my life have always commanded others, have done this transport service for other people? These are arguments that only these judges that don't know anything about the law and life can sustain.[36]

Angela's mafia attitude emerges clearly from this claim of innocence. Interestingly, she was born in 1908 and her position is in contrast with the traditional image of women of her generation who are generally depicted as silent and unaware of their men's activities. In the interview with Marina Pino, Angela talked about her past: brought up like a man, she learnt from her father how to shoot and also the main mafia principles, which she then taught to her five children. The son who turned state witnesses and then retracted his testimony was the one most involved in their illegal family business. He was in charge of flying to Milan and Rome from Palermo, where Angela ran the drug operation from her house in the city centre. When the police discovered the trafficking and arrested the entire family, including four women coming from different generations, Angela played the poor old woman unaware of her son's activities and asked, 'Cocaine, what's that? A detergent?'[37] As mentioned above, Angela's role emerged from her son's confession, which confirmed her position of leadership, already clear from the taped conversations.[38] For mafia association and drug trafficking, Angela was sentenced to five years imprisonment that was commuted to house arrest because of her precarious health and age.[39] The following words show how deeply she believed in the mafia principles, instead of the state:

> God damn these cops, god damn these judges. Nowadays, the law does not exist anymore; they invent the law; they do what they want. These cops that get mixed up in everything; they don't know the truth; if they didn't have informers they

would not be able to do anything; they only investigate if they get a 'tip' and that becomes immediately Gospel, without asking who is talking, what's he saying and why is he saying it. And the same for the judges; these judges disgust me.[40]

By idealizing the mafia of the past, Angela showed the same attitude usually adopted by old mafia bosses when nostalgic for the 'good old mafia':

> ... once upon a time in Palermo there was the law. And this law did not kill a mother's innocent sons. The mafia did not kill anyone if they were not sure of the facts, really sure that it was the right thing to do, really sure of the right law. Of course whoever committed a sin *avia a chianciri* (started to cry), whoever is wrong has to pay, but at that time there was the rule of a warning. The person was warned at least three times: 'Be careful, because *sgarrasti* (you slipped up)'; then if the person kept being wrong and not right, of course he had to disappear and in fact they made him disappear ... At that time there was such a law and such a mafia. There were real men. My father, Don Peppino, was a real man and everybody trembled with fear in his presence, from Torrelunga and Brancaccio all the way to Bagheria.[41]

The family structure of the drug business has also been observed recently in a group that operated in Gela, in the province of Caltanissetta, that is dominated by the Stidda, an organization detached from Cosa Nostra and led by the Emanuello family. The operation *Donne d'onore* (Women of honour) coordinated by the Direzione Distrettuale Antimafia of Caltanissetta in 2017 showed that the more the business is run by groups based on the family, the more women are involved. A boss of the Emanuello clan and his prison companion entrusted their women (wife and fiancé) with managing the drugs' transportation (especially cocaine) and contacts with buyers. The boss' wife turned to her son, who had the task of going to the city of Catania and getting the drugs, to sell it locally through a number of pushers.[42]

The 'Ndrangheta

The Calabria mafia has also engaged women in the drug trade. Generally speaking, from the investigative work done by Prosecutors and law enforcement agencies it has emerged that women are aware of the drug activities carried out by the clan-family, and support them. However, they seem to be involved as little as necessary. Women in positions of leadership are exceptions. This is quite evident if we consider, for example, one of the largest investigative operations conducted in recent times: the 2018 'European 'Ndrangheta connection'. A joint team investigation involving prosecutors and police forces from Italy, the Netherlands and Belgium detected three mafia criminal groups trafficking great quantities of cocaine from South America to Europe. Also, investigators found out that the 'Ndrangheta clans invested illegal money in restaurants and bars both in Germany and Belgium. Out of ninety arrested individuals, three were women: one of them was from Naples and had a central function in the drug networking, yet she did not belong to the 'Ndrangheta; while the other two women were from the 'Ndrangheta, but were charged with crimes not related to drug trafficking. The first, Paola,[43] was charged for supporting her husband, the head of the 'Ndrangheta group, in avoiding the execution of his punishment (he had escaped from prison and lived hidden in his house supported by his family); and the second was charged with the crime of 'abusive exercise of financial activity'.[44]

Even considering from other police operations that have investigated the 'Ndrangheta's involvement in drug trafficking, female engagement in this sector seems to be limited to supporting roles.[45] On the one hand, women are not engaged in the drug sector's front line, but on the other, they are fully aware of the trafficking managed by their family, as has emerged clearly from both direct women's testimonies and from conversations intercepted by the police.

Paola, for example, was aware of the drug business that her family undertook with South American traffickers. This is clear from the fact that she, along with other relatives, showed 'concern for the seizure of material found at the fugitive's hideout, including a sheet indicating a Belgian name, telephone number and address in Colombia'.[46]

Some of the conversations registered during the 'European 'Ndrangheta connection' investigations show clearly that there were women participating in meetings in which their male relatives discussed how to manage international drug trafficking and the conflicts that had arisen among groups or members of the same groups. The girlfriend of the head's son, who was not charged with any crime, was actively present during family meetings in which her relatives talked about issues related to the drug trade. This is because drug trafficking was a common topic of discussion in the family, as much as other ordinary matters. Moreover, she intervened in the dispute between her boyfriend and her father. She tried to calm down her fiancé, who was furious because her father had not returned to him an amount of money he gave him for a batch of drugs, and thus did not want to meet him.

Not surprisingly, even her mother was aware of the trafficking carried out by the men of the family and her daughter's boyfriend. In fact, she acted as a mediator when a conflict between one of her sons and her 'son-in-law' broke out. In an agitated dialogue with his 'mother-in-law', he said: 'if he (her son) doesn't bring me 27,000 Euros, here, tomorrow, I'll cut his head off and throw it in the middle of the road'.[47] Worried about this threat, the woman tried to stimulate an agreement between the two men and during a conversation with both of them in December 2016, she suggested they overcome what they had said to each other by using the metaphor of wind, saying to them:

> Whoever wanted it wanted it, those are just words, blowing in the wind, words, among ourselves ... Later, if it involves ... if it involves people we don't know, people we don't know at all, words do not just blow around in the wind. Now, take the words the two of you have had, and let them blow in the wind.[48]

This way of facing internal problems, proposed by the mother, gives a striking insight into female efforts to keep the extended family united, despite it being characterized by aggressive relationships. She distinguishes between internal and external conflicts. In the first case, according to her view, it is necessary to go beyond offensive words, while in the second case words mattered and therefore it was necessary to act.

Paola, although she was not charged with crimes related to drug trafficking, played a crucial networking function, which proved to be useful for the drug trafficking of her family-clan identified in the European 'Ndrangheta Connection investigation. In 2007 she was detained in Messina Prison, where she developed a friendship with the woman from Naples who had a core role in the drug network arrested in the operation. Based on this friendship, the 'Ndrangheta clan established a business relationship with an influential woman who was able to connect different criminals, including mafiosi and drug brokers.[49]

Some of the women of the 'Ndrangheta groups controlling Lamezia Terme from the 1990s through to the 2000s were also aware of the drug trade carried out by the men of the family, insofar as they had the role of bringing messages from detained men to their companions. The wife of one of the heads of the Giampà family, and a collaborator with justice, described her involvement to magistrates:

> I met (my husband) when I was 16 years old and although I knew that he was the son of the so-called 'Professor' in fact I was not fully aware of what, at the time, was the criminal group Giampà and the 'Ndrangheta in general ...; obviously then with the passage of time I had the opportunity to see him who often wielded guns or dealt with 'cutting' narcotic substances, even in significant quantities, I began to realize the associative context in which I found myself living.[50]

She used to collect the money from the members of the group, who worked in the drug sector as dealers, couriers and pushers, and passed on the orders to their boss. One of the group's adherents, who after the arrest became a collaborator with justice, described how the communication system with his boss on drug issues worked:

> Other episodes that involve me concern the custody and subsequent sale of drugs. In particular the episode related to the custody of four packs containing about 10 kilos of Marijuana that G. had given me before his arrest. Subsequently I asked G., again through his wife who went to the prison visits, what I should do with the drugs. G. sent me the order to divide it between T.A., P.C., and C.P. Therefore, I delivered them one package each, equal to two kilos of drugs per package. Subsequently, the three guys delivered a total of about 15,000.00 to me on a few occasions. From time to time I delivered this money to (his wife). After some time she came to me.[51]

From the testimony of another woman who also collaborated with justice, it emerged that women are aware of the drug trafficking carried out by the men of the family. In 2010 this woman gave prosecutors important information about the Giampà group, in which her father and her brothers were involved from the early 1990s. During the interrogation she declared:

> I always saw . . . come to us, or I heard my brothers saying to each other that he . . . was the one who supplied them with drugs. My brothers who sold drugs were . . . When I had a shop, my brother . . . often came to us and told us that in case police officers came looking for him, my husband and I had to say that he had been there with us to bring bread with Peppone, namely with my husband.[52]

Then she specified: 'Near my brother's house there is land, which my family has appropriated, and on which there was a ruined building. My brothers went on that ground and hid grass, drugs and guns there.'[53]

It is rare to find examples of women leading drug trafficking in the 'Ndrangheta. One well-known case involves Maria Serraino, who was the head, along with her son Emilio Di Giovine, of an organization that trafficked drugs internationally. She belonged to a long-standing mafia family from the Reggio Calabria area,[54] and in the 1960s emigrated with her husband, Rosario Di Giovine, and her numerous sons and daughters, to Milan. Here she began her illegal career of smuggling cigarettes and receiving stolen goods.[55] During the 1970s, her trade shifted from cigarettes to drugs and weapons and involved the whole family. Her older sons, Antonio and Emilio, who dealt in stolen cars, helped to develop the drug trade from their contacts with foreign criminals, thereby transforming their small business into a huge international operation. The family trafficked not only drugs – including hashish, cocaine, heroin and ecstasy – but also arms, which were sent to Calabria where their relatives were involved in a feud that lasted from 1986 to 1991.

Three police operations, called *Belgio* from the name of the street where Maria's house was located, carried out by the DDA, Milan's Direzione Distrettuale Antimafia (Prosecutor office dealing specifically with cases of mafia crimes) in the early 1990s, coordinated by Public Prosecutor Maurizio Romenelli, led to her arrest and to the imprisonment of almost all members of the clan. The investigations relied on wiretapped conversations, arrests of people caught red-handed, seizures of drugs, money and documents, testimonies from collaborators with justice, international requests, and autonomous investigations by criminal offices from other regions.[56] Maria, charged with mafia association and murder, was sentenced with life imprisonment.[57]

The clan exercised military control over the area around *Piazza Prealpi*, a square in the northern periphery of Milan. According to Maria's son-in-law, who became a collaborator with justice, the square was Maria's *feudo* (fiefdom) and her home in Via Belgioioso was the headquarters of the illegal operations. She was particularly charismatic, to the point where she was able to employ many women living in their neighbourhood. She offered them jobs, including storing drugs and weapons in their houses, and offering their houses and phones, which were free from police taps, to organize meetings.

Women were inspired to do these jobs due to the good, easy money, which enabled them to buy goods such as motorbikes for their sons.[58] As with the women from Torretta, their experience might be read through the theories of marginalization and anomie, able to analyse the behaviour of women who, not linked to the mafia through familiar bonds, participate on the lower level of its activities.

The other central operation of the international organization was located in Spain and managed by Maria's son Emilio,[59] who organized narcotics operations between Morocco and England and across the Atlantic from Colombia to Milan. Not surprisingly, he was wanted by the police worldwide.

Maria shared her power with her son Emilio. However, she showed an independent authority over the clan's affiliates. This emerged clearly from a conversation between Maria and one of the criminal group's companions in relation to a drug delivery:

> I don't know what the fuck my son is doing ... because he told me that you have ... you have to organise everything. Now, you are doing it ... but don't fuck with me, if I cancel out Emilio, for me he is done for, because I am already pissed

off ... with my own fucking problems ... you are taking care of your fucking business ... I am the one, me, who has to come when you unload ... I am the one who has to come watch my own fucking business.[60]

The tone of the way in which she spoke to this soldier is indicative of the strong attitude she showed in the criminal sphere, which derived from her personality and from belonging to a traditional and powerful mafia family. Her surname, Serraino, provided her with a sort of 'mafia licence', since the family was considered 'respectable' in the criminal environment. Despite this, she had to share leadership with her son. Even though she had a strong character and was able to exercise real power, she needed her son in order to maintain relationships with other criminal groups. The testimony of a collaborator with justice whom I interviewed is interesting in this sense. As the boss of the neighbouring clan, he had to deal with Maria's organization. In the account he gave me, he stressed, not only in words but also with facial expressions, his irritation in dealing with Maria about mafia business because she was a woman.[61] There is no doubt that to be respected in the mafia criminal field one must be male. This would suggest that women in positions of leadership must always be supported by a male relative. As will be explored later on, women cannot play an authoritative role unless it is supported by or delegated to a male boss.

Economic crimes

By expanding the illegal trade in geographical and quantitative terms, mafia organizations, including Cosa Nostra and the 'Ndrangheta, accumulated so much illegal wealth that they needed to launder it. This was often achieved by investing money in legitimate companies registered under dummy names, which often belonged to women since they were unlikely to be investigated.[62] The role of the figurehead was thus typically female, as most of prosecutors I interviewed pointed out.

The reality of female involvement in the economic sector started to emerge following the approval of the so-called 'Rognoni-La Torre law' in 1982. This law not only defined the characteristics of mafia association, but gave investigators a useful instrument with which to investigate the mafia's methods of investing illegal money. In other words, investigators could seize proprieties registered under clean names yet suspected of belonging to a mafioso. When women are used for illegal financial operations, they are often aware of the fact, as Prosecutor

Teresa Principato pointed out: 'It is impossible for them not to know the provenance of the money or what such companies are for.'[63]

Even by simply taking a quick glance at the newspapers, it is common to find examples of women's names in companies acting as a cover for mafia activities.[64]

The criminal investigation called *Gemini*, from the initials of Gela and Milan, and carried out in the early 1990s discovered a mafia clan of the *Stidda* that continuously transferred people from Gela, a mafia town in the heart of Sicily, to the outskirts of Milan, between San Donato and San Giuliano. The media called this criminal organization the '*mafia rosa*' (pink mafia), as many women were involved. One of them was Chiara,[65] who played a role in the real estate business managed by her boyfriend, who was a member of the Stidda. In 1993, the couple moved from Gela to San Giuliano, as a consequence of the expansion of the mafia's business into northern Italy carried out by the main Stidda group, the Emmanuello family. The Public Prosecutor for this case told me that Chiara was only seventeen years old when her boyfriend registered in her name various flats used by members of the organization for their illegal activities.[66] Chiara's sisters-in-law were in charge of the accounting for the income of the criminal organization and sometimes also investing it.[67]

Even in the Serraino-Di Giovine clan, investing money was entrusted largely to women, in particular to Marisa Di Giovine.[68] The latter was the daughter of Emilio Di Giovine and an English woman, who moved with Marisa to England in order to offer her daughter a childhood and adolescence far from criminal contexts.[69] Marisa, however, when she was eighteen years old, decided to move back to Italy, where she joined her father's criminal organization, becoming a financial mediator in order to launder the income from drug and weapons trafficking. Marisa's financial role was confirmed not only by her bank documents, but also by testimonies given by various collaborators with justice. They described her financial activity and specified that enormous amounts, constituting profits from hashish trafficking, were consigned to her and deposited in an account in a Geneva bank where Maria also had an account showing large transactions.[70] Since the judges took into consideration her youth and psychological dependence on her father, Marisa was charged only with mafia association and sentenced to six years' imprisonment.

The other woman playing a financial role in the Serraino-Di Giovine clan was the wife of one of Maria Serraino's sons. Not only she was involved in the activities of the Serraino-Di Giovine family, but she also managed the bar where 'Ndrangheta members used to meet and organize their major operations. The woman received cheques coming from Italian-American drug deals as the holder of an account in Switzerland and ultimately became the owner of a large real-estate portfolio, valued at nearly fifty million euros, which included shopping centres, houses and shops.[71]

In Cosa Nostra, the wife of the accountant for Cosa Nostra's bosses between the 1970s and early 1990s was apparently involved in her husband's affairs with the criminal organization.[72] Having gained a degree in accounting, in 1971 the woman started to collaborate with her husband in his office, frequently visited by mafia protagonists in the drug trade of the 1970s and '80s. These included Badalamenti, Liggio, Madonia and Vernengo. Mafiosi at large could use a number of properties owned by the accountant's companies.[73] Moreover, the accountant created front companies on behalf of mafiosi who thereby could participate in public bids, which eventually were granted owing to Mandalari's political links (thanks to his membership in the Freemasons). In 1974, the accountant was forced to change his residence for a while (under the programme known as *soggiorno obbligato*) because his activities were under suspicion. Afraid of further investigations, he registered front businesses in his female relatives' names, including his mother-in-law, who was probably unaware that he was using her name. This was not the case with his wife, who was her husband's *factotum*, as various collaborators with justice, previously clients of the accountant's office, told Public Prosecutors. Moreover, she held important positions in numerous companies linked to the mafia.[74] The public prosecutor who dealt with Mandalari's judicial case told Clare Longrigg that the accountant's wife:

> was always there in the office while clients came and went ... She is on the board of a number of companies. If you are on the board you have to know what's going on. It is possible for someone to be on the board in name only but this is very unlikely in this case. We put taps on their phones and found out that she knows her husband's mafia clients and his politician friends personally; when they rang up and he wasn't there, she was always in a position to give them an answer or make a decision. Her role in the firm is the same as his: she knows that you have to do the accounts in a certain way to make it look as though the money has followed certain channels.[75]

From this description it is clear that she was not simply a figurehead, acting as a front on company documents. Her case tells us that female financial involvement becomes more sophisticated when women are well prepared, and that the mafia system soon took advantage of the progress made in education by women. However, the evidence was not sufficient to prove her involvement and thus condemn her. Charged with mafia association, she was later acquitted.

Another interesting example of a woman financially involved in Cosa Nostra concerns the daughter of Giuseppe Lipari, Bernardo Provenzano's lieutenant. In the 1990s most of Provenzano's business revolved around health-care investments. Lipari contributed mostly to building publicly controlled local health offices. While officially a surveyor for ANAS (the Italian motorway company), he was actually an entrepreneur and financial consultant to the head of Cosa Nostra.[76] Journalist Salvo Palazzolo discovered a crucial report (the Corleone *Carabinieri*'s report against Gariffo et al.), which enabled him to understand Provenzano's business. The report, drafted in 1984, gave many details and names in the new mafia business carried out by Provenzano's group. The importance of this report was underestimated by experts and investigators, who neglected it even though it warned: 'We are facing a monopoly ... created by companies seeking to grab bigger and bigger slices of a profitable market given the high cost of modern hospital equipment.'[77] The report also alluded to the role of women in the financial management of this business. Therefore, we can maintain that the mafia as renewed by Provenzano was pioneering not only because it undertook new types of business, but also because it used women at a time when they would not be suspected. For example, Giuseppe Lipari's daughter, who was a lawyer, played a central role within the ranks of Provenzano's organization,[78] as underlined in the *Carabinieri* report:

> The person under investigation (Lipari's daughter), as far back as 1984, managed numerous companies of the Provenzano group and, hence, was one of the main interlocutors in phone calls from and for the related businesses of the mafia association ... .[79]

Indeed, she had close relationships with relevant Provenzano's figureheads, who were pleased to be in touch with a woman and lawyer, rather than with offenders, like Giuseppe Lipari. Her sex and profession meant that she was above suspicion and this reassured the figureheads of Cosa Nostra.[80]

Prosecutors depicted her financial role as follows:

> This lawyer ... in close collaboration with her father, was in charge of collecting, keeping and distributing profits from the management of goods and activities traceable to the fugitive Provenzano and the Corleonesi. She often managed these goods on behalf of her father.[81]

There is no doubt that the growth of mafia wealth, and the corresponding need to invest money coming from illegal operations, opened up job opportunities for women beyond the traditional roles they played in the private sphere, such as transmitting mafia values and encouraging vendetta. These women demonstrated that were aware of their function and position. In relation to a meeting with a figurehead, Lipari's daughter, for instance, 'was not a mere intermediary who took care of organising meetings maybe without knowing what they were for. On the contrary, she was very aware of the fact that during those summits with D. M. (the figurehead) the latter collected … money belonging to the Corleonesi.'[82] Moreover, from another conversation 'it was clear that the woman herself ordered, even contrary to her father's will, that nothing was to be given to …, who had already received 40 million lire on 17 July 1999'.[83]

This new female participation, however, was not matched by progress in women's condition, because they tended to remain dependent on their men and controlled by the entire family.[84]

To illustrate the simultaneous presence of new female roles and enduring male dominance and bonding, it is worthwhile to consider the story of the sister of Giuseppe and Filippo Graviano, Cosa Nostra members sentenced in the early 1990s for the murder of Padre Pino Puglisi and terrorist attacks carried out in 1993. Since Nunzia spoke English, was computer literate and could travel abroad easily, her brothers used her, during their detention, to protect their money from seizures by investing it in international circles.[85] The brothers charged their sister with the task of:

> overseeing the shareholding portfolio, distributed among various banks and owned under various cover names, containing shares in companies including Mediaset, Mondadori, Seat-Pagine Gialle, Merloni, Eni, Fiat, Amga, Pirelli, Montedison, etc.[86]

In the judicial file she is described as 'a point of reference and decision-maker, alongside her imprisoned brothers in managing and investing the assets of the Brancaccio mafia family and the other illicit business carried out by the family'.[87]

Being the 'treasurer' of the group, she recovered and distributed sums of money to members of the clan. She established relations with the figureheads used by the family, property sales, and the video poker business. With this income she was able to cover various expenses, including, as emerged from a conversation she had with the family lawyer, the salaries of the associates and the maintenance of her sisters-in-law.

To carry out her 'financial duties', Nunzia Graviano moved to Montecarlo, where she developed a relationship with a Syrian man. A letter from prison showed that her brothers objected to this relationship: 'What kind of religion does he believe in? There are some traditions that you know very well … I am

Sicilian, you are Sicilian.' Eventually, she split up with the Syrian man.[88] This underlines the fact that even an apparently self-confident woman, like her, who met people at an international level, had to give up her individuality in order to comply with the male rules of her family.[89] The contradictions emerging from her experience provide an interesting contribution to issues related to the persistence of patriarchal mechanisms in contemporary society.

The role of treasurer is still entrusted to women in today's Cosa Nostra, during a negative period for the group due to the measures taken by law enforcement, as in the case of Graviano's group. Patrizia Messina Denaro, for example, after the arrests of some relatives in March 2010 as part of operation *Golem II* – as written in the judicial files – 'intervened repeatedly and with a certain authority to resolve the issues relating to the management of the mafia family's cash even while apparently having no authority to dispose of the income of the companies attributable to the same family'.[90]

In the 'Ndrangheta's traditional division of labour, women are often in charge of keeping the family cash. The 'Califfo 2' investigation, carried out in 2012, found that the so called '*bacinella*', the cash of the group, was entrusted to the oldest women of the Pesce family.

Evidence shows that women are even involved in the mafia's main economic crime, extortion. Twenty years ago, the women of one of the most important 'Ndrangheta groups, the Condello-Imerti, were charged for running the activities of the clan, including racketeering.[91] Police discovered the Condello's activity by intercepting phone calls between a woman and her husband who was the boss of the clan. She was tried and sentenced to fourteen years in prison for mafia association and extortion of money from legitimate business on a regular basis.[92] Racketeering was one of the main criminal activities run by the woman and her sister: 'When a new commercial business opened, they contacted the owner and dictated the terms of payment, then they made their monthly rounds to pick up the money.'

The boss himself recognized that women were frequently better at this job than men, since they could make threats without the use of arms.[93] The point underlined by the boss is illuminating in understanding the nature of female power in a violent environment, such as the mafia, where physical strength is a fundamental feature. Women could run extortion rackets because this did not necessarily involve the immediate use of violence, but only the threat of it. In other words, women could intimidate people by threatening male violence if they did not receive the protection money.

More recently, female participation in the extortion sector managed by 'Ndrangheta groups emerges quite clearly from the *Medusa*, *Chimera* and

Crisalide investigations, that hit the 'Ndrangheta groups governing the territory of Lamezia Terme. This geographical area is quite economically productive compared to other parts of Calabria. The 'Ndrangheta has exploited this feature by demanding money from shops and by forcing entrepreneurs to employ members of the mafia groups.

The extortion business was shared by two groups of clans until 2000, including the Gianpà, Torcasio, Cerra and Gualtieri families. However, with the eruption of the wars between the Gianpà and the other families the peaceful management of racketeering ceased. The women of both formations were quite active in carrying out the extortion against the town's shops.[94] They took the goods they wanted from the shops without paying for them or with a 50% discount. Their threat was implicit. A collaborator with justice recalled this modus operandi carried out by women from the Giampà groups, explaining that:

> shopkeepers cannot refuse to give discounts to these women because they know that they are dealing with women from the Giampà's clan who have the habit of picking up goods from the shops leaving the account open by telling the shopkeepers that their husband will come for the payment.[95]

I identified similar female practices in Sicily twenty years ago while carrying out my doctoral research. I interviewed a high level fashion store owner in Palermo, who told me that every month she received a visit from two mafia women, mother and daughter, dressed in the best Italian designer clothes. During their visits, they took all the dresses they wanted without paying, but above all asked for the mafia tax.

Some of the women of the Gianpà groups also collected money from their companions engaged in the extortion branch of the criminal group. Interestingly, during a prison visit, the wife of the leader complained to her husband because the companions had delivered the extortion money to her mother-in-law rather than to her. Thus, the husband wrote a message in which he ordered that the money be given to his wife and not to his mother.[96] The woman's behaviour showed her willingness to be part of the system and take care of important aspects of the mafia organization, namely those related to finance.

Generally speaking, female engagement in racketeering demonstrates that the active participation of women in the mafia is highly ambiguous. Women who dealt with extortion were not exploited, as was the case seen above with women employed at the bottom of the organization. On the contrary, they wanted a way to show their power, even though it stemmed from being the relatives of mafia bosses.

The mafias' expansion into the financial sector has necessarily required the organizations to use professionals, especially accountants and lawyers. This is particularly true in new areas of expansion, such as northern Italy, where the social capital of mafiosi is more scarce compared to the areas where the mafia is traditionally established. Women, too, have figured among the professionals supporting mafia businesses, and the case of one accountant is exemplary in this sense.[97] The woman, from Reggio Emilia, was totally at the disposal of one of the heads of the 'Ndrangheta group that colonized the territories of Emilia Romegna. In the judicial file related to her case, it is written that she offered:

> consulting for the businesses managed by the *cosca*, introducing the mafia members to other financial operators, even participating on their behalf in meetings for managing the affairs of the *cosca* both in Emilia and in other regions of Northern Italy (above all Veneto and Lombardy).[98]

The magistrate underlined that:

> she was fully aware and willing to make a contribution to an organized group belonging to the 'Ndrangheta (whose associative and operational dynamics she learned in detail) and also sought professional affirmation for herself, externally exploiting this relational capacity as a resource.[99]

The use of services provided by educated women who are not family members is indicative of the mafia's new outlook in terms of gender ideology. This emerges not only from the case mentioned above, but also from a recent case regarding a criminologist who had a significant role in the communication system of the 'Ndrangheta group. She could perform this function thanks to her profession, which gave her the possibility of coming into contact with imprisoned bosses.

In conclusion, it is worth underlining that the mafia has used women since the 1970s, the time when they became more educated and more free to move compared to women of previous generations. Mafias employed them in skilled labour related to the financial sector, as their professional profiles were suitable for new jobs that emerged as a consequence of the need to launder money. The expansion into new areas of activities created new 'opportunities' for women, similarly to what occurred in the legitimate labour market as a consequence of the process of the economy's tertiarization. Moreover, the increasing breakdown of gendered barriers in society partly eliminated prejudices towards women's capacity and ideological obstacles to women's access to criminal activities. Female involvement in economic crime can be read through the lens of Rita Simon's theory that links increasing female participation in crime to the process of female emancipation. She supported the emancipatory theory in relation to the increase in property crimes by women.[100] In her view, this was a consequence of changes in the status of females, including an increase in labour-force participation, education, professions and income. Other scholars contradicted this theory by underlining that the kind of property crimes in which women were becoming more involved were committed by women who had not participated in the liberation process, but were a result of the increasing 'feminization of poverty'. Thus Simon's thesis might be valid only for explaining the increase in white-collar crime, a typical offence deriving from new occupational opportunities. The type of participation analysed in this section, in some circumstances, requested skills and agentic capacities that women have conquered through the feminist revolution. This does not automatically indicate that the women involved in mafia-related economic crimes have achieved equal opportunities with men, nor autonomy. Yet, what we might sustain without objections is that the female emancipation process has had an impact on mafia groups, which are part of society and as such are influenced by the practices seen in the environment in which they flourish.

From Hermes tasks to leadership positions

Couriers of words

In mafia associations, members follow the law of silence to avoid leaking secret information. At the same time, communication cannot be eliminated, especially during mafia wars and when the bosses are under investigation. Therefore, mafias have developed various systems of communication: from the most basic one, passing news from mouth to mouth or through small notes transferred from one person to another (the so-called *pizzini*), to more sophisticated methods, using new information technology, especially non-traceable social media.[101] The first methods are considered more reliable and practicable in cases of communication from prison, and in making them work women are crucial. This is because they are allowed to visit their male relatives in prison. Most of the criminal investigations that have detected female participation in the mafias, including Cosa Nostra and the 'Ndrangheta, have identified women carrying out Hermes tasks, i.e. bringing so-called '*ambasciate*' (messages).

When I interviewed Rosa N. in 1998 she described this role to me, emphasizing that it was typically female. She attributed the reasons for this women's task to the warfare between clans, which occurred in Calabria in the late 1980s and compelled men to stay hidden, and also to the police actions that led to male members of the organization being imprisoned.

In the past, investigators tended to exclude the prospect that even relatives of bosses on the run might be in touch with fugitives, because of the widespread belief, both popular and judicial, that women were unaware of their men's activities. Only in the last twenty years have people seriously considered that women see their men while they are on the run. In this sense, Salvatore Boemi maintained that 'women are the umbilical cord of any fugitive ... if the women of fugitives in Calabria were followed more, we would have fewer fugitives'.[102] Supporting a fugitive is quite an important role, as much as being a courier, because it permits bosses at large to have a safe environment, which facilitates them in carrying on with their illicit activities. The Pelle house, for example, where Antonio was hidden, was equipped with a video surveillance system. His wife and sons obsessively checked the monitors of the video cameras, in order to be sure that were no people around the house. The wife's task, basically, was to protect her husband in order to avoid him being captured by police.[103]

The women of the Giampà family played a crucial role during a period in which the group went through difficult times due to the war against their ex-allies and the effectiveness of police investigations. As emerged from the trial following the *Medusa* investigation, these women acted as '*portalettere*', carrying letters from prison to outside. They collected the messages from the bosses in prison, including Francesco Giampà, nicknamed 'The Professor', and his son Giuseppe, known as 'The President', and delivered them to their companions. One collaborator with justice underlined that 'Giuseppe, in his decisions, always had to account to his father, who directs him and gives him orders from prison, including prison talks with his family, in particular his daughter or his wife'.[104] Women, thus, were at the core of the circle of information going from Francesco Gianpà to his son Giuseppe and vice versa. The judge defined these women as the '*collante*' (glue) between the detained bosses and their men outside. The messages covered many topics, some of which were quite intricate.

Sometimes, some messengers also intervened, expressing their opinion and showing a determined attitude in maintaining their beliefs. The episode of the conflict between Giuseppe Gianpà and his uncle is very relevant for grasping the deep female involvement in mafia affairs, in which criminal business overlaps with family relationships. In November 2011, Giuseppe's sister visited her brother in prison. In that circumstance she communicated the content of the conversation between their father and mother during a prison visit regarding the clash between

Giuseppe and his uncle over the management of extortion activities. Talking with Giuseppe, she underlined that their father had stated to their mother that her brother was 'fucking everything up'. She said: 'he said that you have to stop talking loosely'. Moreover, she recommended that he calm dawn, underlining that 'the family must be united'. And then she reproached and blamed him for the dispute with their uncle. According to her, their uncle had never betrayed them and Giuseppe was wrong, because he did not give him the opportunity to explain himself and clarify his point of view. She underlined his difficult character: 'Shut up, now ... you know what your problem is? When you have a dispute with a person you do not talk with them, as instead you should have before they arrested you. You can see that certain things would not have happened'.[105]

Also she blamed her brother for trusting people that would 'stab him in the back' and for being too interested in money. In her view, the family was more important than money.

She showed a moralist attitude, saying that even if a person is wrong you should not turn your back on them: 'whatever you do, do you think I'm going to turn my back on you? You must be kidding!' At this point Giuseppe replied, saying: 'but this problem ... you're talking about it now? It's always been here, for ten years, what can I do?' Giuseppe kept inveighing against their uncle and, as a reaction, his sister blamed him for destroying everything: 'you have destroyed this, it's your fault'. Giuseppe insisted on blaming their uncle for taking some money coming from extortion. She was disappointed, regretting the fact that in their family the problem had always been that one member clashes against the other: 'you know what the problem is, it's always been the problem of this ... "family", they've always tried to screw each other over'. Then she asked her brother to put aside all their disagreements: 'since we are unable to speak, let's put everything aside, when it's time to discuss it we will, but now let's put everything aside, let's put a stone over these words and our past discussions and let's move on'. Giuseppe agreed with his sister's proposal, with the condition that their uncle had to behave correctly: 'he has to do things like a Christian', meaning that their uncle should behave correctly. He agreed with his sister about the need to make peace in the family. In the end she made a declaration of intense fidelity towards her brother stressing the value of blood relationships:

> You never needed money, you can take my money, I don't give a shit, okay? Okay? For example, if you were greedy and wanted something from me, I wouldn't care, because I've always loved you, I always come to see you, whatever you need I'll always be there, you know what I mean? Because you are my family and my blood, if you treat me badly I will not hold a grudge against you.

She promised that she would talk personally with their uncle in order to facilitate a resolution of this conflict.

Moving to Cosa Nostra, it is useful to illustrate the case of Lipari's daughter, already mentioned in the previous section.[106] Not only did she make an economic contribution to Cosa Nostra, but she also enabled her father to communicate with the mafia organization from prison. Angelo Siino, an important collaborator with justice, called by investigators Cosa Nostra's 'minister of public works', during an interrogation in 1998 said: 'I kept in touch with Lipari through his daughter, ... the lawyer.' The trial documents described her as an essential link between her imprisoned father and the mafia association. The woman was his means of delivering '*pizzini*' (notes) to Cosa Nostra boss Bernardo Provenzano. Not only his daughter, but all family members helped Giuseppe maintain his relations with Cosa Nostra. Trial sources documented this function for Giuseppe Lipari's wife: 'She was the link between her husband, Giuseppe Lipari (as the principal subject administrating Corleonesi assets), fugitive from justice Bernardo Provenzano, and other affiliates and members of the organisation at large. Thereby, she permitted the communication and exchange of news concerning the management of the mafia group's illegal activities.' However, unlike her brother and mother, his daughter's role as a link was special since she was not only Giuseppe's daughter but also and very significantly his lawyer. As the magistrates explained, 'The woman, in fact, as opposed to her brother, who was more suited to unskilled labour, by exploiting her background of legal knowledge and experience gained during her career as a lawyer, ended up making an incomparable contribution to her father's illegal activities.' Being his lawyer, she had preferential access to her father-client who could safely pass her his notes. Therefore, 'by taking advantage of her professional mandate and the relative secrecy given to defence lawyer activities, she often hid whatever her father asked her in the legal folder she brought during the prison meetings, thus bypassing prison controls'. In the transcripts of the electronic surveillance tapes recorded in prison, many episodes appear in which she:

> showed her role as letter carrier for correspondence between Giuseppe Lipari and Bernardo Provenzano. In fact, this woman, via the fully functional folder for trial documents, managed to carry the missives written in prison by her father to the fugitive and, vice versa, bring back the replies from Provenzano.

Therefore, 'defence attorney meetings were obviously the moment when Giuseppe Lipari exercised his administrative activities for Cosa Nostra thanks to the compliance of his daughter'. Even though she played an active role as a criminal when her father was free, it became all the more crucial when he was in prison. As mentioned briefly in the previous section, these documents emphasized that she had always worked for the organization:

> Ms. Lipari's role was not strictly limited to the period of emergency caused by the imprisonment of her father, who could not therefore operate personally. In fact, the woman had already done everything possible in administrating *Corleonesi* assets since as far back as 1984.

Many points in the trial documents stress that she was involved in the organization not only during periods of emergency. However, during difficult times, namely when her father was in prison, her roles and tasks increased.

Women carry messages not only from/to imprisoned bosses, but also from/to those who are in hiding. Despite the huge investigative apparatus involved in the search for Matteo Messina Denaro, he was able to communicate from the places where he was hidden through people close to him. One of his communication enablers was one of his sister who was arrested in 2013 following the investigative operation named *Eden*. She was video-intercepted while talking with her husband during prison visits. In one of these, her husband wanted her to ask her brother whether he had given permission to his own figurehead, who was in prison, to collaborate with justice as a strategy to save the boss' assets; and if not, whether he could beat him. She took these questions to her brother when she met her. Then, a few days later, she went to visit her husband in prison with Matteo Messina Denaro's responses:

> **Woman** No one can touch him! Leave him alone ... he says
>
> **Husband** So, he's right?
>
> **Woman** No, he might do even more harm! More ... ten times ... Husband nods.
>
> **Woman** ... A disaster. He's not right ... he's not right ...
>
> **Husband** Of course!
>
> **Woman** So, if anyone asks you, you have to say: 'leave him alone.' He said ... tell Enzo to get together with him, ... I said to him: 'don't exaggerate.'
>
> **Husband** And put him?
>
> **Woman** With you ... (laughs)
>
> **Husband** They're not going to put us together!
>
> **Woman** I told him: "Just listen, I'd love to, ... but don't exaggerate" (laughs)...[107]

According to the investigators, she saw her brother to get the information her husband needed. This detail, which was very important for the investigators searching for this fugitive, emerged from the fact that, while talking with her husband, she used expressions like 'he said', 'he listened to me' and 'I said to him'.[108]

From the above conversation it is clear that the sister was not a mere messenger. She contributed with her own views, almost placing herself on the same level as her brother. She contradicted him when he proposed that her husband share the jail cell with the figurehead to avoid the risk that other mafia companions in prison beat him. She did not agree with the solution proposed by her brother, considering it an 'exaggeration'.[109]

The prosecutor also proved her role in extortion activities and her underlying threatening attitude, a sign of her capacity to employ mafia methods, as delineated in article 416bis:

> she employed methods in imposition entirely similar to those used in this area by the criminal organisation known as Cosa Nostra. She did so with great skill, giving her intimidations that peculiar force, that leads to increased pressure and coercion, which is objectively part of the operational method typically used by mafia-related criminal associations.[110]

Her contribution was very important, elicit heavy responsibilities, insofar as 'it was meant to ensure her brother maintained an undisputed top position ... and was guaranteed operative capacity, giving him the same timely and full knowledge of the issues interesting the mafia association as well as the exercise of the prerogatives of evaluation and decision related to his recognized top position'.[111]

There is no doubt that in her case, on the one hand her family of origin heavily conditioned her life, while on the other she was ready to assume the role and tasks the family attributed to her.[112] Watching the video of the conversation between the woman and her husband during the prison visit mentioned above, it is not difficult to grasp the complexity of her experience. From the profile illustrated in the judicial file, it is quite evident that the woman was determined and clever in using the secret code based on conventional gestures and words, and endorsed the criminal aims of her family. However, it is not possible to explore the intimate and personal side of her life and feelings. We might try to trace a more complete picture of her by reading the images of the video showing her speaking with her husband. Here, it seems that she was a stressed and tired woman, weighed down by her role and tasks.

Both in Cosa Nostra and in the 'Ndrangheta, the function of transmitting messages makes a great contribution to the continuity of the organization, since it allows the heads of the clan to maintain their positions and their power.

In the Giampà family, the procedure of transmitting messages through women allowed the bosses of the group to keep giving orders and thus maintain their authority intact. In the judicial files, the prosecutor emphasized the element of 'continuity' as a crucial support given by female participation. Describing the role of messenger of the wife of one of the bosses, the Prosecutor wrote that she was the *'longa manus'* (long arm) of her husband.[113] This was confirmed by the conversation intercepted not only between the boss and his wife during prison visits, but also between the boss's wife and the husband's companions.

The Hermes function becomes particularly important during delicate moments in male relatives' leadership. The wife of a former Brancaccio's *capo mandamento*, who was in prison between December 1999 and December 2000, following his arrest in the police operation *Golden Market*,[114] was arrested in December 2002 and charged with mafia association. Her role was discovered in the criminal operation code-named *Ghiaccio*. As is written in the judicial files charging the woman, she was used by her husband in order to 'maintain his relationships with mafiosi on the outside and reinforce his definitive investiture as head of the Brancaccio *mandamento* – but also to absolutely support the latest and current reorganisation of this *mandamento* and the families that composed it'.[115]

Promoting, organizing and leading the clan

Acting as a messenger is often the 'prelude' to a position of female leadership, in which women exercise 'delegated power'.[116] Indeed, to explore the nature of female power at the top of mafia clans, it is necessary to analyse the fusion between acting as couriers when men are on the run or in prison, and giving orders and managing the group. The women's experiences illustrated in this section give us insight into this integration and shows that the 'passage' from being a 'simple' courier to assuming a position of leadership can be traced along a continuous line. Some of these women were sentenced not only for participating in mafia associations, but also for promoting, organizing and leading the clan. Thus they were involved in all the female tasks analysed so far, from drug trafficking to economic crimes.

The evidence collected shows that women are more likely to occupy 'leading' positions in Cosa Nostra than in the 'Ndrangheta. In the latter, they are constantly engaged in their family's criminal affairs, yet rarely in the higher levels of the organization.[117]

Case one

As seen in Chapter Three, Giuseppina Vitale was the sister of two brothers, Leonardo and Vito Vitale, who were the bosses of the Partinico *mandamento* belonging to the Corleonese faction. In the beginning, Giusy was the link between Leonardo, who was in prison, and Vito, who was on the run. Her various tasks ranged from giving orders to members of the clan to bringing lovers to Vito at his hiding place. When Vito was arrested, Giusy's role became more vital as she was the only family member, apart from her nephew Giovanni (Vito's son), able to run the family business. She demonstrated a certain degree of autonomy, as when, contrary to her brothers' wishes, she planned to murder a man who informed the police of Vito's location. The following quote from the court sentence explains Giusy's 'progress' within the organization:

> her activity and the contributions she made to the criminal activities coordinated by her brothers developed from an initial activity of sending and exchanging important messages (in relation to which the woman seemed well aware of the role played by her relatives within the mafia context as well as the meaning those messages had to that organisation) to a subsequent moment when, partially due to the arrest of her brother Vito ... she took personal initiative in relation to deciding and organising serious violent events, which failed only due to external circumstances beyond the defendants' control.[118]

Taped prison conversations revealed that Giusy Vitale was always aware of all changes within the Cosa Nostra organization, so much so that she even gave her opinion about the substitution of a *capo mandamento*. The man indicated by Giusy as the new head of the *mandamento* was arrested. The new name was indicated by her brother Leonardo in a note given to Giusy. By participating in decision-making, Giusy became part of the power syndicate. Finally, she became head of the *mandamento*. In her autobiography, she explains the reason behind her nomination:

> with Vito's arrest, what happened to the Fardazza clan? In these cases inside Cosa Nostra either there is a male relative who takes the whole family and the entire *mandamento* on his shoulders, or one disappears and also becomes a target for all sorts of revenge. The solution was found by Leonardo, who from prison let everyone know that for the Fardazza there was myself, that the *mandamento* was not in disarray and that from prison he and Vito guaranteed for me.[119]

Giusy took on this new task with great determination. There is no doubt that she was heavily oppressed by her brother's orders, as emerges from some of the intercepted conversations in prison, in particular when Leonardo, after giving her each order, said to her as a sort of stock phrase: *U capisti*? ('Got it?'). And she would answer him: '*See*' ('Yes'). Giusy's shift towards an independent decisional role within the organization while her brothers were in prison came as a form of relief to her after years of taking orders from them.[120] However, as we will explore later, her true 'liberation' occurred when she was arrested.

Case two

Maria Filippa Messina, alongside Giusy Vitale, is another good example of the transition from being a courier and receiving orders from her imprisoned husband, to running the clan with a certain degree of independence.[121] Police began suspecting she had taken over the clan led by her husband, Antonino Cintorino, a boss from Calatabiano (a small town near Catania), because the clan's illegal activities continued even after Cintorino and his companions were arrested in 1993. Maria Filippa came from a mafia family; her cousin Salvatore Messina was a Calatabiano boss and was murdered by the rival clan, led by Cintorino, who since then, in the early 1990s, became the local boss. As Catania's investigators explained to me, Calatabiano was a wealthy area, and therefore Cintorino's business was good (extortion, usury, rigged construction bids and drug trafficking).[122] When the entire clan was arrested in 1993, its management was entrusted to Maria Filippa, only twenty-five years old at the time. In the beginning, she acted as a mere link between her husband and the remaining members of the organization, but later became more autonomous when her husband was subjected to the strict prison rules of article 41bis, which made communication with him almost impossible. Maria Filippa inherited a critical situation, since there was a gang war in progress with the rival faction known as Carrapipani. The woman decided, along with other members of Cintorino's group, to organize a massacre of their rivals. Conversations inside Maria Filippa's home, taped by investigators, give insight into the tension among the members, as appears in phrases such as: 'let's crush these four pieces of shit, cut them down, break them up'.

In order to communicate this decision to her husband, on 27 December 1994 Maria Filippa sent him a telegram written in code: 'My love, I wish time would run faster so I could come to you; my love don't worry, the horses are all inside because it is cold here, everything is okay. I love you very much.' The investigators understood this message meant those who were creating problems (*horses*) would have been eliminated (*all inside*). The plan, for which Maria had already employed hit men and ordered weapons from the former Yugoslavia, was halted when the police force arrested Maria Filippa, who was sentenced to fourteen years for mafia association. She was placed in solitary confinement pursuant to article 41bis. Her pivotal role clearly emerges from court documents I was able to consult in Catania. The prosecutors wrote that she was 'the true driving force of the organisation and, as a real boss, she gathered the most prestigious men of the group and with them managed the strategies of the criminal organisation at that moment led by herself'. In some episodes, she showed the skills of a manager; for instance when she wanted to substitute the man in charge of racketeering with a man called Raimondo, since the first was on the run. She 'repeats that she does not need a "boss" who cannot be on the job'. Eventually, when the man on the run was arrested she nominated Raimondo. All these factors indicate that she held real power; however, at a closer glance she appears to be in difficulty when there were issues concerning money. Let's take as an example the following conversation, regarding *la carta* (the piece of paper) containing the list of people extorted by the clan:

> **Maria** They don't even know where to find him, so no one knows. So you know what you have to do, you tell them they have to contact S. You say it's because your *commare* (godmother) wants the piece of paper, just like that, because you know that at the end of the month there is a lot of money to be collected and so you collect it, because Nino (her husband), as you should know already, received another arrest warrant, so he has to get two more lawyers and all the rest, so we need the money. This is the first thing. Then you ask him what he intends to do and also I want him to give me the guns if he has them . . .
>
> **Raimondo** Maria, you have to do something, you have to talk with your husband, when your husband tells you what you have to do, do it, you act accordingly, but if you don't talk to your husband, S. is still responsible . . . when you have the money in your hand, then you can start to raise your voice.'

Raimondo's words clearly underline the fact that Maria Filippa's power was delegated. Indeed, the magistrate accused Cintorino of the crimes carried out by Maria Filippa and his group: 'The role maintained by Cintorino within the organisation, through his wife Maria Filippa Messina, allows us to give him, even though he has been in prison for a long time, responsibility for crimes that were essential to this same organisation such as extortion, and unauthorized possession of firearms'. Maria Filippa is an excellent case of the notion of 'delegated power'. Indeed, the judges wrote:

Another characteristic of the organisation was its highly hierarchical structure. This regards Ms. Messina, who acted as boss *on behalf of her imprisoned husband* ('we are under her, so we have to do what she tells us'), and the investiture of Gaetano Intelisano who was given the role of boss, instead of Rosario Lizzio, who was imprisoned. ('The boss will be Gaetano. Of course, what my husband sends me to tell you, we have to do ... he told me he doesn't want any arguing, so as soon as I hear of any arguing, it will be your fucking problem.')

Case three

In 2017 Eleonora was condemned for promoting, organizing and leading a mafia clan.[123] Her position of leadership was strictly linked to the fact that she was the wife of head of the Porta Nuova *mandamento*, one of the most important of Palermo's mafia districts. Investigators found out that she reported the orders given by her husband from jail to his criminal companions.

As an acute and experienced boss, she was careful to avoid being intercepted by the police. She once stated: 'to whom? ... no ... no, don't call him ... these phones have to be eliminated ... I've never worked with the phone ... I don't call anyone on the phone.' The Prosecutor commented that it seemed that she 'wanted to celebrate her own "professional attitude"'.

Despite her prudence, her conversations with the members of the organization were recorded by the police, who installed a device for intercepting conversations within her house. These conversations revealed her leading role in running the illicit activities of the *mandamento*, including drug trafficking, managing the organization's cash and, more importantly, overseeing the relationship between families and members of the *mandamento* for the sake of the organization's accounting.

The money coming from basic activities such as extortion and loan sharking was invested in the drug sector, which 'brought together the interests of all the families in the *mandamento*'. The drug business was thus shared by all the families. However, due to the huge economic interests at stake, this activity created tensions among the members. She designated, after consulting her imprisoned husband, the person responsible for drug trafficking in the group. He would have the task of activating the supply channels, proceeding with the collection of the capital necessary for purchasing the drugs and overseeing the distribution and marketing network.

The person responsible for drug trafficking had the duty to update the woman about trends in the drug business and also about extortions activities. She gave him orders, as in this conversation:

no, you tell him ... "she wants the money right away because she's behaving like a crazy person" I'll send them to call right away ... what are you doing, can you tell me? I mean, you blocked me, now you want ... you take my money but where is this going? ..., you have to pick him up you have to make me ... you tell him, she is taking pen and paper and writing to him ... Eleonora says that she is writing to her husband.

She also offered him suggestions. For example, she invited him to overlook the discontent shown by other associates in relation to his investiture as responsible for the drug trafficking. The affection that pushed her husband to entrust him with this important role did not preclude her from feeling free to '*accantonare*' (set him aside) if his results were not 'satisfying', as she confessed to her son-in-law. This consideration confirms, according to the judge, that she 'was not a simple spokesperson for her husband, but she had full decision-making and managerial powers in the context of the Mafia *mandamento* to which she belonged'.

The designation of this new person responsible was accepted by the head of the Porta Nuova *mandamento*, who had substituted her husband, yet he led the *mandamento* under the influence of the woman. Thus, formally he was the '*reggente*', yet substantially, the boss in prison still ran the *mandamento* through the shadow function of his wife.

Another important function of the woman was managing the 'cash' of the Porta Nuova *mandamento*. She had to 'update and control the sums related to their illicit activities'. The money came from extortion activities and some of it was used to meet the needs of the families, especially for maintaining the relatives of imprisoned mafiosi. She received a wage that was higher than the contribution the other members receive monthly, because the association recognized her crucial role.

Finally, it is important to mention one of her qualities that led the members to recognize her leading role, namely her abilities in mediating. As is reported in judicial files: 'During her house arrest she received in her home the most important members of the Porta Nuova *mandamento* and gave them her husband's orders, being informed of his criminal strategies.' The members of the organization, moreover, turned to the woman to resolve issues and tensions arising within the *mandamento*. According to the judge, she had the task of doing the accounting for the various members of the organization. For this reason, she was an 'essential figure' in the consortium. She stated that she would be able to keep order and stability within the group even if dangerous individuals were released from prison. As she told a member of the organization, to reassure him:

you know that you walk with my face, because you walked with my face because only for this you can walk and you know it. And then one must tell you all ... he was dead, and now ... as soon as he goes out ... now he goes out it's normal, now that he goes out they will make the winning couple with this, and you know that without me you are lost. This is the truth.

Her vision for the organization was quite lucid. Like any good leader, she was worried about chaos inside the organization. Talking with a fellow she recalled the fact that her husband had left the organization tidy, just before he was arrested, and that the *mandamento*'s division of competences needed to be respected:

it was so clean, he has left it totally clean, that's the truth, but I told him ... you can't just go to the *Vucciria* district and make a mess of everything, while someone else goes to the Zen district ... what would the meaning of that be? But we are also losing face.

Her mediation role also emerged when she intervened to settle a conflict that arose between some members of the mafia organization, relating to the percentage of profit that had to be given to the Porta Nuova *mandamento* following a significant robbery committed in the Friuli Venezia Giulia region.

In conclusion, she acted as a substitute and at the same time exercised independent power over the members of the mafia families composing the *mandamento*. From the intercepted conversations, it seems that the members of the group showed respect towards her not only because she was the wife of their boss, but also because she was clever and able to deal with the different needs and problems the organization had to face.

Case four

Santina was born in 1968 and grew up in a mafia family.[124] Her father was the *reggente* of the *mandamento* of Resuttana, in Palermo, and her brother was the head of the so-called '*gruppo di fuoco di via Strasburgo*'. On her mother's side as well, she had relatives belonging to Cosa Nostra. Moreover, she married a man who belonging to the Madonia family and occupied a leading position in the Resuttana *mandamento*. Her husband was condemned to life imprisonment and was subjected to 41bis. They celebrating their wedding in the *Ucciardone* prison in Palermo on 23 May 1992, the day on which judge Giovanni Falcone was murdered. In 2008 she was arrested during operation *Rebus*, and was charged with mafia association because, according to the evidence gathered by investigators:

she was a channel between the imprisoned leaders of the Resuttana mafia *mandamento* and the associated mafia members in freedom, especially by establishing relationships and establishing contacts, both direct and mediated ... with Lo Piccolo Salvatore, on the run at the time, *reggente* of the of San Lorenzo Tommaso Natale *mandamento* and, since June 2006, head of the entire Cosa Nostra of Palermo (as well as a reference point for the Madonia family in the Resuttana area).

She was in contact with important, well-known mafiosi both through meetings in which she participated personally and also through the consolidated system of the so-called *pizzini*. Moreover, she managed the illicit assets of the Madonia-Di Trapani family both directly and through other associates. She received sums of illicit money, that she redistributed within the Madonia-Di Trapani family nucleus.

When she was released from prison in 2015, she went back to her own environment, intervening in the internal changes the *mandamento* was undergoing during those difficult times. Her plan was to reorganize it. Thus, she called a meeting in order to reinforce the leading role of a man whom other influential members of the organization disliked. From the intercepted conversations among these members, it appears that the convocation of this meeting created some amount of apprehension. Some were not pleased with the leading role taken by her, which was perceived as a sort of 'imposition'. According to them, she should have limited herself to playing her usual role as a mafioso's wife, and – as recorded in a conversation between two members – 'collect the money the organization gave her for her family'. Despite this aversion towards the woman's appointment, they respected her decisions. Later on, when it was quite evident that the man designated was not able to carry a role of responsibility, some of the members started to work towards deposing him. They were aware, however, that *'la gran signora'* (the great lady), as one important member of the clan (who was also her uncle) called her, had to agree with them. And indeed, finally, she realized that the new *reggente* was not up to par.

Due to the difficult times, the soldiers of the *mandamento* were paid not on a monthly basis but with a percentage of each extortion they committed. She arranged for all the members of the organization to receive a monthly wage. Decisions regarding remuneration given to members are typically taken by those at the top of the organization. For this reason, according to the prosecutor, 'she had the typical powers of a top manager'.

In conclusion, it is worth noting that, while the regency of the *mandamento* was not formally given to her, in many circumstances she behaved as though she was the *reggente*. Her sex probably hindered this formal recognition.

Case five

Born in 1954, Daria was active in the C. family for a long time.[125] Her participation was crucial for guaranteeing the continuity of her brothers' power over the area surrounding a small town in the province of Caltanissetta. The C. family was part of Cosa Nostra and supported it in the late 1980s and early 1990s, during Cosa Nostra's war against the rebel faction of the Stidda. This caused it to be involved in blood conflicts. In the early 1990s, her brothers also had to go into hiding due to investigations, which later led to their arrests. However, while they were detained, her role allowed them to keep governing the area until 1996, when she too was arrested and later charged with mafia association. The police found out that she had 'the delicate task of coordinating and managing the illegal activities carried out on the territory of the Mafia family of the town, in particular by maintaining contacts between the brothers who were in hiding and the other affiliates as well as by providing economic support for imprisoned members'.

When she was arrested, responsibility for coordination was given to another brother, who became the *reggente* of the group. Once she was free, in 2003 she started to work in a restaurant. One of her brother obtained this job for her by blackmailing the owner. This was possible because the group controlled the area through intimidation, and many people, afraid of their violent attitude, tended to meet all their requests.

In the early 2000s, the group was in trouble as a consequence of the investigative operation called '*Odessa*', carried out by police in 2003. Later on, it also saw turmoil because of the constitution of a rebel group made up of people complaining about the C. family's management of the economic resources of the clan. However, the brothers were able to face all these challenges and maintain their control over the area. According to the judges, the group's kin structure was a key element in their ability to overcome these difficulties. During times of crisis, for example when her brothers, either imprisoned or in hiding, could not be continuously and physically present, they entrusted the coordination to close relatives, or to trusted people who, however, were supported in managing the clan's power by their relatives.

Delicate decisions about who had the duty to govern the group were taken by the brother in prison and then communicated to the woman, who entrusted the duty of transferring the brother's orders to a third person, who finally passed on the information to those concerned.

Not only was the woman the depository of 'very significant information that concerned the reorganization of the clan in an extremely difficult moment', but she also:

gave adequate support to P. and A. (the two new substitutes of the brothers) in front of the other associates – who had difficulty digesting the appointment of the aforementioned rulers – so that it was clear that behind them there was, in any case, the authoritative presence of the C. brothers. That is, those who have always represented, almost like a sort of family-oriented lordship, the mafia power established in the area surrounding (the town).

Eventually, she received messages whose contents were fundamental for the group. They concerned decisions related to who had to take power on behalf of her brothers, or who had to stand aside. The way she transmitted these decisions was crucial for avoiding their weakening during the 'transfer'. Her role, thus, was important for 'guaranteeing the seamless working of the group'. And this continuity allowed money to be gathered to sustain the members of the family. She was particularly active in the sector of extortion, from which the group's main economic sources stemmed. Not only was she 'the final destination of the sums illicitly accumulated by the criminal group' – so that she could later distribute them to the family members of her brothers, all of whom were confined to prison at the time; but she also 'intervened with determination to block any initiative that could interfere with her crucial role, which consisted in financially supporting their relatives'. When a member of the group who was transferred to Genoa in northern Italy decided to go back to the town, in order to take advantage of the problems faced by the C. family, the woman reacted in order to defend her brothers' territory. In particular, she intervened when she discovered that the man started to collect extortion money on behalf of the C. family. A collaborator with justice, who had spent some time in prison with the man, told a magistrate that 'she had summoned him because she had learnt that he was "going around" to commit extortions on behalf of the C. family and had consequently invited him to "mind his own business"'. The woman had found out that the man was trying to take power from the C. family because some of the people being extorted complained to her and told her that they preferred to bring the money directly to her, as usual, instead of paying it through a person who came to their house. This episode shows quite clearly the significant role she played in the field of extortion, since she was recognized by the people being extorted as a representative of the C. family.

In conclusion, she always played a pivotal role that, however, 'came to the fore above all in situations of temporary crisis experienced by the local mafia family'. The Prosecutor dealing with her case depicted her as a strong woman, *'fuori dal comune'* (unusual),[126] underling that her case was unique in the mafia controlling the area of Nisseno (around the city of Caltanissetta in Sicily). He believed that her acquisition of a leading role was due to both the family structure of the mafia family of that town, led by the C. brothers, and to her own character, that in his view 'was very determined'. He underlined that 'she was almost totally unscrupulous and not afraid of anyone' and that 'her relationship with her brothers was between equals'.

However, it is interesting to note once again, as in the previous cases, that although she transferred delicate organizational messages, was involved in extortion activities and was recognized as a point of reference, given that the members addressed their complaints about the C. management of the money to her, she did not occupy a formal position of leadership. She exercised her authority in the shadow of her brothers' power. All the events in the dispute over the acquisition of power were related to males. In other words, it was taken for granted that men had the right to the formal roles of leadership. In the discussion between the C. brothers and their companions, as reported in the judicial file, there was never any reference to the possibility that she might take on the role of *reggente* and gain effective and concrete authority. Collaborators relayed the fact that – in their own words – 'she is walking', which in mafia slang means that 'she was dealing concretely with managing the illicit activities of the association'. At the same time, significantly, in the conversations among the people affiliated to the group she was always referred to as 'the sister of . . .'.

Case six

Lavinia's life, mentioned in Chapter Four, was marked by the murder of two sons, during the 'Ndrangheta feud that lasted from the 1990s to the 2000s in Lamezia Terme.[127] After this, she took a top role in the organization made up of the group of families, to which her family belonged.

Born in 1939, she was the sister of one of the most important bosses of the confederation, who survived the feud, unlike other leading men of the group. Her brother was influential in the 'Ndrangheta, as is demonstrated by his close relationships with the bosses of important 'Ndrangheta groups operating in northern Italy.

Unusually for a woman, Lavinia participated in the group's meetings as a representative of her family. In these meetings, important decisions were taken 'in order to implement the criminal program of the group'. Indeed, in the trial following the investigative operation on her clan, carried out by the police in 2014, she was condemned for promoting and coordinating the 'Ndrangheta group, along with other bosses, including her brother. The members of the group respected her. She was called by various nicknames, such as 'donna Lavinia' or 'the old woman'. Some collaborators stated that in the 'Ndrangheta environment she was considered a 'woman of honour'. Others declared that she was a 'terrible woman' with 'strong criminal charisma'. One of them maintained that she was able to 'even keep pace with her brother ... as regards the decisions to be taken within the criminal organization'.

According to the judicial files, her contribution to the group's functioning concerned mainly the extortion business and the communication system.

Extortion was a central activity for the Lamezia Terme's 'Ndrangheta groups, as mentioned previously. Not surprisingly, control over extortion was the origin of the feud among the main clans governing the town. Lavinia developed excellent skills in managing this sector, insofar as she coordinated people engaged in racketeering shops, restaurants and small businesses, and received the money from them.

The extortion business, fundamental for the organization's economic stability, flourished even when the bosses of the group were arrested. This was possible thanks to the role of the women who brought orders from the detained heads to their soldiers. Hence, the group could remain active through this female communication chain that went from the prison to the final receivers of the messages. Lavinia was the intermediary of all the *ambasciate* (messages) going from the imprisoned bosses to the Torcasio group's members. She received and passed along information by being in contact with the women of the members. This communication system worked very well not only because women were efficient and smart, but also due to the blood relations linking all the members of the circuit. Being relatives gave easier access to prison visits and made the circle of information airtight.

Much as in other 'Ndrangheta groups, the strength of the confederation of families rested on the kinship created through weddings. An expression used by a collaborator with justice helps us understand the relevance of these kin linkages: the two families 'were *one single thing*, because of their family ties' created through marriages. The expression 'one single thing' renders very well the sort of fusion characterizing relationships among the members of the 'Ndrangheta groups. It is on this feature that the 'Ndrangheta's success and also its female participation are grounded.

Lavinia participated in the criminal sphere of the organization during the period of necessity caused both by the conflict with their former allies and the police investigations that led some of the bosses to be imprisoned. However, it seems that her involvement at a high level of the group was not mainly due to necessity, but above all her own desire, driven by the death of her sons.

A collaborator with justice, who declared that 'Lavinia gave the approval to the decisions made by her sons, and also by the members of the G. family, as well as her brother', stressed that 'for her personality, is to be considered in all respects one of the leaders of the ... group, if not the leading figure, even above her brother'.

The reason provided by this collaborator, explaining how Lavinia acquired the top position, is conceivable. Personality is a key element in understanding what makes the difference when a woman achieves a chief role in an 'Ndrangheta group, which is such a rare event.

More recently, another criminal investigation carried out in 2017, discovered that Lavinia kept playing her leading role from prison, as a respected boss. This was possible because, during prison visits, she transmitted to her twenty-eight-year-old niece important orders, intended for the group's members. On one occasion, she communicated her decision that her niece's husband was to take on a leading role in the family. The fact that she allowed herself to take this kind of decision showed her ability to exercise true authority. Offering a role model for conscious female involvement in the 'Ndrangheta, she represented a strong vehicle transmitting criminal practices to her young niece, who went on to live a life of crime. It is this kind of legacy that guarantees continuity and thus solidity to the 'Ndrangheta.

Female agency meets mafia organizational needs

When can women hold positions of leadership? Who among mafia women has held authority? What is female power like in the mafia? Addressing these three questions is crucial for going beyond the legal and media representations of women charged with law 416bis, which tend to depict them in the same manner as male bosses.

By analysing women's experiences, it is quite clear that they become important tools even at the top of mafia families during emergency periods. In times such as these, mafias need money and communication becomes more important and risky. That is why these organizations need trustworthy people, to take care of the cash and above all transmit delicate messages. The increasing value of the messages entrusted to women and the impossibility for these women to remain constantly in contact with the imprisoned bosses, especially when under harsh prison conditions (41bis), upgraded the female status from couriers to heads on behalf of their men. Women were able to satisfy the organization's requirement of assuming a leading role, thus overcoming their role as mere spokeswomen, and giving orders to mafia companions, thanks to their mafia know-how. Indeed, they demonstrated knowledge of everything regarding mafia companions and activities and showed great skill in running their men's clans. This mafia know-how could surely not have been learnt overnight. These women's knowledge was wide and deep, because those who had been entrusted with such leadership and organizational tasks were women from inside the mafia, either because they had grown up in a mafia family or were the wives of bosses.

The case of the wife of former boss of Brancaccio, mentioned above, is particularly illustrative. The magistrate for her case significantly commented: 'As already demonstrated in relation to the previous conversation, (the woman) showed an immediate understanding of the instructions received and was perfectly aware of both of the nature of interests at work and the roles played by all subjects involved.'[128] The knowledge used by this woman when substituting her husband was the result of a process of accretion.

This example, just as those reported above, concerned Cosa Nostra, which in the last thirty years had to face considerable difficulties, more so than the 'Ndrangheta. Women were used in almost all the *mandamenti* that since the 1990s have had to face significant challenges, posed by prosecutors' offices and law enforcement agencies.[129] The employment of women thus can be read as an organizational response to a turbulent environment. When no close male relatives were available, bosses in hiding or in prison started to entrust leading roles to women.

As already stressed, leading female figures in the 'Ndrangheta have not been common. The reason for this might lie in the fact that during difficult moments this organization can place its trust in a greater number of reliable male workers, given its family structure. In other words, there is always a reserve of trusty men available to substitute bosses in hiding or in prison. Therefore, it does not seem particularly necessary to involve women at the top of the organization. The few cases of women running a clan in the 'Ndrangheta are regarded as anomalous and ambiguous situations, or were strictly linked with peculiar characteristics of a given woman's personality. Maria Serraino exploited her surname, but she also created the group by herself. Her top position was not the result of a male designation. Another example concerns Irene,[130] who did not come from an 'Ndrangheta family, but she was the companion of a powerful boss of the Bellocco clan in Rosarno. Their unofficial relation was not recognized by this criminal group, which, according to the prosecutor dealing with her case, might have driven her to demonstrate that she was, to all intents and purposes, the 'wife of the boss'. In the first stages of the trial she was condemned to a punishment more severe than her companion (the final verdict, however, has not yet been given).

The last case regards Lavinia, who was recognized by the men of the group as 'woman of honour' despite not being formally affiliated. However, as a co-coordinator of the 'Ndrangheta consortium in Lamezia Terme she seems to be an exception. Her strong personality led her to respond to the death of her sons by participating more actively in the 'Ndrangheta family clan. The organization did not prevent her from becoming co-leader of this criminal consortium, since it was convenient given that the clan was quite worn down by the feud against its ex-ally.

The answer to the second question is clear. Women who substituted men at the top of the criminal organization were always relatives of bosses, including sisters or even daughters.[131] Thus, legitimization in the criminal environment came from their family background. Indeed, women could not enter the organization in leading roles unless they were relatives of male mafia bosses who were absent from the criminal scene. The last point brings us to the final question addressing the nature of female power in the mafia.

From the evidence analysed so far, women's power is delegated and temporary,[132] and also onerous and masculine. As such, it entails elements of male exploitation. This new female position was not a result of acknowledged 'advancement', deriving instead from an organization's needs. As much as the couriers of words, heads of mafia clans are used by men to maintain their power, thereby keeping the organization active.

This power was delegated to women by men for the time they were in prison, and thus was temporary. Men 'promoted' women to the top level of the mafia only in emergency situations, because they knew that the concession of power was temporary, i.e. until they were out of prison. This was clear from Lipari's daughter, who had played a supportive role since her youth; when her father was captured, her position progressed in terms of importance, but then, as soon as the father was released, she returned to a secondary position. Men found it convenient to turn over their power to women firstly because women did as much as they could to preserve the men's power, thus defending it from potential internal rivals, and secondly because women are not allowed to acquire formal positions inside the mafia structure. Marisa Di Giovine's effort was paradigmatic; while her father was in prison, she prevented other men from the clan from taking over her father's power. During that time, not only did she deliver messages from Emilio Di Giovine to the other members of the organization but above all defended Emilio's authority against internal attacks, including those coming from Emilio's brother.

The fact that power reverted back to men once they became free brings us to the conclusion that men entrusted their power to their women not only because they were part of the family, and as such trustworthy, but also because entrusting authority to another man would entail the risk of losing it entirely. Since women were excluded from mafia power by definition, giving it to them was meant to ensure that the leadership would always revert to its original owner. These gender dynamics show female subordination in the mafia even at the top of the organization.

Moreover, given the fact that women take over management of the clan during difficult periods, they have to deal with many thorny issues, from scarce economic resources to affiliates' discontents and the related risk of uprisings. It is not rare for women to have to re-modulate the clan's organizational chart, due to the turmoil caused by police investigations.

Finally, women's power in the mafia is masculine. In other words, the way in which women manage the clan has to resemble the male style. As Mintzeberg noted in relation to early women managers, their 'success ... rested on their ability to mask their feminine traits and mimic their male counterparts. They had to forego their personal lives and resign themselves to the fact that the organisation was their family. The more successful they were at concealing any gender differences, the more successful they became at assimilating into the male-dominated professions.'[133]

Such factors regarding the legitimate world have proved to be all the more accentuated in the violent environment of the mafia, where masculinity, in its traditional meaning linked to virility, is a fundamental trait.[134] Therefore, to become leaders women must show those traits society has traditionally linked to masculinity. This was particularly accentuated in the case of Giuseppina Vitale, who adopted male behaviour to play her leadership role on behalf of her brothers. This habit was the result of the 'contradiction of female power in a patriarchal order',[135] and was in line with what anthropologist Anton Blok noted in relation to female rulers: 'women leaders had, and still have, to adapt their appearance and imagery to the pattern of "hegemonic masculinity" and, in the process, help to perpetuate it'.[136]

As Giusy Vitale confessed to sociologist Alessandra Dino, she was compelled to take on a masculine attitude in order to acquire positions that were reserved to men. She wished to be part of the male group and she understood that to satisfy her desire she had to appear masculine:

> to be with them, I knew that a woman up to a certain age does not create problems, and also that with a woman there is a different way of speaking, and that, if they saw that I was a woman it meant that they stopped bringing me with them ... Therefore, I did everything possible to make it look like I was male. I was female but I was equal to them.[137]

Giusy Vitale shaped her gender by adapting it to manliness, since it was the only way for her to participate in the mafia in a position of leadership. She used gender as was convenient in that circumstance. Her case makes the process of gender adaptation that men and women carry out in everyday life quite explicit. Sharply, Dino comments: 'Attracted by her brothers' model of life, she takes on "male" behaviour to gain access to a world more fascinating than the closed and restricted world reserved for girls and, even more, for women.'[138]

Assuming male behaviour to give orders to other men was an act that brought her to neglect her femininity, which later on she regained in prison, as illustrated in the next chapter.

Undoubtedly the strong agency she showed brought about a change, because she assumed a role that used to be exclusively reserved to men. However, her agency contributed to the persistence of male power, which subjugates women. As Dino wrote, analysing Giusy Vitale's willingness to demonstrate that women are able to do the same things that men do:

> She does not realize – or does not want to become aware – that she has identified herself with the male model that oppressed her. She did not rebel; she simply went over to the dominant side, ending up perpetuating the power of which she had been the victim.[139]

In conclusion, when looking at female involvement in criminal activities it seems clear that the mafia system has been able to take advantage of the ongoing process of female emancipation in the legal world, especially with regards to the increase in female education and in women undertaking jobs traditionally considered male. Therefore, from a current mafia perspective, women are more useful nowadays than in the past due to their progress in education and changes in habits.

Women have been ready to face the challenges posed by the mafia system, by participating actively in the criminal sphere. Thus they have showed significant agentic capacities that have brought about many changes that, however, have contributed to perpetuating the male system by maintaining traditional gender dynamics in the intimate sphere. This agency may be seen as an aporia that can be read through the lens of the concept of pseudo-emancipation, able to grasp the contradictions and ambivalence emerging from the experiences of women living in the mafia.

The notion of pseudo-emancipation allows us to underline their exploitation without at the same time justifying or neglecting their responsibility as fundamental contributors to the mafia organization. The notion must be used to understand the long-term historical processes that have seen women in the mafia modify their roles. This term, indeed, helps us to understand their transformation not as an expression of progresses in female status, but as a reproduction of unchanged patterns. Needless to say, it is obvious that the mafia does not provide equal opportunities to women, given that it is based on male chauvinist values. Moreover, as we know from Chapter Two, the process of female emancipation in Italian society has been incomplete and imperfect, and thus it would be foolish to expect a different picture in the mafia. However, the assumption that the shift in women's roles inside the mafia was a sign of 'advancement' in female positions is quite widespread at a popular level and in the media. From what we have analysed so far, this assumption is not a valid hypothesis. In fact, the evidence has shown that women's tasks in mafia businesses are marginal and virtually unpaid. Even at the top level, their leadership is temporary and delegated.

Moreover, constrictions coming from traditional female roles have not disappeared. Gender relations, based on the patriarchal system, persist. Highly controlled, women might experience violence from the male members of their family, as seen in Chapter Three. Even when women do not directly suffer it, they live in a context that is heavily marked by violence.[140] Women are aware that their men constantly deal with violence and when it is latent, it can explode at any time. It is not surprising that they often put themselves in a position of mediation, since they know that even the slightest dispute might give rise to violent conflicts.

Even some of the women holding decision-making positions continued to experience male domination. In this sense, the story of Giusy Vitale and Nunzia Graviano gives some insight. Sisters of mafia bosses, their surname and skills gained them a good reputation in the criminal field, and thus respect from the other members of the mafia family. Yet they remained subjugated to their brothers.

Clearly formulating such an ambiguous condition is quite complex. Renate Siebert defined mafia women as female pseudo-subjects by comparing and contrasting them with female subjects present in the legitimate world. In Siebert's words: 'If the historical development of a female subject, despite the deep wounds that have accompanied the processes of emancipation, can be read as a process of liberation from patriarchal male violence (in intimate as well as public relationships), then the social production of a female pseudo-subject (as in the case of the mafia, or Nazi/Fascist regimes, or of all domination based on patriarchal male chauvinism) should not be misinterpreted as a process of liberation.'[141]

In order to understand better the contradictions inherent in the identity of mafia women it is appropriate to speak of a multi-belonging identity.[142] The definition of multi-belonging identity is also capable of embracing the individual nuances of being a woman in the mafia. Indeed, assuming such a perspective helps us avoid generalizations that reduce women's experience to a few models of behaviour, conditions and feelings. It furthermore permits us to grasp the simultaneous aspects of change and continuity that, generally speaking, characterize the condition of women in the mafia. On the one hand they assume 'modern' features in the external world, in terms of appearance – i.e. they dress in modern clothing – and demonstrate the ability to move freely – i.e. they drive cars and travel. On the other hand, they tend to remain traditional in relation to the internal sphere, as far as they are strictly controlled by the men of their families, experience male oppression and tend to identify womanhood exclusively with marriage and motherhood. In other words, it seems that in the mafia environment, women have acquired the superficial traits of female emancipation rather than those related to equality in gender relations. The tension occurring between the two spheres, external and internal, might explain the conflicting attitude of mafia women, stressed above, that ranges from conscious participation in the mafia to subjugation to male power.

In conclusion, women attaining criminal roles seem to acquire a 'static autonomy'.[143] In other words, the 'competence and mastery that are pursued are in the interests of domination, denied connectedness, and defensive separateness'.[144] On the contrary, as seen in the next chapter, women who have decided to take their distance from the mafia show transformative agency, that leads them to achieve a relational and 'dynamic autonomy', entailing 'competence that promotes an enhanced sense of self'.[145]

6

Transformative Agency: Searching for Autonomous Paths

The strength of vulnerability

Women involved in the mafias are not mere victims. Although they are controlled by men, they are able to express agency not only by participating directly in the mafia system, as analysed so far, but also by distancing themselves from it. In the latter case, they convey a form of agency that is transformative. To grasp their capacity to affirm their will to break away from the mafia, it is best to avoid labelling mafia women as passive and introduce the notion of vulnerability. Despite its complexity and ambiguity, this concept provides us with a useful key to understand better the paths taken by women who decide to leave the mafia. This might occur when, for example, they are arrested by the police and later collaborate with justice; or when they find the environment in which they live unbearable and, as a consequence, decide to become witnesses or follow their children who have been inserted in Youth Court educational programmes.

The details surrounding the decision to run away from the mafia vary with each individual story. However, what these women seem to share is the fact that undertaking a new route in life is not a smooth process, but a conflictual and ambivalent journey that originates from the 'strength of vulnerability'. As vulnerability theorists have amply illustrated, the latter is a force generated by the marginal position one occupies and provides the chance to shift one's own view of the world.[1]

Vulnerability must be understood in two senses: universal and particular. The first has to do with the condition of precariousness that all human beings share, as they are mortal. We live in a condition of constant fragility, because each of us is potentially exposed to injury. As Marta Fieneman puts it: 'Human vulnerability arises in the first place from our embodiment, which carries with it the imminent or ever-present possibility of harm, injury, and misfortune.'[2] This condition of potential injury unites everyone, without distinction of gender, class, ethnicity or age. We are all exposed to the violence of nature. Yet, we experience vulnerability in different ways. Indeed, in its particular meaning, vulnerability modifies according to socio-demographic, economic and cultural variables and depends on the resources of resilience (personal, economical and relational) that everyone has at their disposal. Thus, there is a specific dimension of vulnerability that concerns a certain category of people who are identified in groups such as women, minors, the elderly, the disabled. However, labelling specific groups as vulnerable might give rise to stereotypes. That is why some scholars criticize this use of vulnerability, considering it too vague and nebulous, stating that 'the concept of vulnerability stereotypes whole categories of individuals, without distinguishing between individuals in the group who indeed might have special characteristics that need to be taken into account and those who do not'.[3]

To avoid this risk of stereotyping is worthwhile to employ 'the layers approach', according to which individuals might experience different layers of vulnerability, that might even change over the course of their life.[4] In some circumstances, the layers might increase and thus render vulnerability heavier, while in other they might decrease, making it lighter. In this view, the notion of vulnerability 'is not a category or a label we can simply apply', but it is 'a relational and dynamic one, closely related to the situation under analysis'.[5] The metaphor of layers helps us understand vulnerability as an elastic concept, able to support the assumption that a state of fragility might change according both to individual choice and the opportunities or obstacles posed by the context, as well as the social relationships developed in a given circumstance. This approach allows us to apply the category of vulnerability to women living within the mafia and leaving it, while avoiding, at the same time, portraying them as a homogeneous category of people. The idea of stratified vulnerability is very useful, in order to avoid analysing them indistinctly. Mafia women's stories, indeed, reveal differences that result from various identity sections, which are forged by factors including, for example, the type of relationship they have with the male members of the organizations (i.e. mother, sister, daughter, even wife), the position of the men to whom they are bond, the level of their family in the mafia organization and their origin (whether they are born in a mafia family or not). In other words, various factors may contribute to overlapping the levels of these women's oppression and thus increase the layers of their vulnerability. The latter, for example, increase if they do not follow honour norms or, in the case of witnesses and collaborators with justice, they might change according to the opportunities and concrete help that the state and society offer them.

Ultimately, both universal and contextual vulnerability characterizes the condition of women in the mafia system. The way they experience these types of fragility changes singularly, insofar as the resources they can use to respond might be different. What is worthwhile stressing is the fact that when the layers of vulnerability grow and women recognize them, they feel increasingly helpless and enter a condition of impotence. This, however, paradoxically opens up new possibilities. A sense of powerless might occur, for example, when they experience constant domestic violence or become aware of the risk of being killed by their own relatives, because they have betrayed their husband, breaching the rules of honour.

In the process of gaining awareness of the own condition of subjugation through seeing the oppressive system to which they belong negatively, they come to occupy *any place* – that is, an atopic space – which, as such, becomes ethically determinant. Reaching this space is not immediate. On the contrary, it requires a long, traumatic process that gradually results in developing a critical view and forming a creative and innovative agency able to trigger a concrete and productive change. Vulnerability scholars maintain that vulnerability is a powerful heuristic tool that offers the vulnerable subject a fresh lens to read their own condition and thereby to open up new and generative possibilities of action.[6]

Activist bell hooks, too, underlines that power is formed in the margins of society. She highlights the fertile strength of those subjects occupying a position on the fringe of the social system. The African-American thinker, whose pseudonym bell hooks is made up of her mother's and grandmother's names deliberately written in lowercase in order to rename herself as a gesture of rebellion against the white, masculine and patriarchal order, offers a point that is interesting in understanding the *habitus* of mafia women as subjects colonized by male power.[7]

Being on the edge of the system means surfing the border between inside and outside. This ambivalent position allows vulnerable subjects to form a different view of society, culture, law – one that is alternative to the mainstream vision. Vulnerability theorists link the potentiality of critical thought to the possibility of emancipation. This is quite evident from the new rights this group of people, emerging out of a vulnerable condition, has achieved, by criticizing the status quo and pushing the law forward. Among the examples of critical approaches that have stimulated rights claims with positive effects, various movements involve workers, women, African-Americans, LGBTQ and people with disabilities. They have produced new, innovative narrations of themselves and effective forms of resistance that have led them to conquer rights unthinkable before their actions.[8]

Uncovering the mechanisms underlying these innovative visions and discovering that they are grounded on a condition of vulnerability gives us useful insight in further understanding the female choice of leaving the mafia system. Their transformative action does indeed emerge from the subordinate and oppressed position they occupy in this system. Forced into a state of marginality, in which the ideological and military system of the code of honour collocates them, they transform it in a place of alterity with respect to the male mafia order. This female differential position can become a magnifying glass revealing the oppressive system, and thus allow women to imagine alternative ways of living.

If we read fragility as the female know-how on which the act of rejecting their belonging to the mafia system is founded, there is no doubt that the notion of vulnerability can be strictly connected to that of agency, as Judith Butler suggests: 'Once we understand the way that vulnerability enters into agency, then our understanding of both terms can change, and the binary opposition between them can become undone.'[9] Women who separate themselves from the mafia express a transformative agency showing the ability to distance themselves from their previous context and their consolidated networks of family and social bonds, and affirm their own subjectivity. The latter is the product of something deeper, which has an effect on their responsibility towards themselves, their children and, ultimately, society. Through their choice, these women leave the performative role required by the gender norms of their social group and explore an identity that seems to be more linked to their deeper singular desire, and as such is able to transform their habitus in a revolutionary manner.

New paths and opportunities might become concrete when mafia women find the conditions for self-determination, for instance by developing constructive relationships with actors embodying public institutions or other organizations, including schools, the Youth Court, law enforcement, NGOs or the church. Female action, stemming from the 'power of lacking' can play a transformative function if and when there are contextual conditions required to realize female 'relational autonomy'. To transform an act into an event, it is necessary for the context to offer opportunities to the actor, without neglecting his/her subjectivity.

A woman's decision to leave her kinship group might lead her to take various avenues. Here we will dwell upon those female routes that are more visible to external observers, including becoming a collaborator or witness, or following their own children in the Youth Court's programmes implemented as a consequence of the removal of the father's authority.

Speaking out

Before dealing with the stories of women that have decided to cut their connections with the mafia system, it is worthwhile recalling the so-called '*pentiti* law', that gives people charged with mafia association the opportunity to offer a contribution to justice in exchange for a reduced punishment. This law has enabled investigators to carry out significant criminal actions against mafia associations. The crime of mafia membership is by definition committed by a group of people. Therefore, the testimony of one of the members is valuable in order to discover the secrets of the consortium. The use of *pentiti* has been a controversial. Italian public opinion tends to believe that judges use *pentiti* witnesses as the only evidence in trials. On the contrary, however, these testimonies are always corroborated by other oral sources or 'written' evidence such as intercepted telephone calls, bank documents, etc.

Investigators have always used secret informants; however, in the late 1980s, it became necessary to regulate the use of people talking to the state. The turning point in the regulation of *pentitismo* was the 1991 law (Law 82/91), which stemmed from the witness programme designed by the Italian state to combat terrorism in the late 1970s. At that time, the state offered imprisoned terrorists the opportunity to dissociate themselves from subversive organizations. Given the positive results of that procedure, it was also applied to the crime of mafia association, thus enabling judges to learn more about the workings of the mafia. In this regard, the testimony of Tommaso Buscetta given to judge Giovanni Falcone in 1984 was exemplary.

Under Law 82/91, the state offered mafia defectors reductions in punishment and protection from mafia revenge in exchange for their testimonies.[10] Thus, the law encouraged many mafiosi to leave the mafia and start a new life under state protection.[11] Public prosecutor Maurizio Romenelli, who had long experience in convincing mafiosi to turn state's evidence, observed: 'It was a tiny law, made up of only ten articles, however it had a positive effect on the battle against organised crime.'[12]

The state witness programme is managed by *Commissione* ex-art.10 and the *Servizio Centrale di Protezione*.[13] The first body (made up of politicians, judges and law enforcement) is in charge of deciding whether a given *pentito* is admitted to the witness programme, as requested by the prosecutors. Once the *pentito* is included in the programme, the *Servizio Centrale* deals with the practical aspects of managing his/her life, including protection and assistance.

Whether or not to include a collaborator with justice within the witness programme depends on two factors. First, the extent of the relevance of the *pentito*'s account and his/her reliability must be considered; second, the extent to which the person is in danger. Along with their family, people who become state witnesses run the risk of being murdered by the mafia organization, because vendetta is a basic mafia principle both in practical and symbolic terms. As previously explained, punishing traitors not only cleanses the offended honour, but also acts as a deterrent.

The state witness protection programme includes protection measures (*misure di protezione*), which consist of moving *pentiti* to another place of residence, providing them with false documents (*documenti di copertura*) and, in the most dangerous cases, a change of identity (*cambio delle generalità*), i.e. the creation of new personal data. Moreover, the programme provides assistance measures (*misure di assistenza*) entailing economic support, which varies according to the numbers of relatives considered to be in danger, and prison benefits, which often result in alternatives to prison (*misure alternative al carcere*), including house arrest.[14]

This legislation, thus, was crucial in the judiciary history of the Italian mafias and for mafia members. It allowed individuals, both men and women, to escape from very difficult and risky situations or to avoid long detention. We are not likely to find out the reasons underlying the decision to collaborate with justice. What is certain is that it is an act of speaking out. And this, for people that have grown up in an environment dominated by the law of silence, is a revolutionary act. Especially for women, who in the masculine order are socially educated to talk in private and not in the public arena.

Early testimonies and collaborators with justice

The state's protection system was not yet up and running when, in 1991, seventeen-year-old Rita Atria decided to go to the *Carabinieri* and tell them what she knew about the mafia in her small town in Sicily, Partanna. Rita was the sister-in-law of Piera Aiello, who a few months earlier had gone to the police and become a state witness. Piera took this decision after the tragic death of her young husband, Nicola Atria, who had taken over the clan when his father was shot dead by a rival clan. While her husband was alive, Piera had tried to convince him to collaborate with the justice system, since her *habitus*, shaped in a family with no mafia connections, was not in line with mafia values. Prosecutor Alessandra Camassa explained that:

> Piera Aiello was unusual for a mafia wife because she wanted to find things out; she wanted to know everything. She gave us a lot of detailed information on the

Partanna mafia. It wasn't vendetta she was after; she isn't the type. She didn't have a particularly high opinion of her husband; actually, she thought he was a *cretino* (idiot). She wanted to get away, to start a new life.[15]

The words used by Alessandra Camassa to describe and explain Piera's decision allow us to define her collaboration with justice as one of the shapes that female emancipation can take in the mafia. Talking to the police had a sort of cathartic effect, because it liberated Piera from mafia tyranny and allowed her to become autonomous and behave in line with her ethical views.

Rita Atria followed in the footsteps of her sister-in-law not long after. Unlike Piera, Rita grow up in a mafia family. In fact, for her, collaborating with justice created conflicting feelings, as moving away from her mother and family entailed getting rid of her past cultural structure and assuming a new one. The dichotomy between her world and the one she met appeared quite clearly when she developed a strong bond with Prosecutors Alessandra Camassa and Paolo Borsellino. At the beginning, she stated immediately that her confession was aimed at sending the people guilty of her father and brother's murders to prison. Thus, her action was rooted in her original mafia environment's principles. However, her ongoing relationship with Prosecutor Paolo Borsellino gradually opened her mind, increasingly and painfully shifting her perspective. Her image of her father had always been positive, since she considered him someone to whom needy people went to ask favours. Later on, this image turned negative when she realized he was a criminal. After this discovery, she needed to find a substitute figure of reference, which she found in Paolo Borsellino who became like a surrogate father.

At the beginning of her experience as a witness, she felt frustrated because when she communicated her intention to the *Carabinieri*, they did not believe her testimony. This was because she was a young woman and also belonged to a mafia family. Thus, she had to fight to make herself credible. Later, Prosecutors Camassa and Borsellino started to listen to her testimony, until she received the first threat by the mafia due to her confession. To be protected, she was sent to Rome to live with Piera Aiello who was already living under witness protection. In her diary, Rita described her feelings of living in a big city like Rome, which to her, coming from a small Sicilian village, appeared much bigger than it was in reality. In some moving passages of her diary, she describes her feelings of emptiness provoked by living in hiding and, moreover, without love, since she had been rejected by her mother and also by her sister who lived in Milan. Alessandra Camassa wrote: 'Rita was young, she needed a family environment.

But her mother rejected her for testifying and she rejected her mother for not supporting her. So judge Borsellino intervened. He sought a responsible solution. Rita needed her mother. He arranged many trips to Sicily so Rita could meet her mother. I was present at some meetings. They weren't very nice.'[16]

Rita also suffered due to her impression that her sacrifice would be worthless. As she wrote in her diary:

> I am pretty sure that C. (the Partanna mafia boss whom she accused) will never go to prison. He murdered, stole and cheated; yet no one will be able to find the evidence to lay charges against him and prove I'm telling the truth. I am sure that I will never be able to make the judges believe me; I wish my father were here, because he could find the evidence to make him appear as he really is; that is, C., who is only a cheating murderer; yet obviously the words of a 17-year-old are worthless. I am only a young girl who wants justice and he is a man who plays the role of the good and honest worker very well. I can't live anymore, but he will keep on stealing and concealing that he was the person who carried out Stefano Nastasi's murder. As usual, the person who is better at cheating in life is the one who wins.[17]

Her thoughts were typical of an adolescent who was going through a terrible experience:

> It is almost nine o'clock p.m. and I am sad and discouraged because I am not able to dream anymore; in my eyes, I see only darkness. I am not worried about the fact that I will die but the fact that I will never be loved by anybody. I will never be happy and fulfil my dreams. I would like to have Nicola [her brother] here, to be caressed by him; I need it; but the only thing that I can do is cry. No one can understand the emptiness within myself, that emptiness that has gradually increased, due to everything. I haven't anything anymore; I have only crumbs. I can't distinguish good from bad, because everything is gloomy and miserable. I believed that time could heal all wounds; on the contrary, time opens them up more and more, until you die slowly. When will this nightmare end?[18]

However, she continued dreaming with hope in her future, since she was only seventeen years old. Indeed, she wrote notes about new experiences in Rome. Here, unlike in Partanna, she experienced a new freedom; she had the chance to meet a young man who became her boyfriend. Nonetheless, her world fell apart when her surrogate father Borsellino was killed by the mafia on 19 July 1992, in the so-called 'Via D'Amelio slaughter'. The grief was so unbearable that she decided to jump off her balcony. The suicide note she left said:

> Now that Borsellino is dead, no one can understand the emptiness he left in my life. Everybody is scared, but my only fear is that the mafia state will win and

those stupid people that fight against the mafia will be murdered. Before fighting the mafia you have to examine your conscience and then, after having defeated the mafia that is within yourself, you can combat the mafia that is among your friends; we are the mafia, in our wrong way of behaviour. Borsellino, you died for what you believed in, yet I am dead without you.[19]

Witness Rita Atria was transformed into a powerful symbol of the antimafia movement.[20] Her story is still remembered in schools and at public events.

Turning state's evidence may cause deep grief when there is an overlap between blood family and mafia clan, because speaking out against the mafia automatically means accusing one's closest relatives. This is often the case in the 'Ndrangheta, which has a familiar structure.

A deeply conflicting feeling was experienced by Rosa N., who denounced her relatives belonging to an important 'Ndrangheta family working between Reggio Calabria and Milan.

Arrested in 1993 at the age of thirty-six, in possession of drugs, she decided to collaborate with investigators. She informed them where the members of her clan were hiding drugs and money. Afterward, she revealed details of everything else she knew about the criminal organization in which, moreover, many women were involved. Expressing the ambivalent condition of women, she was an active protagonist in her mafia clan and yet at the same time was subordinate to the men of her family. She became independent from her mafia family by collaborating with the state, thereby constructing a new life based on principles contrary to those at the very core of her family. Her decision was clearly an autonomous choice to live a different life.

The psychological and symbolic violence experienced by Rosa in her family were crucial in her need to change her life. Her decision to collaborate with justice can be understood as a form of 'internal' revenge, which was the starting point of her path to authentic emancipation. Her experience had nothing to do with a typical mafia vendetta, which is an 'external' revenge resulting from the murder of a relative, as is clear from her reply to my first question in the interview she gave me in 1998.[21] The question addressed the reasons behind her decision to leave her usual world and set out on an unknown path under the protection of the traditional 'enemy', i.e. the state:

> The decision came from my heart, because as you know I unfortunately live in a family which is ignoble; it is rich in drugs, weapons and killings; it is rich in working life, but it is not rich in sentimental life; the sentimental life of a person is nothing for them; they don't care; they don't have problems; they live for money that in the end they do not have, for their work, but in the end, what does

it bring? It brings you to selling drugs ... to all of this, not to a quiet future; in the end you do not have anything.

Rosa was thus driven by a sincere desire to turn over a new page, as soon as she realized that the life she had led until then 'was ignoble'. She excluded revenge as a possible explanation: 'I did not collaborate for revenge because revenge is useless; I am already dead inside; I am not keen on sending them (her relatives) to prison; I did it because I felt like doing it, but they cannot come to tell me that it is my fault.'

Not only the violence she experienced, but also the fact her mother did not protect her, influenced her action. Rebelling against the system means the upheaval of a mentality in which masculine domination is sustained by women themselves, who have incorporated it as a natural order. Female submission, as Bourdieu pointed out, is produced by symbolic violence and is both spontaneous and extorted.[22] Here lie the ambivalent traits of female submission that young women strive to decode, when they see their mothers enforcing male power against themselves. This enigmatic reproductive mechanism disorients women themselves.

Though Rosa did not need proper revenge, she was still looking for a way to leave the people who treated her badly. Even more so, she was fed up with living in the underworld: which meant living on the run, having her house searched, seeing people (including relatives) die from drugs, constant violence and so on.[23] As she put it, 'after a long story, you see that and you arrive at the point at which you say "we cannot go on here anymore"'.

Describing her past, despite the nostalgia she felt for the luxurious aspects of her life, Rosa admitted: 'life was worthless; people themselves were worthless ... I was fed up with watching my seven-year-old daughter see my sister dead in the toilet, and having to run and call the ambulance and try to resuscitate my sister. This was traumatic for my daughter. These kinds of episodes went on until I decided to give up.' The future of her children was among the reasons prodding her. Unfortunately, there was no hope of saving her elder son, born out of her incestuous relationship with her father, because he was much too deeply involved in the criminal environment. The other two, a 19-year-old daughter and 10-year-old son, however, were taken away from that violent world.

When speaking with me, she stressed that her decision was not driven by an opportunistic calculation, since she did not know anything about the state's benefits for collaborators with justice:

When I made this decision I did not know that there was the witness program ... Nobody asked me anything; nobody compelled me; they were really kind; the only thing I said ... it was three in the morning; they let me rest then they told me 'just relax here;' I looked them in the face, after calling the *maresciallo*, and said, 'I intend to talk; I will tell you what I know' ... Just like that ... I did it instinctively. He replied to me, 'Are you sure?' And I said, 'At the moment I am sure; I don't know later; if tomorrow I wake up badly, I don't know.' One night in the police station, the day after I started calmly without anybody ever asking me anything. In fact, they did not believe what I told them since it seemed impossible that I had started to talk.

Whether the choice on which female collaboration with justice is based results from a calculation or arises as a spontaneous act, it is strictly linked to women's marginal position, which ends up becoming a crucial factor in the process of female separation from mafia families.

Rosa N.'s collaboration entailed denouncing the criminal involvement of all the members of her blood family, including herself. If she did not collaborate with justice, she could have expected a light sentence. On the contrary, she preferred risking a harsher sentence so she could leave her 'dirty' life. Later on, she learned about the reduction of punishment offered by the state in exchange for her information. As she told me: 'I had a reduced sentence; I must be honest; I got a lot of reductions in my punishment because I was sentenced to two years and five months, but I served all those years.'

Despite the positive aspects of a less severe punishment, her decision involved a drastic change in her life and habitus, which at the beginning caused her suffering. Her new situation, moreover, produced the constant risk of being murdered by members of her clan who remained free, such as her Calabrian relatives. When I asked her if she was afraid of death she replied:

> I swear to you, ever since I made this choice, I've been aware of its positive and negative implications; I know that from one day to the next, I should expect to see somebody in front of me; because I have this person always in front of my mind; I always see somebody, because unfortunately I am known, therefore eventually I always run into somebody; but, it does not matter much to me, because I know that sooner or later, if they want to ... they'll find you, even in America; so you shouldn't be scared of death, otherwise you stop living.

The fear of dying did not stop her from undertaking a path of collaboration with justice, and yet it is important to note that this time the circumstances were favourable, unlike in the past. In fact, Rosa N. had already thought of a possible collaboration in case she was arrested, but she did not act on it, due to her lack of trust in the state. As she told me:

> It crossed my mind in 1985, yet I did not trust anybody, otherwise I would have already given up a long time ago. The courage to go to the police station and say, 'Arrest me, I am here': no, I couldn't do this because I was always scared; and then, I had young children, even if I wasn't a good mother ... In 1986, when my sister died, I decided if somebody came – since I was the one with the drugs – and caught me, if I trust ... The thing is I didn't trust the law, or anything.

Trust in public officials makes the difference in the chance of developing a fruitful relationship between the person who has turned state's witness and the criminal justice system. All the *pentiti* I met stressed this point. Rosa N. remembered that meeting people who respected her was crucial. Until she was arrested her experience with public officials was negative, not only because she committed crimes, but as she explained to me:

> When I went to the police station to report that my car was stolen, the first thing they said was: 'Hey, ... [surname of her family] is here'. It was not my fault my car was stolen; even if I belong to the ... family, I needed to report the theft; in that case they push you away, even if you had the instinct to say another word, only to feel their arrogance ... also knowing that there were corrupt officials in that police station made you angry. I have always been a polite person with everybody; I have never turned impolitely to anyone who stopped me, never; I have always treated people with politeness and kindness; therefore one day I said, 'Detective, I respect you for your job and you respect me as a person. I have never done anything against you, so you saying in a disrespectful way "the ..." like you were saying "piece of shit" is intolerable, unfortunately I am one of the ... family, but if someone has stolen my car, can't I report it? ...' We were really far away from the law because they treated us like this; I found the trust to collaborate when they arrested me on 31 March, five years ago in Verona because of the way I felt I was treated. By chance, it was a *maresciallo* that in reality is a police inspector, I don't know, I don't know how to explain it to you, he had a trustworthy face.

The encounter with a prosecutor from the Milan DDA was particularly significant for Rosa N., as she told me:

> When I saw Prosecutore R. for the first time, he had such a nice face, so friendly that I said 'Yes, this would be the right moment'. I had had dealings with other Prosecutors but I can guarantee you that as soon as I saw them I panicked, I was terrified ... when I saw R. the first time I remember him saying to me, 'Madame, you are not obliged to do anything'. And I replied to him that this wasn't a problem because I had decided. And he said: 'If you feel ready we can start'.

Similarly, Giacoma Filippello said to Clare Longrigg about Prosecutor Paolo Borsellino: 'He was a lovely person, so understanding. I felt very close to him. When he talked to you, you never felt he was the big man behind the desk. He was a real friend to me. I suppose he made me believe in the legal system.'[24] Piera Aiello had a similar impression of Prosecutor Paolo Borsellino, who, as we have already seen, developed a special relationship with Rita Atria.

Rosa N.'s reflections over her rapport with the state and the law throw light on what was going on within the mind of a woman who had been accustomed to considering the habits and rules of her clan to be right and, by comparison, state law to be wrong. It reminds us that the notion of 'normality' is relative; we consider whatever we are accustomed to as 'normal'. When a mafioso sincerely becomes a *pentito*, he/she has to modify his/her her habitus – the representation of the world in which he/she was brought up, that she reckons 'normal' – and hence the content of words such as good and bad, right and wrong. This much is clear when reading the following passages of the interview in relation of the transmission of a certain mentality, explored above in Chapter Four. Indeed, Rosa N. explained to me what it means to be born in an environment in which adults have taught you that illegality is normal ever since you were a child:

> When somebody has a family such as mine, no one can stop you. You can understand that it is wrong, and disagree with everything. However, you are there, you have to do it and that's it. I do not have the chance to say 'I am going far away from here'; I did not have an escape route, I have no money, I was always dependent on my mum.

This reflection brought her to justify her criminal deeds insomuch as she did not feel guilty: 'if you think carefully, I do not have any guilt to expiate, I did not do anything abnormal, unfortunately living in that family I was doing a job'. From the point of view of her regular life, her criminal behaviour was normal. When I asked her for an explanation regarding drug trafficking or other illegal businesses, Rosa apologized for the fact she forgot that I am 'not normal'. 'Sorry Ombretta, I talk to you as if I were talking with a normal person. This happens to me even with lawyers; we often simply do things, therefore it is very easy for us to talk about them.' In other words, she had difficulties making herself clear when talking with people not belonging to the criminal world.

Despite the fact the criminal world was understood by Rosa to be normal, she confessed to feeling distinct from that normality. In fact, she recalled that she was considered 'bizarre' by her family or was called 'the black sheep' of the family:

> I think I was born different, in fact in my house they called me crazy because I had a different mentality from them ... My mum kept saying that I was not her daughter, she told me that I was found under a plant ... No one in my family will collaborate with the state ... I am the black sheep of the family. I have been always like that.

She maintained that although she shared a way of life with them, she felt a stranger to certain aspects of the criminal organization. For instance, she ignored the formal rules of the 'Ndrangheta and tried to rebel against male violence, unlike other women who supported it in silence; she refused to cut drugs in a potentially lethal way; she was against the death sentences the clan sometimes passed; she rejected typical mafia values such as *omertá* and vendetta. Perhaps this 'diversity' found expression in her subsequent decision to collaborate with the law. An alternative analysis of this self-presentation, as being 'different' from the other criminal members of her family, might be that she presented herself from her new perspective. This is a clear example of her present influencing her self-perception of the past. In looking back to her past she was searching for clues helping her to link her new identity (free from criminal behaviour) with her past. This has to do with the difficulties that *pentiti* experience in changing their own identity. Indeed, by talking with Rosa N. I understood how tough and painful it is to realize that the value system upon which you used to gauge your life only contains negative values when compared to a nonviolent value system that shows respect for the liberty of other human beings. A process of subversion of values, which obviously varies according to one's personality, occurs in any sincere *pentito*.

At the time I met Rosa N., she had not yet developed a definitive identity; hers was still hovering between past and present. This emerged from her words so much that when looking back she not only underlined the atrocity and violence of her life but also felt nostalgia for certain moments. She missed her comfortable life, even while recognizing that it was not earned honestly. Much as in the tales told by other *pentiti*, Rosa N.'s words and gestures revealed a sort of pride for having achieved a life of material comfort and consumer goods: 'I was doing fine, I had a housemaid, furs, gold jewellery, mobile phones; I was not short of anything; in my house, I never had to take an ashtray and move it; I was always served and revered.' Later, the new Rosa added to the argument presented by the old Rosa: 'However, it was not clean money.'

On many occasions, Rosa N. disclosed this internal and intimate process of transformation of a value system by showing two contradictory and clashing identities. At times one prevailed over the other and vice-versa. By observing her gestures and later analysing her words, I could discern the two identities, which were the result of the transition from an illegal mentality to a legal one, and from a busy life to an empty and solitary one. There is no doubt the passage was difficult, rough and full of conflicts. Contrasting opinions about her past life emerged continually, throughout our encounters: 'I described what really was my life, a life which was a hell, but also a heaven since you did not have to suffer hunger; there were 12 children and we never suffered hunger.' This nostalgia was not only due to the luxurious aspects of her life, but also for some particulars that were part of her everyday life: 'I was in love with my house, my furniture, my staff; I was crazy about them, just remembering them makes me cry; how can I explain it to you? Nowadays I wouldn't do my house up that way, however I still have it inside myself.'

Finally, her new identity prevailed, since she kept telling me she would make the same choice again. Also, when she remembered with nostalgia and regret the comforts of life she used to have, immediately she underlined their illicit origin. And more than this, she stressed the fact that she would prefer having family love and a regular life instead of those comforts: 'You can have all the fur coats you wish; I had twelve of them, I'm not bragging, I'm just saying; I had jewellery, I had cars, but they weren't worth anything because what I needed was just one caress from my mother...' Undoubtedly, Rosa left many material advantages in her past life. 'I was never at home; I was always running around, always in movement.' But she preferred her new life because it was clean, even though she felt alone.

Rosa's two identities corresponded to her two names: her real name and the new one, which was chosen by the state and obviously kept secret. It must be very hard to change one's own name at the age of 36, because on paper you get rid of your past life, even though it was an illegal one. The parts of the interview in which we addressed the delicate and intimate questions surrounding identity revealed the feelings of a collaborator with justice. The following quotation is from the last part of the interview, which was characterized by an empathetic atmosphere:

Q   Do you still feel like the same person or did you create a new identity?

A   I have created another person. You cannot cancel your past, even Jesus Christ cannot cancel that.

Q   Would you like to cancel it?

A No. I would like to cancel certain years of my life, but those are the years you can never cancel; but not everything because of course it is your life, from when I was one month old until I was 36, that was my life; you cannot cancel it; however inside myself, I feel like another person. I call myself by my true name when I get angry; I swear, it's weird; even in my mum's house she called me 'Maria Rosa' when she was angry at me, that is, with my true name; if she called me 'Rosa' it meant she was calm; even now when I call myself by my real name it means I am angry, whereas I call myself with my second name when I am relaxed.

Q So, your new name is your positive side?

A Yes, my second name is really important, my second life.

As she told me, Rosa could not cancel the past and the present was dominated by uncertainty and fear, because she could not reveal her true identity to anybody. This situation entailed difficulties in terms of human relationships:

> I have some friends but you have to understand that in my condition I cannot reveal who I am; I always have to invent things and unfortunately the invention, the lie brings about some limits. You have to limit yourself, you cannot overcome the limits, that is why I stay indoors.
>
> **Q** Can you invite your friends home?
>
> **A** Yes, yes, I can invite them but they have jobs; I told them I work. So I phone them after seven, that is, after work. I told them I was a civil servant. My one vice is the phone. I spend half a million lire every two months. I know that it is bad, but it is my only diversion. When it is half past eight in the evening my heart starts to open up and I start, and I can't tell you with my daughter.

Even in terms of a romantic relationship, living as a *pentita* presents problems:

> If I meet a guy I should tell him the truth because in the end he will find out. I would like to start a romantic relationship, but this will never happen, because of my character; I am a bit hard, but if I have to start something with a guy I want to base the relationship on sincerity not lies; it is useless for me to invent who I am ... because later maybe one day you bump into somebody who will say: "Look, it's Rosa, what are you doing here?" No I am sorry. And even this is an obstacle to meeting a guy.

Indeed when I interviewed her, in 1998, she was in a phase of her witness programme where she had new documents yet was still testifying at the hearing, so she could not work. Therefore, she spent all her time indoors without the possibility of talking with anybody. She defined her life as a parasite, a vegetable:

> Lately, I've become a vegetable. I don't recognise myself. I disgust myself this way. Sometimes I do get out of bed, I could say, why get up, I have my coffee, a whole three-cup coffee maker, I dust, I look at the house and I say to myself, "sure, nobody ever comes here anyway." It is always clean, but what do I have to do? Every morning I dust ... and clean. Then if you have something to read, I am crazy about books, I read many of them. I hate my bed, I hate it, I hate it. For two months I just go: living room, toilet and bed. Can you believe the skin on my back is ruined from staying in bed all the time, because what can you do? You go out, you are alone, I am not compelled to stay indoors, but I am alone and where do you go?

She wanted to work in order not to feel dependent on the state and spend her time doing something. This would have also contributed to her 'redemption':

> It seems to me that I'm stealing money that is not mine and then for my mind as well, because to me the most beautiful thing for a human being is having something to do, not living as a vegetable ... In my view, it would be better if they found me a job and I earned the money ... Anyway, to me anything is fine, I do not care, being a cleaning woman, a waitress, making beds, I don't care, it's not that I am a lady ... I told you that I have always been waited on, but I have always said that I wanted to work and not stay at home. When I was a child I dreamt of going to work in a factory; imagine this mania I had of punching a clock, but it was something that touched my soul; I used to see my neighbours coming back from the factory and punching the time-clock and I used to say, 'When I grow up I will go work in a factory.' I've had this ever since I was a child. I don't know; I have never said that I would go work in a bank. Or be a policewoman, you know? This is another hidden dream, but not just for me, for my daughter too. When she was a child and she saw the movies she'd say, 'Mamma, I'm going to be a policewoman.'

Once again, her words reveal her self-perception of the past, and as such they need to be interpreted with caution. In fact, what we are observing is Rosa N.'s attempt to seek traces of a lawful mentality in order to create the roots for building her new 'clean' identity. This mental process is much more understandable if we consider that in 1998, Rosa N. was sure her life was a tunnel with no way out. 'What can I expect of the future? You, or my daughter, can expect something but not me ... unfortunately; I am in a tunnel and it is very hard to get out ... I got out of the scene but I'm still inside this tunnel and I will never have a different life.'

This detailed description of Rosa N.'s feelings and life gives us a clear idea of the early stages of her *pentimento*, thus permitting us to understand the extent of her further progress. At the time I met Rosa, N. her strong and brave character led people who were close to her, including her lawyer, the prosecutor and myself, to believe she would be able to regenerate and construct her future. During the collaboration, she had already demonstrated an acute intelligence, to the extent that her lawyer had procured her some books. In a short time, she became a keen reader. This allowed her to gain a good level of ability in oral expression. Her dream in 1998 was to learn to write properly:

> Writing is my handicap. Unfortunately, I only completed the second year of secondary school; I have to thank books for what I've learned and the way I can express myself, otherwise ... I do not know how to spell, I have to ask ... to me this is something that I cannot tolerate. I tried to enrol in night school, but you have to pay. I cannot go to any school, and also in my area there is only one school and then they want your name and at that point you avoid it. I would like so much to write; it is something that I love, but I can't write; I have to write in block letters to be able to understand what I write.

From our encounter in 1998 to the present, she has made great progress and aligned herself with the positive pole of her *pentimento*. Once she obtained the official change of identity, she enrolled in a school and gained a diploma. Then, she worked as a volunteer helping people with disabilities. Finally, as provided by the state witness programme, she received state money – referred to as '*capitalizzazione*' – to buy a shop, since she was in the last stage of the programme. Today, she has just started her new business; hopefully, she will manage to live by herself without the state's help.

From prison to collaboration with justice

For some woman charged with mafia-related crimes, prison might become a place to discover themselves and their own desires, beyond the strict male rules that had driven their lives in their family.[25] For example, they can start to dress as they wish, unlike in the past when they were strictly controlled by their male relatives. During the time she spent in prison, Giusy Vitale, who had been raised as if she were a man, totally controlled by her brothers, as described above in Chapter Three, started to express another side of herself, more feminine, which she had to deny as an adolescent and while working for the criminal organization. As the prosecutor dealing with her case told me, in prison Giusy Vitale started to care about her appearance and education.[26] Her attention to dressing up, and appearing aesthetically 'female', and getting an education might be read as an expression of a sort of liberation from previous constrictions. This was confirmed by Giusy herself: 'Probably, you won't believe it, but I felt freer in prison than when I was really free, because in prison I rediscovered myself and now I know what I have to do.'[27]

After a while, Giusy decided to collaborate with magistrates. As she underlined, this decision was driven by her love for her new partner and also for her children:

> One of the reasons I decided to collaborate with justice is that G.A. (her partner) made me understand that it was the only way to really get out of this life and truly be able to have a life, not only for myself but also for my children, to make them grow up in a better life ... I had already thought about collaborating ... in July 2004 ... (but I postponed it) because ... I felt alone, up against the whole world, so automatically I thought of my family, I said, if I move away from them I have no one, but I was also thinking of my children, so it was quite troubling.[28]

However, her collaboration showed signs of ambiguity as it is clear from her statement:

> What do I regret? What am I supposed to say to people's families, did I really turn state's witness because I killed someone's father? Or their husband? ... What good would that be? It would be a joke! I'd be despicable if I did, and that's not part of my personality, not at all.

Probably her collaboration with justice was more a question of convenience rather than the result of an inner change, given the benefits she received for her collaboration.[29]

Despite the ambiguities of the motivations, her choice directed her towards a path of self-affirmation, more and more away from her brothers.

For other women, being arrested and spending time in prison might be experienced both as an opportunity for protection from family violence, if they had breached the mafia code of conduct, and as a chance to think critically about their past. After being arrested, Giusy Pesce distanced herself from her family, specifying to Prosecutor Alessandra Cerreti: 'I wanted to see you because I feel like I'm a victim ... of this family context that does not belong to me'.[30] Life in prison was not easy. Also she was aware that her family repudiated her for the shame she brought upon them by collaborating with justice, and she missed her three children very much. That is why she decided to retract her testimony and quit the protection programme. Afterwards, she changed her mind again. She asked to be reintroduced within the protection programme, as she wanted to offer her contribution to justice and above all to save her children from a mafia education. It is quite evident that this gradual passage towards moving away from her family was the product of a process that was rooted in the vulnerable position she formerly occupied in the mafia system. This emerges clearly from the letter she sent to the magistrates when she decided to collaborate with them:

> On October 14, 2010, I expressed my desire to start this process, driven by love as a mother and also by the desire to have a better life, far from the environment in which we were born and raised. I was – and am still – convinced that this is the right choice. Due to the choice of lifestyle made by family and relatives, we have always been marked by a life of suffering, hardship, and above all, a lack of courage for fear of consequences; whereas, each one of us should be able to do and choose what is right and wrong.[31]

The last words clearly show the nature of her gesture. Usually it is the code of honour that establishes what is right and what is wrong. Here she goes against the mafia law, returning the right of choice to the subject.

Giuseppina's story shows the ambivalence underlying both the female presence in the mafia and these women's decision of changing radically their own path in life, abandoning their familiar environment and undertaking an unknown avenue. This sort of ambivalence is common in the other stories of witnesses and collaborators illustrated below.

Uncertain and thorny paths of autonomy

When women living in the mafia are under oppressive protection, they also experience an isolation that makes it more difficult to escape, not only for logistical problems but also due to emotional and intimate reasons. The testimony of Maria Stefanelli explains female vulnerability in the mafia environment by linking it to a situation of isolation: "This is what makes us weak, atomizes us, leaves us each on our own way, even more vulnerable to the abuse of men and the organization. If you suffer violence, shut up, because you see that it is the same for the others, you know that nobody can help you".[32]

Testifying and collaborating with justice is not a linear process, but an uncertain, contradictory and complex undertaking. It can even bring women's lives to a tragic end, as in the cases of Maria Concetta Cacciola and Lea Garofalo. Both women entered the protection programme and both at a certain point decided to leave it. Maria Concetta Cacciola wished to reunite with her children, and Lea Garofalo was worried about her daughter's economic situation and future. Driven by these desires and concerns, they both trusted their relatives: Maria Concetta her parents, Lea Garofalo her ex-husband. This trust was fatal for both, as we know from Chapter Three.

Once Maria Concetta was back at home, she lived with the constant fear of being killed. She was already scared of her brother before becoming a witness. He was searching for proof about her extra-conjugal affair and, as she told the magistrates, she was sure that as soon as he found the evidence, he would have killed her and her lover: 'I knew that soon or later he would have come to me and tell me "come with me" and for sure he would make me disappear.'

When Maria Concetta's relatives discovered her love affair she was really scared, because she knew what kind of punishment female betrayers received. As is written in the judicial file, the relatives 'make burnt earth around her, creating an intimidating situation for her friends who could have provided her with logistical help if she had intended to run away'.[33]

She had bought some travel tickets but eventually she did not find the courage to escape due to her fear of being killed.

As shown by recordings of her mobile phone, which the police examined, she was so scared that in April 2011 she called the anti-violence centre's number (*Centro contro la Violenza alle donne*, 'Pink Phone Line' for Calabria) for listening to and supporting victims of violence, yet she disconnected the phone before somebody replied to her. After one month, she went to a police station, because her elder son was given a fine when riding his motorbike. There she met a policewoman with whom she started to talk about her personal life and the violence she suffered in the household. This encounter opened up the possibility to become a witness and, as such, to live under state protection.

As is written in the judicial file concerning the abuses perpetrated by Maria Concetta's family towards her:

> Violently beaten, forced to live with the fear that at any moment her brother would kill her for reasons of honour, constantly monitored by her mother and followed by her brother ... and her cousins, Maria Concetta Cacciola decided to turn to the police and provide statements regarding 'underworld discussions that she was forced to listen and that she didn't like' as she had confessed to her lover some time before.

In May she was inserted in the protection programme. The police took her from Rosarno and transferred her to a protected location. There is no doubt that her decision to start along this path was motivated by 'the fear of being killed for having blemished the family honour'.

Before leaving the house, she wrote a letter to her mother, in which she tried to explain why she had decided to leave the family and entrusted her three children to her.

I don't know where to begin and I can't find the words that might justify what I have done. Mum, you're my mum and only you can understand, a son or a daughter ... I know that I'm causing you great pain. If I explain everything to you, at least you'll have an explanation for everything ... I didn't want to leave you without saying a thing. I wanted to speak with you so many times, but I couldn't, so as not to give you any pain. I hid all my pain beneath a mask and turned it into aggressiveness, but unfortunately I couldn't release it, so I got angry with the person I loved the most, you. This is why I am putting my children in your care, since I wasn't up to it ... I beg you one thing and one thing only, don't make the same mistake I made ... give them a better life than the one I had, married at 13 to get a bit of freedom ... I thought I could do anything, but I ruined my life because he didn't love me and I don't love him, as you know. I beg you, don't make with them the same mistake you made with me ... give them room to live in ... if you lock the door, it's easy to go wrong, because they feel like prisoners on account of everything. Give them what you did not give me. I can't go on like this anymore, I only want to tell you to forgive me, mum, for the shame I've brought on you. Slowly, I have realised that I'm alone, alone with everyone and everything. I didn't want luxury, I didn't want money ... it was the peace, the love that you feel when you make a sacrifice. I never had any satisfaction in life, only pain, and the most beautiful thing are my children, they'll always be in my heart and it's so painful to leave them, no one will ever make up for this pain. Don't get discouraged you can't make my children understand this, be strong for them, don't give them to their father, he isn't worth them, stay close to A. because in the end he was just unlucky, he's been treated that way since he was a child ... that's why his character is the way it is, I know the little girls listen to you, so I'm not worried about them, but be more careful about him ... he's weaker. I will live as long as God allows, but I want to find out how I can find peace with myself. Mum, forgive me, please, I beg you, for all the terrible things I'm bringing upon you. All I can tell you is that where I'm going, I will live in peace, don't come looking for me, because you'll get in trouble. And I don't want to do what other people have done, just to find peace. I can't talk anymore now, only I know what happened and how I'm writing about it, but I couldn't leave you without telling you, and saying goodbye, I know I'll never be able to hug you nor see you but all I see in my eyes, before me, are you and my children. I love you ... mum, hug my children like you always have, and talk about me to them, don't leave them in their hands, they aren't worthy of them or anyone. Mum, farewell, and forgive me, forgive me if you can. I know I'll never see you, because this is what the family's honour calls for, this is why you have lost a daughter. Farewell, I will always love you. Forgive me, I beg you, forgive me. Farewell.

Maria Concetta's letter shows her intimate and profound desire for a kind and loving relationship with her parents. Strength and despair alternate in invoking her mother to understand her act of rupture. From her words, it seems that she turns to her mother as a woman, when she hints at a female complicity by asking her to talk about her children and 'not to leave them to them'. By the second 'them' she means the men of the family, including her father and her brother. She is searching to be defined as female, as though she was saying quite clearly: 'We are the females, they are the males'. This letter provides us with a rare glimpse into a mafia family, showing its strict division between men and women, and also some traces of female solidarity, which however is scarcely feasible in such a male-dominated system. After many years of life outside the mafia environment, Maria Stefanelli understood the attitude shown by her mother, who did not defend her from male violence:

> I realized that she had not been able to protect even herself from the legacies of the false code of honour to which she was bent, and that the pain and bewilderment she felt were equal to ours: the weight of life had overwhelmed her, removing them any ability to react, cancelling her maternal instinct. She barely had the survival spirit left, but in the end, that too was gone.

Men obtain female submission partly by exercising symbolic violence that is more subtle and less evident than the physical type, but equally powerful and effective. Bourdieu explains that to understand the form of domination achieved through symbolic violence it is necessary 'to move beyond the forced choice between constraint (by forces) and consent (to reasons), between mechanical coercion and voluntary, free, deliberate, even calculated submission'.[34] He specifies that 'the effect of symbolic domination ... is exerted not in the pure logic of knowing consciousnesses but through the schemes of perception, appreciation and action that are constitutive of habitus and which, below the level of the decisions of consciousness and the controls of the will, set up a cognitive relationship that is profoundly obscure to itself'.

Maria Concetta's mother was aware of the peril to which her daughter was exposed. As is written in the judicial file, 'She felt the need to warn her about the risk, telling her "you know, they (her husband and son) know everything; ... you see, daughter, they have your phone call's printout ... they have all the printouts of your conversation with another person"'. She attempted to reduce the risk that Maria Concetta's betrayal and 'damnation' might bring her in the name of honour. However, she was not in a position to defend her daughter. Actually, after Maria Cacciola started to collaborate with justice, she become totally complicit with male power, acting in conformity with mafia norms. The limits of female solidarity are not only due to the concrete difficulty involved in rebelling, but also to women's attachment to the male cultural system, that has been incorporated by women themselves. Female complicity seems to remain a mirage in this family context.

Eventually, Maria Concetta's mother, along with other relatives, used the woman's children as blackmail tools, in order to convince her to retract her confession and to return home. The family succeeded. As emerged from the intercepted phone calls, Maria Concetta begged forgiveness from her mum and dad, even if they were responsible for her segregation and they had not helped her when she was victim of domestic violence. Finally she was back, therefore, in what the magistrates defined a 'domestic prison'.

Paradoxically, she felt that she was in the wrong, because she considered becoming a witness while repudiating her family identity, the one that was shaped in the household where her primary socialization occurred.

As was clear from the phone conversation with her best friend and the letter to her mother quoted above, Maria Concetta's feelings were not only an expression of her fear of being killed, but were also closely linked to a sense of fault and shame. The latter were the result of the symbolic violence exercised on her by the context where she grew up and her family. Following Bourdieu's theoretical framework,[35] it is clear that Maria Concetta embodied the cultural norms and gender expectations established by the family and the clan, insofar as she perceived her behaviour as negative and wrong. Therefore, she felt guilty.

Not only the fear of being separated from her children, but also her deep bond with her family become the main obstacle in her path toward a new life. When she was back at home, her life ended tragically.

Lea, too, trusted her husband when he proposed economic help for their daughter's sustenance. Disappointed by the state's treatment and by the experience of continuously changing names and protected locations, she decided to leave the protection programme. She wanted to be independent. However, she felt alone and scared, as is clear from the letter she wrote to the President of the Republic, and ultimately never sent to him.[36] Despite the recommendations made by a lawyer working for the antimafia association Libera, who had tried to dissuade her from meeting her ex-husband, Lea Garofalo was determined and went to a meeting that proved to be a trap intended to kill her. Courage, dignity and aspiration for justice led her ethical action in opposing 'Ndrangheta dominance, represented by her husband and the environment in which she grew up. This suggests us that her agency was deeply marked by innovative features.

Following their own children

Women escape from the mafia system not only by asking to be inserted in the protection programme, intended for collaborators with justice and witnesses, but also by following their children that have been monitored by the Youth Court (*Tribunale per i minorenni*), because they have committed a crime or because they risk becoming juvenile delinquents. In the last ten years, the number of mothers that have left the mafia system thanks to the Youth Court's interventions with their children has increased. No official data exists, yet the NGO Libera, involved in supporting the Youth Court and supplying children and women with an assistance network, maintains that there are around fifty.

The head of Libera, don Luigi Ciotti, defines this path as 'the third way' for women intending to leave the mafia. Basically, this avenue has become an option for those women who want to cut themselves off from the mafia, but do not have information to exchange with the state, in order to become collaborators with justice or witnesses. Through the 'third way' they take advantage of the possibilities that the Youth Court offers their children. In some cases, they even encourage the Court to become interested in their children's situation, hoping it will intervene, as emerges in many cases of procedural documents.[37] Children, thus, become a channel for liberation from the oppressive mafia environment.

The Youth Court intervenes by revoking parental authority to parents belonging to the 'Ndrangheta only when there is serious proof of abuse (*maltrattamento*) in upbringing and education. This practice has become increasingly systematic over the last ten years. President of the Reggio Calabria Youth Court, Roberto Di Bella, started to use articles 330 and 333 of the Civil Code in order to revoke parental authority in situations in which no one could take care of the child, because the parents, or one of them, or even close relatives (such as grandparents) were arrested (this situation is not rare given that in the 'Ndrangheta the mafia clan and the extended family overlap); or if a minor belonging to a mafia family ran the risk of becoming a juvenile delinquent.

Di Bella started to introduce actions aimed at taking care of children living in 'Ndrangheta families, since he kept observing that the juvenile delinquents he arrested for mafia-related crimes always belonged to the same families.[38] In other words, year after year the majority of the young people imprisoned in Calabria came from the same most important 'Ndrangheta families, which basically were a factory producing juvenile delinquents. Moreover, the prosecutor was worried about the children of witnesses or collaborators with justice. The tragic experience of Maria Concetta Cacciola contributed to the necessity to increase the state's interventions towards witnesses' children. As seen above, Maria Concetta went back to her parents' home due to the fear of being definitively separated from her children, who had been used by her parents as a tool for blackmail. The same occurred with Giuseppina Pesce's children, that were used instrumentally by the woman's relatives, in order to convince her to retract her confession to magistrates. The family, functioning as a device of the mafia system, disciplines its members and places them in a given position. In the cases mentioned above it treated minors as a means for extortion. Recalling these experiences, Di Bella was keen on trying a method for preventing the children of those who decided to collaborate from being used by the extended families as a means to catch those who ran away from the system. He wanted to prevent other minors from being compelled to live in ambiguous and unpleasant situations similar to those that Cacciola and Pesce's children had to bear.[39]

After the first proceedings revoking parental authority, Di Bella's interventions gradually attracted attention in public opinion. Some observers criticized him, thinking that his interventions regarded 'Ndrangheta families in general, while others supported his action.

Owing to the difficulties in planning educational programmes for minors due to the lack of regional social services and the scarcity of jobs in Calabria, since 2015 the Youth Court of Reggio Calabria has started to sign a series of official protocols with other judiciary offices (i.e. DDA), Ministries, NGOs such as *Libera*, and also with Catholic Church bodies like the *Conferenza Episcopale Italiana*. These protocols gave a formal basis to the project '*Liberi di scegliere*' ('Free to choose'), whose aim is to facilitate the coordination of interventions among institutions and the third sector involved in planning programmes for an alternative life for minors coming from mafia families and caught up in Youth Court proceedings, and in some circumstances even for their mothers and their entire family.

These programmes intend to take care of the youths by offering them psychological support and educational opportunities. The tendency is to send them outside of Calabria, collocating them in youth centres, families, or providing their mothers with a job and a house.

What the Youth Court proceedings establish, however, is not always definitive, insofar as the Court hopes to save the family relationship. When the revocation is temporary, children can return to their family, if the parents demonstrate they have undertaken deep changes. These measures are not intended to counter the mafia directly, through a frontal and conflictual approach, looking instead towards the single persons involved in the mafia by offering them a chance of redefining their lives.

The driving principle underlying the innovative judicial practices implemented by the Youth Court of Reggio Calabria is 'the best interest of the child', on which international conventions for children are grounded. In its premise, the 1989 Convention on the Rights of the Child states 'that, in the Universal Declaration of Human Rights, the United Nations has proclaimed that childhood is entitled to special care and assistance'; it underlines that 'the family, as the fundamental group of society and the natural environment for the growth and well-being of all its members and particularly children, should be afforded the necessary protection and assistance so that it can fully assume its responsibilities within the community'; it recognizes 'that the child, for the full and harmonious development of his or her personality, should grow up in a family environment, in an atmosphere of happiness, love and understanding'; it states that 'parents must educate the child to become a useful member of society and develop his sense of moral and social responsibility', and 'that the child should be fully prepared to live an individual life in society, and brought up in the spirit of the ideals proclaimed in the Charter of the United Nations, and in particular in the spirit of peace, dignity, tolerance, freedom, equality and solidarity'.[40] In particular, Article 3 states that 'in all actions concerning children, whether undertaken by public or private social welfare institutions, courts of law, administrative authorities or legislative bodies, the best interests of the child shall be a primary consideration'.[41]

According to the Italian Constitution (art. 30), the state must guarantee that minors have got the right to grow up in their family, yet at the same time it ought to intervene in situations of prejudice. That is why youth judges sometimes decide to revoke parental authority or to separate children from their parents, when, on the basis of the social worker's reports, they observe that in the families the upbringing given to minors by their relatives is lacking and contrary to 'the best interest of the child'. In one Youth Court file, the judges justified their intervention underling that the parents' actions 'are not only relevant for criminal law, but also represent a clear disparagement of the most elementary rules of education and assistance of a minor, as well as being concrete violations of the duties given to parents by the law'.[42]

The Youth Court's intervention intends to prevent children from assuming roles that their families assign them. For example, girls will not be compelled to be an object of exchange in arranged marriages or to bring messages from one mafia member to another, nor to transport arms, etc.

According to Di Bella, the new approach of the Youth Court has encouraged women to come to him to find support, in order to leave their families and to guarantee their children protection and the opportunity to live in a new environment, free from the mafia's influence. In the following letter addressed to Di Bella, a mother asked him to separate her son from their family:

> Please send my son away from our town; send him to a region other than Calabria, where he can escape the negative influence of the environmental and family context. My husband and his relatives are people with serious criminal records [related to 'Ndrangheta]. I fear that my son will take a bad road and may end up involved in mafia affairs. I fear for his safety, also for the delicate age that makes him easily impressionable. I also fear for my own safety, for all these things that I am denouncing in the interest of my son and I ask to be helped, if possible, to go with my children. I want to go away and be with them to give them all the emotional support they need, raising them in compliance with the law, something that in recent years he has not been able to do because of his father. I make this personal sacrifice because I would like to assure my children a peaceful life, which by staying here in ... they certainly would not have. I ask to be helped, I will do everything that the Court will requires of me. Sincerely.[43]

Testimonies like this highlight that women have power as transformative agents.[44] This power remains embryonic until it finds institutions that, embodied by trusty and caring subjects, offer women the conditions for fulfilling their capacities as agents. This is true even for collaborators with justice, as narrated above when describing the crucial relationships between witnesses and Prosecutors.

According to key observers, working in the project *Liberi di Scegliere*, these women are not only terrified by the potential reaction of their husbands, but also afraid of becoming autonomous.[45] Projects supporting these women and their children have to consider this dimension of their experience, in order to plan programmes to help them to take their distance from oppressive relatives by balancing care and protection. This will facility the process of acquiring authentic autonomy, understood – as specified later – not idealistically as proposed by liberalism,[46] but as conceptualized by relational autonomy theorists.

The ethical impact

When women belonging to the mafia take the decision to make a deal with the state, they have to face their relatives' 'contempt', as seen above. While talking about her daughter with a nephew, Giuseppina Pesce's mother used the following words:

Leave her alone. If she calls you, don't answer. If she insists, or if you happen to be picking up the phone, you have to tell her: 'for me you are dead, you no longer exist', that's what you have to tell her. Tell her that your grandmother and your aunt are in jail on account of her and while we are going to jail with our heads held high, she is the most miserable... she is not going to jail... she is the most miserable. But tell her that I don't give a shit, I'm in jail now and I don't care, when you hear from her on the phone you have to tell her: your mom said to forget you have a mom, full stop, your mom is gone, no, no, don't cry, it's the truth.[47]

This is one of the many instances of disowning exercised by families of collaborators with justice or witnesses, who eventually run the risk of being killed by their relatives. Emilio Di Giovine wanted to kill her sister Rita, because she had collaborated with justice in 1993. As he told me:

My sister Rita has also been in danger several times, they wanted to kill her... Before I too thought that the collaborators were ignoble, unworthy, I thought my sister was a poor wretched drug addict, that's what I thought of her. That's right, that's the truth, I was getting her killed.[48]

It is not surprising, then, that for security reasons collaborators have to change identity documents and use cover names. Also they have to change place of residence and they cannot reveal to anybody their true identity. Suddenly they find themselves living in a new context, where no one knows them. They have a small wage from the state and they have many restrictions concerning the possibility of working.

A collaborator with justice told me: 'It was easier to be a mafioso than a *pentito*'.[49] He told me that it was quite difficult for him, who used to be a 'man of honour', to bear the humiliation of being called '*infame*' (betrayer) by his former companions during the trial, in which he testified against them. Significantly, his wife dressed in black, pretending he was dead.

Becoming a *pentito* is a conflicting and painful experience, that however for many women might be the beginning of affirming themselves in an authentic way. As previously discussed, by discovering the strength lying within their fragility, they develop powerful capacities for agency that contribute to forming a critical view of mafia norms. Shifting their view and taking concrete measures to find new possibilities for their future triggers profound short- and long-term changes at different levels, including individual, family and societal.

First of all, women turning state's evidence furnish important investigative elements to law enforcement agencies. The information given by Maria Concetta

Cacciola in 2011 was used even after her death, since it gave significant input for the investigations that led police to carry out, in 2013, the operation called 'Tramonto'.

Moreover, at an individual level, women leaving the mafia acquire autonomy for the first time or achieve a new type of autonomy, an authentic one. The latter is different from the autonomy shown by women engaged in active roles in the mafia criminal sphere that, as seen in Chapter Five, are the results of agentic capacities directed towards perpetuating the mafia system. On the contrary, women taking their distance from the mafia pursue a 'genuine' autonomy. This is demonstrated by the fact that their agential self-governance is close to meeting some criteria of authentic autonomy, that, according to philosopher Meyers, correspond to a series of emotional, imaginative and critical skills. Emotional ability renders the agent capable of reading and regulating their own emotions; imaginative capacity allows the subject to understand the consequences of their own decisions and foresee other possibilities of acting; and critical skills provide the subject with the capacity to criticize social norms and values. These abilities allow women to achieve self-discovery (understanding themselves), self-definition (defining their values and commitments) and self-direction (directing their life).[50]

Oppressive environments and the internalization of an oppressed condition as 'normal' and right, justified by the context's normative system, deteriorate or hinder the emerging of these skills, which 'enable individuals to construct their own self-portraits and self-narratives and that thereby enable them to take charge of their lives'.[51] When women acquire an authentic autonomy, they can finally appreciate the feeling of self-realization. This is what makes the difference with respect to the form of autonomy 'conquered' by women staying in mafia organizations, that are by definition male-centred and male chauvinist. Interestingly, Meyers poses a question that challenges feminist theorists and also our analysis: 'If women's professed desires are products of their inferior position, should we give credence to those desires? If so, we seem to be capitulating to institutionalized injustice by gratifying warped desires. If not, we seem to be perpetuating injustice by showing disrespect for those individuals.'[52] Mackenzie and Stoljar clarify this answer by underling that, according to Meyers: 'not all desires should be afforded equal credence or weight. Autonomous desires, namely, those that express our "authentic selves," as developed through the exercise of skills of self-discovery, self-definition, and self-direction, are more worthy of satisfaction than desires that merely reflect uncritical acceptance of social norms or expectations.'[53] Women working in mafia criminality might perceive engaging in new functions as a response to their own desires of autonomy, while they satisfy the needs of the mafia organization. As a matter of fact, this form of autonomy is other-directed and also does not bring women recognition in terms of power, nor does it hinder male dominance. On the contrary, women who refuse to meet the needs of the criminal organization and undertake a different strategy of autonomy, which is more complex and risky, are rewarded in terms of self-realization, 'that is crucial for self-respect'.

Defining autonomy on the grounds of specific competences allows us to grasp the process according to which women refusing the mafia value system produce a change in intergenerational terms. As mothers, they replace the transmission of mafia values, including male dominance over women, honour, vendetta and the code of silence, with teaching skills leading to authentic autonomy. This means that not only a simple change of the transmission's content occurs, but also critical and self-realization practices.

Rosa's relationship with her daughter is highly indicative in this sense. In the beginning, she refused to accept her mother's decision, because she considered her an *infame* for betraying their family. Later on, she understood what that decision meant, as Rosa proudly told me:

> Finally, she got it, after three and a half years ... At the beginning she wasn't happy, so she talked to me just because she was compelled to, to her I was a shitty mother because I should not have done what I did ... Seven months ago my daughter finally said to me, 'Mamma, you did the right thing and if anything bad ever happens to you, I will carry on along your path.'[54]

A generational transmission, which breaks a deeply rooted cultural model, needs reciprocity in a relationship. To Rosa, in fact, her daughter's support was fundamental in order to keep believing that her choice was right:

> I saved my children by making this choice, because now I can say that I saved my daughter; I talk to her every night and I can guarantee you she is wonderful, and she keeps telling me, 'Thanks mum for what you did;' I'll never hear any such thing from my elder son; he is 25 years old and he won't say 'thanks mum' to me because he doesn't recognise me as his mother.[55]

When Rosa talked to me about her daughter, her eyes filled with joy:

> She is studying to be a cook. This is her last year then I hope the school will find her a job. She likes the gym; she loves everything; she is a volcano; I don't know how that girl can manage; she gets up at six, goes to school, comes back from school, goes to the gym, comes back from the gym, goes to the meeting ... dear

daughter, I cannot recognise you; you are not like your mother. This is beautiful, very beautiful ... then it helps you understand you made the right choice ... at least having the satisfaction that your daughter says to you, 'you did the right thing; *if something happens to you, I will go on*', 'Where do you think you're going? Calm down!'. However, it is fantastic after everything I've been through, I think it is the greatest satisfaction.[56]

Nothing happened to Rosa, unlike another collaborator, Lea Garofalo. As we know, she was killed by her husband because she left him and became a witness. Her daughter Denise (born in 1998) decided to continue her mother's fight against the 'Ndrangheta's principles and achieve justice for her. She found the courage to testify in the trial against her father, charged with her mother's murder.[57] Denise, who had learned from her mother the value of speaking out, offers public opinion living evidence of a female 'emancipated voice', expressing the capacity to speak out publicly with an affirmative, ethical and transformative purpose.

Denise's action had both concrete and symbolic impact. Her testimony was crucial for her father's condemnation. Also, along with her mother, she became one of the female symbols of the antimafia movement. Their story makes people more conscious and aware of the mafia problem. NGOs, local administrations, schools and citizens have organized various public initiatives to maintain Lea Garofalo's memory.[58]

It is evident, thus, that motherhood is a key dimension for grasping the ethical impact on a transgenerational level created by the women leaving the mafia. At the same time, it must be treated with caution, since public opinion tends to attribute a woman's choice to leave the mafia system to instinctive maternal love. This argument is risky, because it reduces the complexity whereby this kind of decision is taken and make women fall back into a stereotyped representation linking femininity to this biological function.[59] On the contrary, motherhood becomes a valuable heuristic tool in this analysis if we consider it as a relational and practical model. In order to understand the ethical reach of women's choice of rejecting the tenets underlying the mafia, it is necessary to overcome the biological meaning of motherhood and understand it as work.[60] In particular, it is necessary to focus on a mother's training of her child to meet the third of the children's demands identified by Ruddick, that is social acceptability, explored above in Chapter Four.

An ambivalence might characterize mothers' role in training, when there is a conflict between the social group's values and what the mothers think is right for their children: 'If the group demands acceptable behaviour that, in a mother's eyes, contradicts her children's need for protection and nurturance, then the mother will be caught in painful and self-fragmenting conflict. Nonetheless, however alienated they feel, mothers seem to recognize the demand to train their children as an ineluctable demand made on them as mothers.'[61]

When mothers are capable of responding to the child's demand for social acceptance by training them not according to the mafia system's expectations, they quit working at the service of the mafia's values and reaffirm their authentic maternal authority to the benefit of society. In these cases, motherhood or better mothering might become a revolutionary practice. A woman, the wife of a 'Ndrangheta member and son of a man charged by the Youth Court, explicitly confessed to Prosecutor Di Bella her hope to regain her maternal authority by leaving her family and asking help from public institutions. She introduced her situation by telling him:

> I am the mother of Rosario, who is 15, and I am also Alessandro's sister, whom the Juvenile Court of Reggio Calabria judged for murder in the 1990s and who is now serving life imprisonment for another murder; I am the sister of Francesco, condemned for having killed a carabiniere, Umberto and Antonio's daughter, who were recently killed in a mafia ambush. I came here on the occasion of the criminal trial that will be held today against my son Rosario, to report my strong maternal concern for the destiny of my children and, in particular, for Rosario and his younger brother aged 13. My son is already in the courtroom, but he doesn't know I'm here, President. I fear that they may end up in prison or killed like my father and brother Umberto or my father-in-law. My family has been involved in numerous local feuds in a 'Ndrangheta context, with several people murdered. My cousin and eleven-year-old son were also killed. My two children are rebellious, violent, have bad friends, are fascinated by the 'Ndrangheta and attracted, despite their age, to weapons. I fear they will commit crimes and go down a road of no return. My son Rosario thinks that going to prison is an honour and he thinks it can give him respect, but in reality he doesn't know what prison is and what could happen to him in there.

Interestingly, then she underlined that she had lost her maternal authority when she stated:

> I am unable to control my children, despite my best efforts, and I ask the Juvenile Court for help so that they can have a different destiny from that of my father, my husband and my brothers. Please, send my children away from Reggio Calabria, I would like them to have strong rules because otherwise they have no respect for anything and I cannot exercise my maternal authority.

The price for regaining maternal authority is high, as she underlines that the decision to turn to the Public prosecutor was not easy:

> Please understand how painful my decision is, which I communicate to a judge for the first time, but it is the only solution because I would like my children to have a peaceful and different life from my family's and mine. There is nobody in my family, nobody I can trust.[62]

Her needs spanned a number of areas, from symbolic to material:

> I would like to go away from Reggio Calabria, a context unsuitable for the growth and future of my children ... I would like to ... build a new life elsewhere with my children ... I ask you for help, President, the Juvenile Court and the Libera association to go away and have a life following and protecting my children. I need to find a home, a job to be able to support myself and I need help finding a school for my children ... I have tried to alleviate the 'heavy' situation in our house, due to the constant absence of my husband, who was always in and out of prison. I have always worked to keep my children from lacking anything. I would like to go away, and begin planning immediately, according to the needs of my youngest children, to do this towards September 2018, when the school year will begin.[63]

Women leaving the mafia teach their children the power of female fragility and the value of words. As pointed out above, vulnerability is not a drawback, it is a valuable resource making women capable of responding to the violence suffered through an act of life, namely choosing to distance themselves and their own children from the culture of death promoted by the mafia system. By demonstrating the value of words against the mafia's law of silence, by interrupting the intergenerational transmission of mafia principles, and by teaching their children skills for acquiring authentic autonomy, women show care towards themselves, their children and society.

Their ethical decision becomes a political event revealing that vulnerability can be exploited as an agentic lever when the institutional context is favourable. The choices made by individuals, supported by institutions, can have wide socio-cultural resonance, profoundly affecting the fabric of society.

Appendix: Lea Garofalo's letter to the President of the Italian Republic

28 April 2009

Dear President,

I am writing to you as a desperate young mother, psychically and mentally exhausted by years of daily torture, due to a total lack of adequate support from certain professional figures, such as my current legal assistant, who says he is willing to help me but does not even answer my phone calls. For about 7 years, we have been in a temporary protection programme. Normally, the temporary programme lasts approximately 1 year, but in this case no reasonable amount of time exists anymore. If I may, no sense of limit exists either, given that our fundamental rights, guaranteed by European laws, are violated each and every day.

The lawyer assigned to me made me appear as a collaborator with justice, using this term even though I have never, I repeat never, committed any crime in my entire life. I am a woman who has always taken responsibility for herself, and who, quite some time ago, decided to break off all ties with her family and her companion. I am trying to begin a new life, with my daughter and with full respect for legality and justice. After receiving numerous psychic, verbal and mental threats, I reported all of them. One month after making my statement, a magistrate listened to me, along with a police officer and the legal assistant assigned to me. I was told I would have to wait until they could find a judge who is not corrupt. After spending more than a month running from one city to another, afraid for obvious reasons and with a young daughter, the police took us to the Public Prosecutor's office in C., where I spoke, accompanied by a lawyer assigned to me by the office itself.

They told me I would appear as a collaborator with justice. I must start by saying that I have no knowledge of the law, and therefore this term, for an uninformed person such as myself, was correct in the sense that I was collaborating in order to have mafioso criminals arrested. After about three years, my case passed to another magistrate, from whom I learned that I had been poorly represented by my legal assistant.

Today, my daughter and I are isolated from everything and everyone. I have lost everything, my family, my job (even though I had a temporary contract), my home, more friends than I can count, and all hope for the future. But I realised this would be the case, I knew what was in store for me when I made my decision. What I did not realise, and could not imagine in any way, not only because I am a poor uneducated person who only barely made it through middle school, but also because I sincerely thought that reporting them was the only way I could put an end to the continuous abuse and, probably, make some poor wretch change his mind, sincerely. I don't even know where I got this spirit, or perhaps I do, considering the sad precedent represented by the many members of my family, who were perfectly honest, and yet lost their trials! People who even sold the house they live in, to pay their lawyers and above all to pursue an idea of justice that has never existed, on the contrary! Today, after all these precedents, I wonder how I could have even thought that something similar to justice might really exist in Italy, above all after the disastrous precedents like the ones my family lived through firsthand.

Maybe it's because history repeats itself and genetics doesn't change, but I am repeating, step after step, what already happened in my family, and do you know what the worst part is? The worst part is that I already know what fate has in store for me, after being hit hard, materially and emotionally, I am going to die! Death, unexpected, ignoble, inexorable and above all without any satisfaction: for some people in my family, this was quite natural, if I may say so, for a person to die because they want to drown their pain in alcohol, trying to forget their children, who were killed because they refused to be blackmailed by the first mafioso that came along. For another it was certainly more atrocious than you can imagine, slowly, because on account of the previous negative results, he carried out justice on himself and, like everyone knows, when you get into vicious circles it's almost impossible to get out unharmed. And all this because the institutions turn a deaf ear!

Now, with this letter, I am presumptuous enough to want to change the course of my sad story, because I absolutely never want anyone, one day, feel like they have the authority to do what the law must do, sacrificing, even though it's for a just cause, their own lives and those of their beloved, to pursue an idea of justice that no longer has anything to do with what's right, if one does it alone, and in the cheapest of ways. I would like, Mr. President, for you, with this request I am making for help, to answer me and the dozens, if not hundreds of people who are now in the same situation as me. Right now, I honestly don't know how many of us has never committed any crime and, after having reported various criminal acts find themselves catalogued as collaborator with justice, thus belonging to that well-known bunch of swine that go by this name in Italy, rather than witnesses of criminal acts. I can assure you, because I have personally lived through all this, that there are people who, even though they have wound up in such situations, manage not to compromise themselves in any way and to give their lives dignity and hope, in addition to justice. You, today, Mr. President, can change the course of history. If you want, you can help those who, even though no one knows why or how, are still able to believe it is possible to live properly even in this country, in spite of everything! Mr. President, I beg you, give us a sign of hope, this is all we, and experts on civil and penal law, are waiting for. You as well must give your support to those who are wrongly experiencing difficulty!

Personally, I do not believe that someone exists who can do miracles, but I believe in people and their will, because I have been through this in the first person, and for those who are close to me. So: if some lawyer reads this article and wants to pursue an idea of justice, settling for what they receive for free legal aid, but also gaining huge satisfaction and the immense gratitude of a young mother who still believes in something vaguely real, today, in this country, let him come forward. I need help, someone help us. Please!

Notes

Introduction

1 Raimondo Catanzaro, *Il delitto come impresa. Storia sociale della mafia* (Milan, 1991).
2 Armao, Fabio, *Il sistema mafia. Dall'economia-mondo al dominio locale* (Turin, 2000).
3 Kimberle W. Crenshaw, *On Intersectionality: Essential Writing* (New York, 2017).
4 On the use of biography as research method see the special issue of *Rassegna italiana di Sociologia* edited by Monica Massari and Roswitha Breckner, 1 (2019). In particular: Monica Massari and Roswitha Breckner, 'Biography and Society in Transnational Europe and Beyond. An Introduction', in *Rassegna italiana di Sociologia*, 1 (2019).
5 Daniel Bertaux, *L'enquête et ses méthodes: le récit de vie* (Paris, 2000).
6 Diana T. Meyers, *Gender in the Mirror. Cultural Imagery and Women's Agency* (Oxford, 2002), p. 10.
7 For a reflection on a critical approach to judiciary sources in mafia studies, see Ombretta Ingrascì, 'Le fonti giudiziarie nello studio delle mafie. Riflessioni per un dibattito', in *Rivista di Studi e Ricerche sulla Criminalità Organizzata*, 4 (4) (2018), pp. 28–40.
8 'Collaborators with justice' known also as *pentiti* (literally 'someone who repents') refers to those who confess all their criminal involvement and give investigators information about criminal events and people; *testimoni* (witnesses) refers to those who have committed no crime but were witnesses to a crime or demonstrated knowledge about a crime. The last chapter gives information about the law that envisages the protection programme for those mafiosi who intend to collaborate with the State.
9 Interview with Rosa N. (pseudonym), Milan, 28 April 1998.
10 The men I interviewed were ex-members of Cosa Nostra and 'Ndrangheta, and belonged to different generations. In this work I will quote the following interviews: Interview with Antonio N., pseudonym of former 'Ndrangheta member and collaborator with justice, Modena, 5 May 2004; Interview with Giuseppe C., pseudonym of former Cosa Nostra member and collaborator with justice, Bologna, 2 April 2004; Interviews with Emilio Di Giovine, former 'Ndrangheta boss and collaborator with justice (in different places between 2008 and 2011).
11 Alessandro Portelli, 'Oral History as Genre', in M. Chamberlain and P. Thompson (eds.), *Narrative and Genre* (London, 1998), p. 30.

12 Joan Acker, Kate Barry and Johanna Esseveled, 'Objectivity and Truth. Problems in Doing Feminist Research', in M. M. Fonow and J. A. Cook (eds.), *Beyond Methodology. Feminist scholarship as lived research* (Indiana, 1991), p. 136.
13 Ibid.
14 Loraine Gelsthorpe and Allison Morris, *Feminist Perspectives in Criminology* (Milton Keynes, 1990), p. 91.
15 The research activity ended in March 2020.
16 Ombretta Ingrascì, *Le donne, la mafia: nuove ipotesi di ricerca* (Milan, 1999); Ombretta Ingrascì, *Mafia Women in Contemporary Italy. The Changing Role of Women in the Italian Mafia since 1945* (London, 2006).
17 Ombretta Ingrascì, *Donne d'onore. Storie di mafia al femminile* (Milan, 2007). The literature on the mafia women on which my research was grounded dated back to the first work on the subject-matter carried out by independent scholars, journalists, and academics: Anna Cascio and Anna Puglisi (eds.), *Con e contro. Le donne nell'organizzazione mafiosa e nella lotta contro la mafia*, Centro siciliano di documentazione Giuseppe Impastato (Palermo, 1987); Giovanna Fiume, "Ci sono donne nella mafia?", in *Meridiana*, n. 7–8 (1990); Liliana Madeo, *Donne di mafia. Vittime, complici, protagoniste* (Milan, 1994); Renate Siebert, *Secrets of Life and Death* (London, 1996; first edition *Le donne e la mafia*, Milan, 1994); Teresa Principato and Alessandra Dino, *Mafia donna. Le vestali del sacro e dell'onore* (Palermo, 1997); Clare Longrigg, *Mafia Women* (London, 1997); Anna Puglisi, *Donne, mafia e antimafia*, CSD appunti, Quaderni 7–8 del Centro Impastato (Palermo, 1998).

Significant work on mafia women can be found in the special issue of Meridiana, Donne di mafia. *Meridiana. Rivista di storia e scienze sociali* n. 67 (2011).

For the role of women in international mafias see Jana Arsovska and Felia Allum, 'Introduction: Women and Transnational Organized Crime', in *Trends in Organized Crime*, 17 (2014), pp. 1–15. Dina Siegel, 'Women in Transnational Organized Crime', in *Trends in Organized Crime*, 17 (2014), pp. 52–5.

Recent reference on mafia women can be found in John Dickie, 'Mafia and prostitution in Calabria, c.1880–c.1940', in *Past and Present*, 232, N(1) (2016), pp. 203–36; Federico Varese, *Mafia Life* (Oxford, 2018).

For a complete review on the literature concerning women in organized crime, including mafias, see Rossella Selmini, 'Women in Organized Crime', in M. Tonry and P. Reuter, *Organizing Crime: Mafias, Markets and Networks, Crime and Justice*, vol. 49 (Chicago and London, 2020).
18 This concept has been used in other work: see the special issue of the Journal *Meridiana* entitled *Donne di mafia*, N. 67 (2011); and Milka Kahn and Anne Véron, *Women of Honour. Madonnas, Godmothers and Informers in the Italian Mafia* (London, 2018).
19 In the analysis of mafia women's agencies my work has been influenced in particular by the following work: Meyers, *Gender in the Mirror*; Sherry B. Ortner, *Making*

Gender: The Politics and Erotics of Culture (Boston, 1996); Catriona Mackenzie and Natalie Stoljar (eds.), Relational Autonomy. Feminist Perspectives on Autonomy, Agency, and the Social Self (Oxford, 2000).
20 Susan Sonstang, Regarding the Pain of Others (New York, 2004).

Chapter 1

1 For a comprehensive analysis of the mafia's use of violence see Monica Massari and Vittorio Martone, Mafia Violence. Political, Symbolic, and Economic Forms of Violence in Camorra Clans (London, 2019).
2 Maurizio Catino, Mafia Organisations. The Visible Hand of Criminal Enterprises (Cambridge, 2019), p. 145; Alessandro Coletti, 'The Welfare System of Italian Mafias', in F. Allum, I. Clough Marinaro and R. Sciarrone, Italian Mafias Today. Territory, Business and Politics (Cheltenham, Northampton, 2019).
3 Camorra clans have shown a more noticeable recourse to violence. Massari and Martone's book, mentioned in the previous footnote, reports the results of a specific study on the wide use of violence by the Camorra's clans and its traumatic impact on local communities.
4 Anton Block distinguished between two types of criminal syndicates in his work on organized crime operating in New York in the 1930s and 1940s: 'One is the enterprise syndicate which operates exclusively in the arena of illicit enterprise such as prostitution, gambling, bootlegging, and narcotics. The second type I call the power syndicate, its forte is extortion not enterprise. The power syndicate operates both in the arena of illicit enterprise and in the industrial world specifically in labor-management disputes and relations', Anton Block, East Side, West Side: Organizing Crime in New York 1930–1950 (Cardiff, 1980), p. 129. This conceptualization has been widely used by scholars studying the mafias (see Salvatore Lupo, Storia della mafia dalle origini ai giorni nostri (Rome, 2004; first edition 1996).
5 Gambetta has studied this mechanism of production of the need for protection, calling the Sicilian mafia an industry of private protection. Diego Gambetta, The Sicilian Mafia. The Business of Private Protection (Cambridge, 1993).
6 Paul Ginsborg, A History of Contemporary Italy: 1943–1980 (London, 1990); Paul Ginsborg, Italy and its Discontents (London, 2001); Donald Sassoon, Contemporary Italy (London, 1997).
7 For the history of Cosa Nostra, see Lupo, Storia della mafia; John Dickie, Cosa Nostra. A history of the Sicilian Mafia (London, 2004); for the history of the 'Ndrangheta see Enzo Ciconte, 'Ndrangheta. Dall'Unita a oggi (Rome-Bari, 1992). For

a history of Cosa Nostra, 'Ndrangheta and Camorra, see John Dickie, *Blood Brotherhoods: A History of Italy's Three Mafias* (London, 2014).

8   Enzo Ciconte, "'Ndrangheta: A (Post-)Modern Mafia with Ancient Roots', in F. Allum, I. Clough Marinaro and R. Sciarrone (eds.), *Italian Mafias Today. Territory, Business and Politics* (Cheltenham, Northampton, 2019), p. 48.

9   For the involvement of the 'Ndrangheta in drug trafficking, see Francesco Calderoni, 'The Structure of Drug Trafficking Mafias: The 'Ndrangheta and Cocaine', in *Crime, Law and Social Change*, 58, 3 (2012), pp. 321–49; Anna Sergi and Anita Lavorgna, *'Ndrangheta: the Glocal Dimensions of the Most Powerful Italian Mafia* (London, 2016); Nicola Gratteri and Antonio Nicaso, *Oro bianco* (Milan, 2015).

10 Interview with Public Prosecutor, DDA Reggio Calabria, Reggio Calabria, 20 February 2006.

11 Relazione del Ministero dell'Interno al Parlamento sull'attività svolta e sui risultati conseguiti dalla Direzione Investigativa Antimafia (first semester 1999), pp. 99–100.

12 Coletti, *The Welfare System*, p. 115.

13 See figure 8.1 in ibid. p. 117.

14 Ibid.

15 Cross, Università degli Studi di Milan, *Secondo rapporto trimestrale sulle aree settentrionali per la presidenza della Commissione parlamentare d'inchiesta sul fenomeno mafioso* (Milan, 2015).

16 Ibid.

17 Rocco Sciarrone, *Mafie vecchie, mafie nuove. Radicamento ed espansione* (Donzelli, 2009); Rocco Sciarrone and Luca Storti, 'Complicità trasversali tra mafia ed economia. Servizi, garanzie e regolazione', in *Stato e Mercato*, 3 (2016), pp. 353–90; Rocco Sciarrone (ed.), *Alleanze nell'ombra. Mafie ed economie locali in Sicilia e nel Mezzogiorno* (Rome, 2011); Alessandra Dino, *Criminalità dei potenti e metodo mafioso* (Milan, 2009); Maurizio Catino, 'Colletti bianchi e mafie. Le relazioni pericolose nell'economia del Nord Italia', in *Stato e Mercato*, 112 (2018); Rocco Sciarrone, 'The Economic Dimension of Mafias, Social Capital and the "Grey Area"', in F. Allum, I. Clough Marinaro and R. Sciarrone (eds.), *Italian Mafias Today. Territory, Business and Politics* (Cheltenham, Northampton, 2019); Vittorio Mete and Rocco Sciarrone, 'The Boundaries of Mafias: Relationships and Business in the "Grey Area"', in S. Carnevale, S. Forlati and O. Giolo (eds.), *Redefining Organised Crime: A Challenge for the European Union?* (Oxford, 2017).

18 For the role of lawyers, see Ombretta Ingrascì 'Organised Crime's Lawyers, from Lawful Defence to the "Bridge Function": The Case of the Sicilian Mafia', in P. Van Duyne et al., *Criminal Defiance in Europe and Beyond. From Organized Crime to Crime-Terror Nexus* (The Netherlands, 2020).

19 Ibid., p. 18, Sciarrone, "'Ndrangheta: A Reticular Organization'.

20 Sciarrone, "'Ndrangheta: A Reticular Organization'.

21 Ombretta Ingrascì, 'Donne, 'ndrangheta, 'ndrine. Gli spazi femminili nelle fonti giudiziarie', in *Meridiana. Rivista di Storia e Scienze Sociali*, n. 67 (2011), pp. 35-54.
22 Catino, *Mafia Organizations*, p. 85.
23 Ibid., p. 217.
24 Sciarrone, ''Ndrangheta: A Reticular Organization', p. 94.
25 For a list of characteristics the candidate must show, see Guido Lo Forte, 'The Sicilian Mafia: A Profile Based on Judicially Confirmed Evidence', in *Modern Italy*, 9, 1 (May 2004), p. 70.
26 For descriptions of mafia rituals provided by informers from 1877 to the present day, Gambetta, *The Sicilian Mafia*, pp. 262-70.
27 Catino, *Mafia Organizations*, p. 90.
28 Archivio di Stato di Catanzaro 1892, p. 336, quoted in Ciconte, *'Ndrangheta*.
29 Ibid., p. 81.
30 Sciarrone, ''Ndrangheta: A Reticular Organization'.
31 Alessandra Dino, *Mutazioni. Etnografia del mondo di Cosa Nostra* (Palermo, 2002); Letizia Paoli, *Mafia Brotherhoods: Organized Crime, Italian Style* (Oxford, 2003); Catino, *Mafia Organizations*.
32 Umberto Santino has divided the analyses of the Mafia historically into two periods, pre-Buscetta and post-Buscetta. Umberto Santino, *La mafia interpretata. Dilemmi, stereotipi, paradigmi* (Soveria Mannelli, 1995), p. 15. Letizia Paoli, 'The Pentiti's Contribution to the Conceptualisation of the Mafia Phenomenon', in Vincenzo Ruggiero, Nigel South and Ian Taylor (eds.), *The New European Criminology. Crime and Social Order in Europe*, Routledge, London, 1998, p. 266.
33 See for example: Henner Hess, *Mafia* (Bari, 1973); Jane Schneider and Peter Schneider, *Culture and Political Economy in Western Sicily* (London, 1976); Anton, Blok, *The Mafia of a Sicilian Village 1860-1960* (New York, 1975). For a critique to Hess, Lupo, *Storia della mafia*, pp. 31-2, and Maurice Aymard and Giuseppe Giarrizzo (eds.), *La Sicilia* (Turin, 1987), p. 954. On the importance of not neglecting the cultural dimension in the study of the mafia, Marco Santoro, *La voce del padrino. Mafia, cultura, politica* (Verona, 2007)
34 Lupo, *Storia della mafia*, p. 266. Marco Santoro rightly stresses that the study of the mafia has to keep giving relevance to the cultural aspects of the phenomenon, at the same time avoiding a culturalistic approach, Marco Santoro, *La voce del padrino. Mafia, cultura, politica* (Verona, 2007).
35 For a detailed historical reconstruction of the trial concerning the *stoppaghieri*, see the excellent work by Amelia Crisantino, *Della segreta e operosa associazione. Una setta all'origine della mafia* (Palermo, 2000).
36 Lupo has amplied analysed this report, as much as other scholars including John Dickie, *Cosa Nostra.*, and Umberto Santino, *La mafia dimenticata. La criminalità organizzata in Sicilia* (Milan, 2017).

37 For a description of hierarchically structured criminal associations in the fascist period, Paolo Pezzino, *Mafia: industria della violenza* (Florence, 1995), p. 172, and Salvatore Lupo, *Storia della mafia*, pp. 43–63.
38 Corte d'assise d'appello di Trapani, *Sentenza* n. 5/96.
39 For Terranova's early understanding of the mafia's structure see Giuseppe Di Lello, *Giudici* (Palermo, 1996).
40 For a description of Cosa Nostra's organization, see Lo Forte, *The Sicilian Mafia*.
41 Unlike Tommaso Buscetta, many informers spoke of this meeting. For details on the meeting, Alfio Caruso, *Da cosa nasce cosa* (Milan, 2000), pp. 92–8.
42 Commissione Parlamentare d'inchiesta sul fenomeno della mafia (legge 20 dicembre 1962, n.1720), *Relazione sul traffico mafioso di tabacchi e stupefacenti nonché sui rapporti tra mafia e gangsterismo italo-americano* (relatore senatore M. Zuccalà), VI legislatura, doc.XXIII, n. 2, Rome 1976, pp. 283–91, in Tranfaglia, Nicola, *Mafia, politica e affari 1943–2000* (Rome-Bari, 1992), p. 160.
43 Michele Pantaleone, *The Mafia and Politics* (London, 1966).
44 Giuseppe Carlo Marino, *Storia della mafia* (Rome, 2000), p. 214.
45 For details on the 'first mafia war', Caruso, *Da cosa*, pp. 146–59.
46 Nando dalla Chiesa, *Passaggio a Nord. La colonizzazione mafiosa* (Turin, 2016).
47 See Buscetta's testimony, Pino Arlacchi, *Addio Cosa Nostra* (Milan, 1994), pp. 142–3.
48 Marino, *Storia della mafia*, p. 250.
49 Lupo, *Storia della mafia*, p. 237.
50 Marino, *Storia della mafia*, p. 252.
51 See, for instance, the kidnapping of Nino Salvo's father-in-law, Luigi Corleo, which was condemned by Palermo families because the Salvo cousins were their fundamental link with political power.
52 Santino, *Storia*, p. 247.
53 Ginsborg, *Italy and its Discontents*, p. 200.
54 According to article 416bis of the Italian penal code, a mafia-type association is defined by 'those who form part of it making use of an associational tie of intimidating force and methods of subjugation and a conspiracy of silence that derive from them, in order to achieve, either directly or indirectly, management or, in whatever manner, control of economic activities, concessions, authorizations, sub-contracts and public services, so as to realize illicit profits or advantages for themselves or others'.
55 Ginsborg, *Italy and its Discontents*, p. 207.
56 Alexander Stille, *Excellent Cadavers: The Mafia and the Death of the First Italian Republic* (London, 1996), p. 210.
57 Falcone Giovanni, 'Che cosa è la mafia', in Giovanni Falcone, *Interventi e proposte (1982–1992)* (Milan, 1994), p. 347.
58 Lupo, *Storia della mafia*, p. 260.

59 For a description of how this system worked, i.e. how politicians were able to extract illegal payment from firms, see Ginsborg, *Italy and its Discontents*, pp. 181-2. According to Marino the mafia lost, after the fall of the Berlin wall, its conservative function against the Left.
60 Maurizio Romenelli, *I collaboratori di giustizia. L'esperienza italiana* (Zurigo, 2003), p. 362.
Angela Della Bella, *Il regime detentivo speciale del 41 bis: quale prevenzione speciale nei confronti della criminalità organizzata?* (Milan, 2012).
61 Alessandra Dino, 'Waiting for a New Leader: Eras and Transitions in Cosa nostra', in F. Allum, I. Clough Marinaro and R. Sciarrone (eds.), *Italian Mafias Today. Territory, Business and Politics*. Cheltenam, Northampton, 2019, p. 20.
62 Dino, 'Waiting for a New Leader'.
63 Ibid., p. 24.
64 The slaughter that occurred in German town of Duisburg in 2007 made the world aware of the criminal organization's global reach.
65 Sciarrone, ''Ndrangheta: A Reticular Organization'.
66 Nicola Gratteri and Antonio Nicaso, *Fratelli di sangue* (Cosenza, 2006), p. 27; Enzo Ciconte, *Processo alla 'Ndrangheta* (Bari, 1996), p. 17.
67 For detail on positions and ranks see Catino, *Mafia organizations*, pp. 162-3.
68 Tribunale di Milano, *Sentenza*, Proc. n. 8317/92 R.G.N.R. For a summary, see Ombretta Ingrascì, 'Como: il clan dei Mazzaferro', in *Omicron/35*, 10/11 (2001), pp. 4-5.
69 Antonio Zagari, *Ammazzare stanca* (Cosenza, 1992), p. 12.
70 Gratteri, Nicaso, *Fratelli di sangue*, p. 31.
71 Ciconte, *'Ndrangheta*, p. 36; Gratteri, Nicaso *Fratelli di sangue*, p. 24; *Sentenza del processo relativo all'indagine Fiori nella notte di San Vito, procedimento penale n. 8317/92 RGNR*, Tribunale di Milano.
72 Sciarrone, *Mafie vecchie, mafie nuove*, p. 138, Ingrascì, *Donne, 'ndrangheta, 'ndrine*.
73 Francesco Forgione, *'Ndrangheta. Boss luoghi e affari della mafia più potente al mondo. La relazione della Commissione Parlamentare Antimafia* (Milan, 2009), p. 23. For a detailed reconstruction of the higher-level bodies of coordination in the 'Ndrangheta see Catino, *Mafia Organizations*.
74 Sciarrone, *Mafie vecchie, mafie nuove*, p. 143.
75 Commissione Parlamentare Antimafia, *Relazione di maggioranza*, 2006.
76 Ingrascì, *'Donne, 'ndrangheta, 'ndrine*.
77 Procura della Repubblica di Reggio Calabria, Direzione distrettuale antimafia, *Decreto di fermo di indiziato di delitto, Agostino Anna Maria + 155*, luglio 2010.
78 Ibid.
79 Historian Truzolillo backdates the existence of central coordinating body within the 'Ndrangheta to the Fascist era. This body had, among other things, the role of

resolving kinship disputes; Fabio Truzolillo, 'La struttura unitaria della 'ndrangheta dale origini', in *Meridiana*, N. 77 (2013).
80 Procura della Repubblica di Reggio Calabria, Direzione Distrettuale Antimafia, *Decreto di fermo di indiziato di delitto, Agostino Anna Maria + 155*, luglio 2010.
81 Ibid.
82 Sergi and Anita Lavorgna, *'Ndrangheta*, p. 4.
83 Ciconte, in *'Ndrangheta: A (post-) modern mafia*, p. 53.

Chapter 2

1 Flavia Pristinger, 'Il lavoro delle donne: passato e presente', in S. Ulivieri (ed.), *Educazione e ruolo femminile: la condizione delle donne in Italia dal dopoguerra a oggi* (Scandicci, 1992), p. 144. Francesca Bettio, *The Sexual Division of Labour. The Italian Case* (Oxford, 1988), pp. 48–9.
2 Gloria Chianese, *Storia sociale della donna in Italia (1800–1890)* (Napoli, 1980), p. 51.
3 Ibid., p. 95.
4 Pristinger, 'Il lavoro delle donne', in Ulivieri, *Educazione e ruolo*, p. 147.
5 Chianese, *Storia sociale*, p. 51.
6 Anna Garofalo, *L'Italiana in Italia* (Bari, 1956), p. 47. For article 37 see Caldwell, *Italian Family*, p. 65.
7 Bettio, *The Sexual Division*, p. 50.
8 Pristinger, *Il lavoro delle donne*, p. 148; Caldwell, *Italian Family*, p. 116.
9 Ibid., p. 72.
10 Manuela Frari (ed.), *Sociologia della famiglia, sull'emancipazione* (Venezia, 1979), p. 70. A. Victoria Goddard, *Gender, Family and Work in Naples* (Oxford, 1996), pp. 10–11.
11 Frari, *Sociologia*, p. 70.
12 Sassoon, *Contemporary Italy*, p. 65. Goddard, *Gender, Family and Work*, p. 13.
13 Pristinger, *Il lavoro delle donne*, p. 149.
14 Ibid., p. 151.
15 Ibid., p. 75.
16 Maria Cutrufelli, *Disoccupata con onore. Lavoro e condizione della donna* (Milan, 1975), p. 64.
17 Interview with Antonio N., Modena, 4 May 2004.
18 Pristinger, *Il lavoro delle donne*, p. 149.
19 Ibid., p. 153.
20 Ibid., p. 150.
21 Georges, Duby, and Perrot, Michelle, *A History of Women in the West. Toward a Cultural Identity of Women in the Twentieth Century* (London, 1993), p. 473.
22 Pristinger, *Il lavoro delle donne*, p. 1.

23 Sassoon, *Contemporary Italy*, p. 109.
24 Ibid., p. 110.
25 Ibid., pp. 110–11.
26 Cutrufelli, *Disoccupata con onore*, p. 88.
27 Dunnage, *Twentieth Century*, p. 203.
28 Duby and Perrot, *A History of Women*, p. 473.
29 Sassoon, *Contemporary Italy*, p. 112.
30 Ulivieri, *Educazione e ruolo*, p. 3.
31 Duby and Perrot, *A History of Women*, p. 468.
32 Laura Balbo, 'La doppia presenza', in *Inchiesta*, 32 (1978).
33 Pristinger, Il lavoro delle donne, p. 160.
34 Ibid., p. 159.
35 Ibid., p. 158.
36 Alessandra Pescarolo, *Il lavoro delle donne nell'Italia contemporanea* (Rome, 2019).
37 Francesca Bettio and Alina Verashchagina, *Gender Segregation in the Labour Market: Roots, Implications and Policy Responses*, Denmark Report to European Commission, Directorate-General for Employment, Social Affairs and Equal Opportunities, Unit G. 1 (September 2008). According to data gathered for the Gender Equality Index 2019, in Italy women continue to experience work segregation: Around 26% of women work in education, health and social work, compared to 7% of men. 6% of women work in science, technology, engineering and mathematics (STEM) occupations compared to 31% of men. European Institute for Gender Equality, *Gender Equality Index 2019: Italy* (Vilnius, 2019).
38 Michela Cozza and Francesca Gennai, *Il genere nelle organizzazioni* (Rome, 2009).
39 Pescarolo, *Il lavoro delle donne*, p. 317.
40 Lesley Caldwell, *Italian Family Matters. Women, Politics and Legal Reform* (London, 1991). p. 8. For a clear explanation of the cultural context of Italy see the collection edited by David Forgacs and Robert Lumley, *Italian Cultural Studies: An Introduction*, Oxford University Press, Oxford, 1996.
41 See ibid.
42 Non-institutional involvement characterized Italian feminism. Paola Bono and Sandra Kemp (eds.), *Italian Feminist Thought* (London, 1991), p. 2.
43 Ada Trasferri (ed.), *Donna. Women in Italian Culture* (Ottawa, 1989), p. 23.
44 Garofalo, *L'Italiana*, p. 65.
45 Ibid., p. 69.
46 Ibid., p. 71.
47 Ibid., p. 45.
48 Ibid., p. 7.
49 For a detailed description of the Church and state's attitude, Caldwell, *Italian Family*, and also Dunnage, *Twentieth Century*, p. 160.

50 For the role of television in this propaganda, ibid., p. 167.
51 Chianese, *Storia sociale*, p. 69 and p. 197. Bravo, Pelaja, Pescarolo, Scaraffia, *Storia sociale*, p. 69. Maria Goretti's lived in the early twentieth century. When twelve years old, she was almost raped and forgave the culprit.
52 For a brief analysis of women in the 1950s, Chianese, *Storia sociale*, p. 71 and, Caldwell, *Italian Family*.
53 Gabriella Parca, *Le italiane si confessano* (Florence, 1959).
54 Ibid., p. 65.
55 Bravo, Pelaja, Pescarolo, Scaraffia, *Storia sociale*, pp. 201–2.
56 Paul Ginsborg, *A History of Contemporary Italy*, p. 215.
57 Ibid., p. 216.
58 For statistics on the number of family members, ibid., p. 243 and pp. 427.
59 VV.AA, *Il Novecento delle italiane* (Rome, 2001), p. 233.
60 Duby and Perrot, *A History of Women*, p. 328.
61 Donald Meger, *Sex and Power. The Rise of Women in America, Russia, Sweden and Italy* (Middletown, 1983), p. 38.
62 VV.AA., *Il Novecento delle italiane*, pp. 109–10.
63 Ibid., pp. 109–10.
64 Luisa Passerini, 'The Women's Movement in Italy and the Events of 1968', in Marina Cicioni and Nicole Prunster (eds.), *Vision and Revision, Women in Italian Culture* (Oxford, 1993).
65 Ibid.
66 VV. AA.VV., *Il Novecento delle italiane*, p. 253.
67 Ginsborg, *A History of Contemporary Italy*, p. 244.
68 Ibid., p. 259.
69 For a brief description of the students protests see Dunnage, *Twentieth Century*, pp. 171–4.
70 Franco Restaino and Adriana Cavarero, *Le filosofie femministe* (Turin, 1999), p. 51.
71 VV.AA., *Il Novecento delle italiane*, p. 9.
72 Meger, *Sex and Power*, p. 40. For detailed data on the spread of mass education see Dunnage, *Twentieth Century*, pp. 160–1.
73 VV.AA., *Il Novecento delle italiane*, p. 243.
74 Chianese, *Storia sociale*, p. 123.
75 VV.AA., *Il Novecento delle italiane*, p. 276.
76 Ibid., p. 279.
77 Ibid., p. 281.
78 Marina Ingrascì, *Le responsabilità penali nel diritto di famiglia* (Turin, 2004), p. 16.
79 Gabriella Parca, *I sultani, mentalità e comportamento del maschio italiano* (Milan, 1965), pp. 5–6.
80 Bravo, Pelaja, Pescarolo, Scaraffia, *Storia sociale*, p. 75.

81 Bono and Kemp, *Italian Feminist*, pp. 211–12.
82 VV.AA, *Il Novecento delle italiane*, p. 377. For details on 194 bill, Tamar Pitch, *Un diritto per due. La costruzione giuridica di genere, sesso e sessualità* (Milan, 1998). For a discussion on abortion, Claudia Mancina, *Oltre il femminismo* (Bologna, 2002), pp. 85–103.
83 VV.AA., *Il Novecento delle Italiane*, p. 444.
84 Duby and Perrot, *A History of Women*, p. 400.
85 For a brief and clear history of women and marriage, Bravo, Pelaja, Pescarolo, Scaraffia, *Storia sociale*, p. 202.
86 Simonetta Piccone Stella, *Ragazze del Sud* (Rome, 1979). The interviews, from which the patriarchal model emerged, were carried out in 1975 and 1976. Maria Cutrufelli, *Disoccupata con onore. Lavoro e condizione della donna* (Milan, 1975), p. 74. Simona Mafai (ed.), *Essere donna in Sicilia* (Rome, 1976), p. 17. It is important to take into account, as Giovanna Fiume warns us, that when analysing 'male patronage', it is also necessary to seek those 'constellations of unequal relations that tie together men and women by investigating exchange, interdependence, reciprocal conditioning ... rather than the unrealistic and simplistic opposition between domination and oppression' Giovanna Fiume, 'Making Women Visible in the History of the Mezzogiorno', in E. Dal Lago and R. Halpernn (eds.), *The American South and the Italian Mezzogiorno* (London, 2002), p. 173.
87 Giovanna Capizzi, *Essere donna in Sicilia* (Palermo, 1996), p. 11.
88 Fiume, 'Making Women Visible in the History of the Mezzogiorno'.
89 Ginsborg, *A History of Contemporary Italy*, p. 417.
90 Chianese, *Storia sociale*, p. 76.
91 See for example the sentence for a rape case at the Court of Bolzano, AA.VV., *Il Novecento delle italiane*, p. 373. Even recently there have been court cases showing a indulgent attitude towards the perpetrator of the rape, justifying their act as a consequence of female provocative behaviour. For a discussion on 'the victim in court', see the interesting essay by Jennifer Temkin, 'Women, Rape and Law Reform', in M. Evans (ed.), *The Woman Question* (London, 1994), pp. 277–96.
92 Bono and Kemp, *Italian Feminist*, p. 212.
93 For the iter of the law, ibid., p. 212.
94 Servizio Studi del Senato, *Violenza di genere e femminicidio: dalla ratifica della Convenzione di Istanbul all'istituzione di una Commissione di inchiesta ad hoc*, nota breve n. 153 (February 2017).
95 Eures, Ricerche economiche e sociali, *Femminicidio e violenza di genere in Italia* (Rome, 2019).
96 Osservatorio regionale contro la violenza di genere, *Primo rapporto sulla violenza di genere in Calabria e documentazione*, Consiglio Regionale della Calabria (2019).
97 For a recent feminist discussion on the deterioration of the public imaginary about women and the consequent women's reaction through the participation into the

worldwide feminist movement 'NiUnaMeno' see Ida Dominijanni, 'Un/Domesticated Feminism', in *Soft Power. Revista euro-americana de teoría e historia de la política y del derecho*, 4(2) (June–December 2017). This essay introduces interesting articles related to the status of feminism facing the neo-liberal discourse. See also Rossella Ghigi and Roberta Sassatelli, *Corpo, genere e società* (Bologna, 2018).

98 Balbo, 'La doppia presenza'.
99 For a reflection on women's identity and dual role, Franca Bimbi, 'Three Generations of Women: Transformations of Female Identity Models in Italy', in M. Cicioni and N. Prunster (eds.), *Vision and Revision*, p. 79; For empiric research, Laura Balbo, M. Pia May and Giuseppe A. Micheli, *Vincoli e strategie nella vita quotidiana* (Milan, 1990).
100 Ginsborg, *Italy and its Discontents*, p. 71.
101 Chiara Saraceno, 'The Italian Family from the 1960s to the Present', *Modern Italy*, 9, 1 (May 2004).
102 Giulia Fuochi, Letizia Mencarini and Cristina Solera, 'I padri coinvolti e i mariti egalitari: per scelta o per vincoli? Uno sguardo alle coppie italiane con figli piccoli', in *About Gender. International Journal of Gender Studies*, 3, (6) (2014), pp. 54–86.

Chapter 3

1 On the gender norms in the mafia see Valeria Pezzini Gambetta, 'Gender Norms in the Sicilian Mafia', in M. Arnot and C. Usborne (eds.), *Gender and Crime in Modern Europe* (London, 1999); 'John Dickie, Mafia and prostitution in Calabria, c. 1880-c. 1940', in *Past and Present*, 1, 232 (2016), pp. 203–36.
2 Gabriella Gribaudi, 'The Use of Violence and Gender Dynamics within Camorra Clans', in M. Massari and V. Martone, *Mafia Violence. Political, Symbolic, and Economic Forms of Violence in Camorra Clans* (London, 2019), p. 247.
3 Martina Panzarasa, *Donne di mafia e carcere. Cultura, esperienze e pratiche in una sezione di alta sicurezza*, Università degli Studi di Milano, Università degli Studi di Torino, PhD thesis (Milan, Turin, 2018); Felia Allum and Irene Marchi, 'Analyzing the Role of Women in Italian Mafias: the Case of the Neapolitan Camorra', in *Qualitative Sociology*, 41 (2018), pp. 361–80.
4 Carmelo Lisòn Tolosana, 'The Ever-Changing Faces of Honour', in A. Dionigi, A. Blok and C. Bromberger (eds.), *L'anthropologie de la Méditerranée* (Paris, 2001), p. 133. The concept of honour was amply explored in the 1950s and 1960s by anthropologists dealing with the so-called Mediterranean culture. Although they were rightly criticized for their homogenous portrayal of cultures and passive representation of women (see in particular Goddard, *Gender, Family and Work*),

they remain an essential theoretical and empirical reference for studying the legacy of honour codes in Southern Italy and, in particular, in the mafias (Ingrascì, *Donne d'onore*, 2017).

5   Pieter Spierenburg (ed.), *Men and Violence* (Columbus, 1998).
6   Aisha K. Gill, Carolyn Strange and Karl Roberts (eds.), *Honour Killing and Violence: Theory, Policy and Practice* (UK, 2014), p. 1038; Unni Wikan, *In Honour of Fadime: Murder and Shame* (Chicago and London, 2008).
7   Interview with Rosa, Florence, 13 November 2003.
8   For the code of honour in Sicilian agro-towns in the early XX century see Linda Reeder, *Women in White. Migration and Transformation of Rural Italian Women, 1880–1920* (London, 2003), pp. 37–54.
9   Peter L. Berger, Brigitte L. Berger and Kellner Hansfried, *The Homeless Mind* (London, 1974). Giovanna Fiume agrees with Berger's argument, Giovanna Fiume (ed.), *Onore e storia nelle società mediterranee* (Palermo, 1989), p. 10.
10 Tor Aase (ed.), *Tournaments of Power, Honour and Revenge in the Contemporary World* (Ashgate, 2002), p. 2.
11 John Thrasher and Toby Handfield, 'Honour and Violence. An Account of Feuds, Duels, and Honour Killings', *Human Nature*, 29 (2018), pp. 371–89.
12 Floya Anthias, 'The Material and the Symbolic in Theorizing Social Stratification', in *British Journal of Sociology*, 52(3) (2001).
13 Gill, Strange and Roberts, *Honour and Violence*, p. 4.
14 See Antonino Calderone's description of his initiation in Gambetta, *The Sicilian Mafia*, pp. 267–68.
15 Historian Paolo Pezzino elaborated the '*paradigma dell'omertà*' to explain the manipulation of the code as a political product: Paolo Pezzino, 'Stato violenza società. Nascita e sviluppo del paradigma mafioso', in Aymard and Giarrizzo, *La Sicilia*, pp. 234–5.
16 Similar mechanisms regard gangs in prison, in which the code of honour is used for regulating relationships among prisoners. According to Sharbek: "Each gang is responsible for their members' actions, so they have an incentive to monitor their members to ensure they maintain their collective reputation". David Skarbek, *The Social Order of the Underworld: How Prison Gangs Govern the American Penal System* (Oxford, 2014), p. 83.
17 Gresham M. Sykes and David Matza, 'Techniques of Neutralization: A Theory of Delinquency', in *American Sociological Review*, Vol. 22, No. 6 (1957), pp. 664–70.
18 Thrasher and Handfield, *Honour and Violence*, p. 386.
19 Ciconte, *'Ndrangheta. Dall'Unita a oggi*, p. 17.
20 Gambetta, *The Sicilian Mafia*, p. 40. For the use of reputation in the mafia industry see ibid., pp. 119–12.
21 Gill, Strange and Roberts, *'Honour' Killing and Violence*.

22 Magdalena A. Grzyb, 'An Explanation of Honour-related Killings of Women in Europe through Bourdieu's Concept of Symbolic Violence and Masculine Domination', in *Current Sociology*, 64 (7) (2016), p. 1043.
23 Barbacetto, Gianni and Milosa, Davide, *Le mani sulla città. I boss della 'Ndrangheta vivono tra noi e controllano Milano* (Milan, 2011), p. 424.
24 Corte d'Assise di Trapani, *Sentenza* n. 4/2001, issued on 17 May 2001.
25 Pierre Bourdieu, *Masculine Domination* (Stanford, 2001).
26 Fiume, *Onore e storia*, p. 12.
27 Ibid., p. 12.
28 Interview with Giuseppe C., Bologna, 2 April 2004. Salvatore Lupo uses the example of *ragionamento* to underline that the code of honour tend to be disregarded, Salvatore Lupo, 'La mafia: definizione e uso di un modello virilista', *Genesis*, II/1 (2003), p. 55.
29 Giovanni Raffaele, 'Il concetto di onore in alcune tipologie criminali nella Sicilia rurale dell'Ottocento', in Fiume, *Onore e storia*, p. 207.
30 Interview with Public Prosecutor, Milan DDA, Milan, 15 November 2017.
31 Roberta Torre, *Angela*, Rita Rusic Company, Movie Web, Sister Film, Italy, 2002.
32 Barbacetto and Milosa, *Le mani sulla città*, p. 441.
33 Interview with Public Prosecutor, Milan DDA, Milan, 15 November 2017.
34 Ibid.
35 Reddy Rupa, 'Domestic Violence or Cultural Tradition? Approaches to "Honour Killing" as Species and Suspecies in English Legal Practice', in Gill, Strange and Roberts, *'Honour' Killing and Violence*, p. 30.
36 Interview with Rosa N., Milan, 28 April 1998.
37 Lirio Abbate, *Fimmine ribelli*, p. 60.
38 Ibid., p. 60.
39 Giusy Vitale with Camilla Costanzo, *Ero cosa loro. L'amore di una madre può sconfiggere la mafia*, (Milan, 2009).
40 Ibid.
41 Gill, Strange and Roberts, *'Honour' Killing and Violence*.
42 Interview with Emilio Di Giovine quoted in Ingrascì, *Confessioni di un padre*, p. 138.
43 Interview with Giuseppe C., Bologna, 2 April 2004.
44 Piero Colaprico and Luca Fazzo, *Manager Calibro 9* (Milan, 1995).
45 This is a pseudonym.
46 Corte d' Assise di Palmi, *Sentenza*, issued on 6 April 2016.
47 Grzyb, *An Explanation of Honour-Related Killing of Women*, p. 6; Martin Rew, Geetanjali Gangoli and Aisha K. Gill, 'Violence between Female In-Laws in India', in *International Journal of Women Studies*, 14(1) (2013), pp. 147–60; Purna Sen, 'Crimes of Honour: Value and Meaning', in L. Welchman and S. Hossain (eds.), *Honour: Crimes, Paradigms and Violence against Women* (London, 2005).

48 Siebert, *Secrets of Life and Death*; Panzarasa, *Donne di mafia e carcere*.
49 Deniz, Kandiyoti, 'Bargaining with Patriarchy', in *Gender and Society*, 2, (3) (Sep., 1988), pp. 274–90.
50 Bourdieu, *Male Dominance*, p. 35.
51 Interview with Antonio N., Modena, 4 May 2004.
52 Maria Stefanelli and Manuela Mareso, *Loro mi cercano ancora. Il coraggio di dire no alla 'Ndrangheta e il prezzo che ho dovuto pagare* (Milan, 2014), p. 12.
53 Ibid., p. 21.
54 Ibid.
55 Ibid., p. 90.
56 Ibid., p. 8.
57 Salvo Palazzolo, "Messina Denaro ritratto di famiglia 'Noi casta di nobiltà', in *la Repubblica* (11 May 2017).
58 Salvo Palazzolo, 'Messina Denaro, liti senza fine a casa del boss', *la Repubblica* (25 November 2014).
59 Gill, Strange and Roberts, *Honour killing and Violence*, p. 1.
60 Ibid.
61 Ibid., p. 389.
62 Reddy in Grzyb, 'An Explanation of Honour-Related Killings of Women'.
63 Rupa, 'Domestic Violence or Cultural Tradition', p. 41.
64 Grzyb, 'An Explanation of Honour-Related Killings of Women', p. 1039.
65 Ibid., p. 1038.
66 Gill, Strange and Roberts, *'Honour' Killing and Violence*, p. 4.
67 According to Sen, it is important to take into consideration both similarities and differences in honour killings across cultures, Sen, *Crimes of Honour*.
68 Thrasher and Handfield, *Honor and Violence*, p. 381.
69 Alessandra Dolci, *Unpublished Relation to the Summer School on Organized Crime, Mafia and Women*, University of Milan.
70 Salvo Palazzolo, *E la mafia sentenziò 'Tradisce il marito boss quella donna va uccisa'*, in *la Repubblica* (10 February 2016).
71 The father was acquitted, even though the reconstruction by journalist Salvatore Palazzolo and the victim's son seems to be in line with Onorato's tale, Alessio Cordaro and Salvo Palazzolo, *Se muoio, sopravvivimi. La storia di mia madre che non voleva essere più la figlia di un mafioso* (Milan, 2012).
72 A report issued by Association *Da Sud* collected many cases of honour killing related to the mafias: Irene Cortese, Sara Di Bella and Cinzia Paolillo. *Sdisonorate. Le mafie uccidono le donne*, Associazione da Sud (Rome, 2011).
73 Alessandra Cerreti, 'Il coraggio della verità', in E. Ciconte, F. Forgione and I. Sales (eds), *Atlante delle mafie volume secondo*, Rubbettino, Soveria Mannelli, 2013.

74 The quotations related to the case of Maria Concetta Cacciola are taken from the following judicial files: Tribunale di Palmi, *Sentenza* n. 6357/15, issued on 11 May 2017; Tribunale di Palmi, *Sentenza* n. 612/15, issued on 24 May 2015; Corte d'Assise di Palmi, Prima sezione, *Sentenza*, issued on 13 July 2013.

75 Ibid., p. 57.

76 For details of Lea Garofalo's story and the trial against the culprits of her killing see Marika Demaria, *La scelta di Lea. La ribellione di una donna alla 'ndrangheta* (Milan, 2013). The trial has been transmitted in television, see: Raiplay, *Un giorno in pretura*. Sangue lava sangue, https://www.raiplay.it/video/2016/04/Lea-Garofalo-Sangue-lava-sangue---Un-giorno-in-pretura-del-17042016-fb319132-7203-4095-8ccd-b517fbca1cb1.html.

77 In honour society these two motivations are interrelated, Thrasher and Handfield, *Honor and Violence*, p. 372.

78 He was the cousin of Maria Concetta Cacciola's father.

79 The case of Francesca Bellocco was reconstructed through the following judicial files: Tribunale di Reggio Calabria, ufficio del giudice per le indagini preliminari, *Ordinanza di applicazione di misure cautelari* n. 452/13, issued on 25 March 2013; Corte d'Assise di, Prima sezione, *Sentenza*, issued on 7 September 2019; Corte di Assise d'Appello di Reggio Calabria, *Sentenza*, issued on 1 February 2019. The quotations in the texts are taken from the above judicial files.

80 Francesca Bellocco's killing was reconstructed and her son was sentenced with murder, while Domenico Cacciola's has remained unpunished.

81 Pantaleone Sergi, 'Agguato d'onore alla moglie del boss', in *la Repubblica* (6 August 1997).

82 Grzyb, 'An Explanation of Honour-Related Killings of Women', p. 1047.

83 Cerreti, Alessandra, *Unpublished Relation at the Summer School on Organized Crime Mafia and Women*, University of Milan, September 2019.

84 Sabrina Garofalo and Ludovica Ioppolo reconstructed honour killings of men who had a love affair with women 'belonging' to mafia families. Sabrina Garofalo and Ludovica Ioppolo, *Onore e dignitudine. Storie di donne e di uomini in terra di 'ndrangheta* (Cosenza, 2015).

85 Quoted in ibid., p. 50.

86 Interview with Public Prosecutor, DDA Caltanissetta, Caltanissetta, 22 October 2019.

87 Thrasher and Handfield, *Honor and Violence*.

88 For a broad history of marriage in Europe see Jack Goody, *The Development of the Family and Marriage in Europe* (Cambridge, 1983).

89 Ibid., p. 213.

90 Maria Minicuci, *Qui e altrove. Famiglie di Calabria e di Argentina* (Milan, 1994), pp. 246–7; Vincenzo Masini, *Sociologia di Sagunto* (Milan,1984), pp. 150–1.

91 Ibid.

92 Anton Blok, *Honour and Violence* (Oxford, 2001), p. 89.
93 Cutrufelli, *Disoccupata con onore*, p. 80.
94 Pino Arlacchi, *Mafia Business* (Oxford, 1988), p. 140.
95 See the recent study by Maurizio Catino et al., 'Blood(y) Relationships: Interfamily Marriages and Kinship Networks in 'Ndrangheta', Unpublished paper presented at SISEC Conference (Turin, 20 January 2020).
96 Piero Colaprico and Luca Fazzo, *Manager Calibro 9* (Milan 1995), p. 100.
97 Ciconte, *Processo alla 'Ndrangheta*, p. 26; Interview with Public Prosecutor, DDA Reggio Calabria, Reggio Calabria, 16 September 2003.
98 Michele Prestipino and Giuseppe Pignatone, *Il contagio. Come la 'Ndrangheta ha infettato l'Italia* (Rome-Bari, 2012), p. 49.
99 Ibid.
100 Nucleo investigativo Carabinieri, Gruppo di Monza, 'Infinito'. Annotazione riassuntiva sui matrimoni e funerali a cui hanno partecipato i soggetti indagati e sulle 'regole' che presiedono agli inviti e alla partecipazione a tali cerimonie.
101 See the testimony of priest Pino De Masi in 'Storiacce', *Television transmission, Sposa-bambina, per patto di 'ndrangheta'*, Radio 24 (28 November 2015) at http://212.45.99.237/programma/storiacce/trasmissione-novembre-2015-220421-gSLAVnMpRB.
102 For the Riina-Bagarella family tree see Blok, *Honour and Violence*, p. 68.
103 Attilio Bolzoni and Giuseppe D'Avanzo, *Il capo dei capi. Vita e carriera criminale di Totò Riina* (Milan, 1993), pp. 30–1.
104 Goody, *The Development*, p. 214.
105 Blok, *Honour and Violence*, p. 90.
106 Quoted in Ginsborg, *Italy and its Discontents*, p. 197.
107 Siebert, *Secrets of Life and Death*, p. 29.
108 Part of Leonardo Messina's confession to the antimafia commission is quoted in Pezzino, *Mafia*, p. 281.
109 Principato, Dino, *Mafia Donna*, p. 54.
110 See the previous section of this chapter.
111 Ciconte, *'Ndrangheta. Dall'Unità a oggi*, p. 38.
112 Stephen Wilson, *Feuding, Conflict and Banditry in Nineteenth-Century Corsica* (Cambridge, 1988).
113 Cagnetta Franco, *Bandits d'Orgosolo*, 1954, quoted in Blok, *Honour and Violence*, p. 95; Blok, *Honour and Violence*, p. 89.
114 Procura della Repubblica di Reggio Calabria, Direzione Distrettuale Antimafia, *Decreto di fermo di indiziato di delitto Agostino Annamaria + 155*, 2010.
115 Gruppo di Monza, Nucleo investigativo Carabinieri, *'Infinito'*, Annotazione riassuntiva sui matrimoni e funerali a cui hanno partecipato i soggetti indagati e sulle 'regole'che presiedono agli inviti e alla partecipazione a tali cerimonie.

116 Corte d' Assise di Milano, Terza sezione, *Sentenza* n. 20/98, issued on 28 April 1998.
117 Ingrascì, *Confessioni di un padre*, p. 30.
118 For a psychological and psychoanalytical analysis of the mechanisms behind mafia fundamentalism see Lo Verso, *La mafia dentro*, p. 28.

Chapter 4

1 Gambetta, *The Sicilian Mafia*, pp. 57–8. Franco Di Maria, 'Identità e sentire mafioso. Percorsi per leggere le trasformazioni', in Girolamo Lo Verso, *La mafia dentro*, p. 42.
2 Gabriella Gribaudi, 'Familismo e famiglia a Napoli e nel Mezzogiorno', *Meridiana*, 17 (1993), p. 13.
3 A synthesis of the debate on Italian southern family is to be found in Nicholas J. Esposito, *Italian Family Structure* (New York, 1989).
4 For the literature on familism see AA.VV., *Dopo il familismo cosa?* (Milan, 1992).
5 Edward Banfield, *The Moral Basis of a Backward Society* (Chicago, 1958). For a synthesis of the history of the term and its critiques, Alessio Colombi, 'L'invenzione del familismo amorale', in AA.VV., *Dopo il familismo*, pp. 201–12.
6 Gribaudi, *Familismo e famiglia*, p. 13.
7 *Meridiana*, n. 17 (May 1993).
8 Gribaudi, *Familismo e famiglia*, p. 14.
9 Masini, *Sociologia di Sagunto*, p. 110.
10 Cutrufelli, *Disoccupata con onore*, p. 71.
11 Masini, *Sociologia di Sagunto*, p. 112.
12 See the work by Martina Panzarasa who has borrowed the expression 'greedy institution' from Lewis Coser, Panzarasa, *Donne di mafia e carcere*, p. 106.
13 Peter L. Berger and Thomas Luckmann, *The Social Construction of Reality: A Treatise in the Sociology of Knowledge* (New York, 1966).
14 Ibid.
15 Ibid.
16 For a detailed account of this story, Bianca Stancanelli, *A testa alta* (Turin, 2003), and Francesco Deliziosi, *Don Pino Puglisi. Vita del prete pugliese ucciso dalla mafia* (Milan, 2001).
17 Melford Spiro, *Gender Ideology and Psychological Reality: An Essay in Cultural Reproduction* (Cambridge, 1997).
18 Interview with Giuseppe C., Bologna, 2 April 2004.
19 Spiro, *Gender Ideology and Psychological Reality*, p. 177.
20 Ibid.
21 Sandra Ruddick, *Maternal Thinking. Towards a Politics of Peace* (Boston, 1995).
22 Ibid., p. 110.

23 Sandra Ruddick, 'Maternal Thinking' in A. O' Reilly (ed.), *Maternal Theory. Essential Readings* (Brafford, Canada, 2007) p. 104.
24 Siebert, *Secrets of Life and Death*.
25 This reduction of the importance of the female role might be connected to the narrow prevailing interpretation in Italian society of womanhood as motherhood, influenced by Catholicism, Goddard, *Gender, Family and Work*, p. 194.
26 Siebert, *Secrets of Life and Death*.
27 Ibid., p. 336.
28 Paola Corso, 'Alle donne non è consentita l'aggressività', in AA.VV., *Dal materno al mafioso – Ruoli delle donne nella cultura delle mafie*, n. 1 (Florence, 1996).
29 Siebert, *Secrets of Life and Death*.
30 According to Paul Ginsborg, relationship between mother and son is one of main features characterizing Italian family, Ginsborg, *Italy and its Discontents*, p. 79.
31 Siebert, *Secrets of Life and Deatch*, pp. 58–9.
32 Panzarasa, *Donne di mafia e carcere*, p. 112.
33 Siebert, *Secrets of Life*, p. 59.
34 Interview with Rosa N., Milan, 28 April 1998.
35 Giuseppe Casarubbea and Pia Blandano, *L'educazione mafiosa* (Palermo,1991), p. 134.
36 Ruddick, *Maternal Thinking. Towards a Politics of Peace*, p. 111.
37 For an analysis of this process in families where fathers emigrated, Piccone Stella, *Ragazze del Sud*.
38 Alessandra Camassa, 'Lo psichismo mafioso femminile. Una testimonianza', in Lo Verso, *La mafia dentro*, p. 121.
39 Panzarasa, *Donne di mafia e carcere*.
40 Ruddick, *Maternal thinking*, p. 104.
41 On the concept of masculinity see Robert W. Connell, *Masculinities* (Berkeley, 2005).
42 David D. Gilmore, *Manhood in the Making. Cultural Concepts of Masculinity* (New Haven, 1990), quoted in Connell, *Masculinities*, p. 32.
43 Casarrubea, Blandano, *L'educazione mafiosa*, p. 131.
44 Ingrascì, *Confessioni di un padre*, p. 59.
45 Nancy Lindisfarne, 'Variant Masculinities, Variant Virginities: Rethinking "Honour and Shame"', in A. Cornwall and N. Lindisfarne (eds.), *Dislocating Masculinity: comparative ethnography* (London, 1994), p. 32.
46 Abbate, *Fimmini ribelli*, pp. 71, 61.
47 Ruddik, *Maternal Thinking*.
48 Tribunale di Reggio Calabria, Sezione G.I.P.-G.U.P., *Ordinanza di custodia cautelare* n. 52/18 (Proc. n. 6089/2015 R.G.N.R.), issued on 6 November 2018.
49 The Youth Court's statement is quoted in ibid.

50 Interview with Rosa N., Milan, 28 April 1998.
51 Abbate, *Fimmini ribelli*, 71.
52 Interview with Emilio Di Giovine quoted in Ingrascì, *Confessioni di un padre*, 2013, pp. 64–5.
53 Interview with Public Prosecutor, DDA Palermo, Palermo, 22 October 2019.
54 Tribunale di Palermo, Sezione dei giudici per le indagini preliminari, *Ordinanza di applicazione di misure cautelari personali e contestuale decreto di sequestro preventivo*, (Proc. n. 10944/08 R.G.N.R.), p. 62.
55 Ibid., p. 12.
56 Michelle Foucault, *Microfisica del potere. Interventi politici* (Turin, 1977).
57 In 1959, Antonio Pigliaru wrote a remarkable book on vendetta in Barbagia – a region of Sardinia. His interest in customs that became law and those that remained tradition prompted him to study the practice of vendetta and to translate the oral principles of vendetta into a written code. This 'translation', based on newspapers, popular literature on Sardinia bandits and oral sources, is a valuable tool for understanding the popular institution of vendetta, not only in Sardinia. Antonio Pigliaru, *La vendetta barbaricina come ordinamento giuridico* (Nuoro, 2000; first edition: Milan, 1959).
58 Ibid.
59 Ibid., p. 149.
60 For the vendetta custom in traditional Calabria, Luigi M. Lombardi Satriani and Mariano Meligrana, *Il ponte di San Giacomo* (Milan, 1987), pp. 327–51.
61 Unpublished Renate Siebert interview with Salvatore Boemi, April 2002. For other passages of this interview concerning the vendetta in the 'Ndrangheta see Renate Siebert, 'Mafia Women: The Affirmation of a Female Pseudo-Subject. The Case of the 'Ndrangheta', in G. Fiandaca (ed.), *Women and the Mafia: Female Roles in Organised Crime Structure* (New York, 2007).
62 Ciconte, *Processo alla 'Ndrangheta*, pp. 142–3.
63 Siebert, *Secrets of Life and Death*; Dino and Principato, *Mafia donna*; Camassa, *Lo psichismo mafioso femminile*.
64 Lupo, *Storia della mafia*, p. 163.
65 Lombardi Satriani, Meligrana, *Il ponte di San Giacomo*, p. 339.
66 Ibid., p. 339.
67 Siebert, *Donne di mafia*, p. 31.
68 Interview with Rosa N., Milan, 28 April 1998.
69 Longrigg, *Mafia Women*, p. 87.
70 Blok, *Honour and Violence*, p. 97.
71 Ibid., p. 96.
72 Siebert, *Secrets of Life and Death*, p. 38.
73 Ciconte, *'Ndrangheta. Dall'Unità a oggi*, p. 63.

74 Satriani, Meligrana, *Il ponte di San Giacomo*, p. 343.
75 Camassa, *Lo psichismo mafioso femminile*, p. 122.
76 For the mafia feud in which Stefano Leale was involved see the Documents of Antimafia Commission which made reference also to Serafina Battaglia's testimony. Archivio italiano, *Testo integrale della Relazione della Commissione Parlamentare d'inchiesta sul fenomeno della mafia*, Volume terzo doc. 2332, 476 (Rome, 1973).
77 Madeo, *Donne di mafia*, p. 190.
78 'Serafina Battaglia accusa e Marco Semilia si discolpa', in *Giornale di Sicilia* (10 December 1970).
79 Lo Verso, *La mafia dentro*, pp. 142–3.
80 Ingrascì, *Donne, 'ndrangheta, 'ndrine*.
81 Tribunale di Reggio Calabria, Ufficio del giudice per le indagini preliminari, *Ordinanza di custodia cautelare* n. 3926/08. p. 250.
82 Ibid.
83 Ibid., p. 179.
84 Laura is a pseudonym.
85 Interview via email with Public Prosecutor, DDA Catanzaro, 27 March 2020.
86 Corte d'appello di Catanzaro, Seconda sezione penale, *Sentenza* issued on 20 July 2017, pp. 363.
87 Interview via email with Public Prosecutor, DDA Catanzaro, 27 March 2020.
88 Corte d'Appello di Catanzaro, Seconda sezione penale, *Sentenza*, issued on 20 July 2017, pp. 363–4.
89 'Ritorna in Assise la vedova della mafia. Dal 9 dicembre nuovo processo ad Ancona', in *Giornale di Sicilia* (6 December 1970).
90 Puglisi, *Donne, mafia e antimafia*, p. 91.
91 Siebert, *Le donne, la mafia*, p. 294.
92 For a detailed and colourful description of Giacoma Filippello's story see Longrigg, *Mafia Women*, pp. 223–9.
93 Madeo, *Donne di mafia*, p. 58.
94 Ibid., p. 189.
95 Longrigg, *Mafia Women*, p. 228.
96 Giueseppe Fava, *Mafia* (Rome, 1984).
97 Blok, *Honour and Violence*, p. 100.
98 Joseph S. Nye, *Bound to Lead: The Changing Nature of American Power* (New York, 1990).
99 Joseph S. Nye, *Soft Power: The Means to Success in World Politics* (New York, 2004), p. 7.
100 Siebert, *Secret of Life and Death*.

Chapter 5

1. Vincenzo Ruggiero, *Crime and Markets. Essays in Anti-Criminology* (Oxford, 2001), p. 17.
2. Inquiry into the drug economy from a gender perspective goes beyond the purpose of this work. For a review of the most relevant work on female involvement in drug trafficking, see a Selmini, *Women in Organized Crime*.
3. Howard Campbell, 'Female drug smugglers on the U.S.-Mexico border: gender, crime and empowerment', in *Anthropological Quarterly* 81 (1) (2008), pp. 233–67. Tammy Anderson, 'Dimension of Women's Power in the Illicit Drug Economy', in *Theoretical Criminology*, 9(4) (2005), pp. 371–400.
4. With the Camorra the picture is different, as far as there is great female involvement in the drug trade. Gabriella Gribaudi 'Donne di camorra e identità di genere', in *Meridiana: Rivista di storia e scienze sociali*, (Vol. 67) (2010); Gribaudi, 'The Use of Violence and Gender Dynamics within Camorra Clans', in Massari and Martone, *Mafia Violence*.
5. Marina Pino, *Le signore della droga* (Palermo, 1998).
6. Ibid., p. 7.
7. Siebert, *Secrets of Life and Death*, p. 131.
8. Pino, *Le signore della droga*, p. 8.
9. Ibid., p. 14.
10. Ibid., p. 9.
11. Interviews with Giuseppe C., 2 April 2004, and with Antonio N., Modena, 4 May 2004.
12. Pino, *Le signore della droga*, p. 21.
13. Longrigg, *Mafia Women*, p. 133.
14. Ibid., p. 15.
15. Pino, *Le signore della droga*, p. 9.
16. Ibid., p. 16.
17. Ibid., p. 10 and p. 13.
18. Ibid., p. 14.
19. Longrigg, *Mafia Women*, p. 134.
20. Ibid., p. 135.
21. Pino, *Le signore della droga*, p. 28.
22. Ibid., p. 32.
23. Ibid., p. 33.
24. Ibid., pp. 71–6.
25. Ibid., pp. 38–9.
26. Ibid., p. 42.
27. Ibid., pp. 36–7.

28 Ibid., pp. 49, 60.
29 Siebert, *Secrets of Life*, p. 132.
30 Pino, *Le signore della droga*, p. 55.
31 Madeo, *Donne di mafia*, p. 197.
32 Pino, *Le signore della droga*, p. 50.
33 Puglisi, *Donne, mafia e antimafia*, p. 74.
34 Pino, *Le signore della droga*, p. 91.
35 Ibid., p. 98.
36 Ibid., p. 79. Puglisi, *Donne, mafia e antimafia*.
37 Ibid., p. 138.
38 For Angela Russo's story see Pino, *Le signore della droga*, cap. VI–VII.
39 Principato, Dino, *Mafia donna*, p. 65.
40 Pino, *Le signore della droga*, p. 78.
41 Ibid., p. 80.
42 Interview with Public Prosecutor, DDA Caltanissetta, Palermo, 23 October 2019.
43 This is a pseudonym.
44 Tribunale di Reggio Calabria, Sezione G.I.P. – G.U.P., *Ordinanza di custodia cautelare in carcere* N. 52/2018, 6 November 2018, p. 29.
45 This does not indicate that women are not involved, since their role might be invisible and police are not likely to detect it, or prosecutors and police might have a chivalric attitude towards the female components of the criminal organizations, as it was in the past, Ingrascì, *Donne d'onore*, pp. 93–122.
46 Tribunale di Reggio Calabria, Sezione G.I.P. – G.U.P., *Ordinanza di custodia cautelare in carcere* n. 52/2018, issued on 6 November 2018, p. 347.
47 Ibid., p. 369.
48 Ibid., pp. 390–1.
49 Ibid., p. 24.
50 Tribunale di Catanzaro, Ufficio del giudice per le indagini preliminari, *Ordinanza di custodia cautelare*, issued on 21 June 2012.
51 Ibid.
52 Procura della Repubblica di Catanzaro, Direzione distrettuale antimafia, *Verbale di sommarie informazioni*, Proc. n. . 1846/2009 R.G.N.R:, 2 July 2010.
53 Ibid.
54 For Serraino-Di Giovine clan see Ingrascì O., 'Women in the 'Ndrnagheta: the Serraino-Di Giovine case', in Fiandaca, *Women and the Mafia*.
55 For the criminal context in Milan and for a description of the relationship between Serraino-Di Giovine clan and other mafia clans, Portanova, Rossi, Stefanoni, *Mafia a Milano*; Ingrascì, *Confessioni di un padre*.
56 Ibid.; Ciconte, *Processo alla 'Ndrangheta*, p. 193.
57 Tribunale di Milano, Sentenza n. 16/94.

58 Interview with Public Prosecutor, DDA Milan, Milan, 9 June 2001.
59 Tribunale di Milano, Sentenza n. 16/94.
60 Ibid.
61 Interview with Antonio N., Modena, 4 May 2004.
62 Siebert, *Secrets of Life*, p. 115; Teresa, Principato 'La donna nell'universo mafioso', in *Segno*, 183 (1997).
63 Teresa Principato interviewed by Marina Terragni, *Il Venerdì della Repubblica*, (Luglio 1997).
64 Ernesto Oliva and Salvo Palazzolo, *L'altra mafia* (Soveria Mannelli, 2001), p. 70.
65 This is a pseudonym.
66 Interview with Public Prosecutor, DDA Milan, 17 September 2002.
67 Ombretta Ingrascì, 'Operazione Gemini e i collaboratori di giustizia', in *Omicron /38* (November 2002).
68 This is a pseudonym.
69 Marisa Di Giovine, *Mafia Princess. They're Lawless, They're Criminal, They're Family* (UK, 2010).
70 Procura della Repubblica di Milano, Direzione Distrettuale Antimafia, *Richiesta di rinvio a giudizio*, Proc. n. 3760/93 R.G.N.R.
71 Ibid.
72 For the case see Principato, Dino, *Mafia donna*, pp. 51–3.
73 Longrigg, *Mafia Women*, p. 148.
74 Principato, Dino, *Mafia donna*, p. 52.
75 Longrigg, *Mafia Women*, pp. 152–3.
76 Ibid., p. 89.
77 Legione dei carabinieri di Palermo, Gruppo di Palermo – Nucleo operativo – prima sezione, Rapporto giudiziario N. 3033/16-1983 del 10/04/1984 a carico di Gariffo Carmelo + 29, pp. 46 e ss., reported and quoted in Oliva, Palazzolo, *L'altra mafia*, p. 89.
78 Interview with Public Prosecutor, DDA Palermo, Palermo, 10 September 2003.
79 The report is quoted in the judicial files related to accusation with mafia crimes against the woman: Procura della Repubblica di Palermo, Direzione Distrettuale Antimafia, *Richiesta delle misure di custodia cautelare in carcere*, Proc. N. 3157/98 R.G.N.R.
80 Ibid.
81 Ibid.
82 Ibid.
83 Annotazione della Squadra Mobile della Questura di Palermo, 8 febbraio 2001, all. 176, in ibid.
84 Siebert, *Secrets of Life*, p. 116.

85 Tribunale di Palermo, Ufficio del giudice per l'udienza preliminare, *Sentenza*, issued on 27 November 2000.
86 Ibid.
87 Ibid.
88 Attilio Bolzoni, 'Le signore del crimine nuovi boss della mafia', in *la Repubblica* (28 May 2002). Interview with Public Prosecutor, DDA Palermo, 10 September 2003.
89 Ibid.
90 Tribunale di Palermo, Sezione dei giudici per le indagini preliminari, *Ordinanza di applicazione di misure cautelari personali e contestuale decreto di sequestro preventivo*, Proc. n. 10944/08 R.G.N.R, p. 64.
91 Siebert, *Secrets of Life*, p. 115.
92 Ibid., p. 89.
93 Ibid., p. 88.
94 Some of them were acquitted in the last phase of the trial.
95 Tribunale di Catanzaro, Sezione GIP-GUP, *Sentenza*, issued on 17 May 2013, pp. 443–4.
96 Tribunale di Catanzaro, Ufficio delle indagini preliminari, *Ordinanza di custodia cautelare* (Proc. n. 1846/09 R.G.N.R.) issued on 21 June 2012, p. 541.
97 Federica Cabras and Nando dalla Chiesa, *Rosso Mafia* (Milan, 2019), pp. 124–7; Catino, *Colletti bianchi e mafie*.
98 Tribunale di Bologna, Giudice per le indagini preliminari, *Ordinanza di applicazione di misure cautelari* n. 17375, issued on 15 January 2015, p. 5.
99 Ibid.
100 Rita Simon, *Women and Crime* (MA, 1975).
101 Enzo Ciconte, *Dall'omertà ai social. Come cambia la comunicazione della mafia* (Pavia, 2017).
102 Siebert, *Secrets of Life and Death*, p. 257.
103 Tribunale di Reggio Calabria, *Ordinanza di custodia cautelare* n. 52/18 (Proc. n. 6089/2015 R.G.N.R.), issued on 6 November 2018, pp. 348–51.
104 Tribunale di Catanzaro, Sezione GIP-GUP, *Sentenza*, issued on 17 May 2013, p. 515.
105 Conversations between brother and sister reported in the work are quoted from Ibid.
106 The quotations related to Pino Lipari's daughter are taken from the following judicial file: Procura della Repubblica di Palermo, Direzione Distrettuale Antimafia di Palermo, *Richiesta per l'applicazione delle misure cautelari*, Proc. n. 3157/98 R.G.N.R.
107 Tribunale di Palermo, Sezione dei giudici per le indagini preliminari, *Ordinanza di applicazione di misure cautelari personali e contestuale decreto di sequestro preventivo*, Proc n. 10944/08 R.G.N.R.
108 Interview with Public Prosecutor, DDA Palermo, 22 October 2019.

109 Tribunale di Palermo, Ufficio del giudicil per le indagini preliminari, *Ordinanza di applicazione di misure cautelari personali e contestuale decreto di sequestro preventivo*, Proc n. 10944/08 R.G.N.R., p. 75.
110 Ibid., p. 60.
111 Tribunale di Palermo, Ufficio del giudicil per le indagini preliminari, *Ordinanza di applicazione di misure cautelari personali e contestuale decreto di sequestro preventivo*, n. 10944/08 R.G.N.R., pp. 63–4.
112 Interview with Public Prosecutor, DDA Palermo, 22 October 2019.
113 Tribunale di Catanzaro, Sezione GIP/GUP, *Sentenza*, issued on 17 May 2013, p. 685.
114 Procura della Repubblica di Palermo, Direzione Distrettuale Antimafia, *Richiesta per l'applicazione di misure cautelari*, Proc. n. 16676/01 R.G.N.R.
115 Ibid.
116 Dino and Principato, *Mafia donna*, pp. 68–9.
117 Ingrascì, *Donne, 'ndrangheta, 'ndrine*.
118 Tribunale di Palermo, Sez. II Penale, *Sentenza* N. 2370/2001.
119 Vitale with Costanzo, *Ero cosa loro*.
120 Interview with Public Prosecutor, DDA Palermo, Palermo, 5 July 2001.
121 The quotations relative to Maria Filippa Messina's case are taken from the following judicial file: Corte d'Assise di Catania, Seconda Sezione, *Sentenza* n. 33/96.
122 Interview with Public Prosecutor, DDA Catania, 11 September 2003.
123 Eleonora is a pseudonym. The judicial quotations relative to this case are from the following document: Tribunale di Palermo, Ufficio del Giudice per le ingagini preliminari, *Sentenza a seguito di giudizio abbreviato*, issued on 27 September 2017.
124 Santina is a pseudonym. The judicial quotations relative to this case are from the following judicial files: Tribunale di Palermo, Ufficio del Giudice per le ingagini preliminari, *Ordinanza di custodia cautelare in carcere* (Proc. n. 1942 R.G.N.R.), issued on 30 November 2011.
125 Daria is a pseudonym. All the quotations related to this case are from the following judicial files: Procura della Repubblica di Caltanissetta, Direzione Distrettuale Antimafia, *Richiesta per l'applicazione di misura cautelare*, Proc. n. 1409/18 R.G.N.R.; Tribunale di Caltanissetta, Sezione GIP-GUP, *Ordinanza di misure cautelari* (Proc. n. 109/2014 R.G.N.R) issued on 25 June 2018.
126 Interview with Public Prosecutor, Caltanissetta DDA, 22 October 2019.
127 Lavinia is a pseudonym. The quotations relative to this case are from the following judicial files: Tribunale di Catanzaro, Ufficio del giudice per le indagini preliminari, *Ordinanza di custodia cautelare* (Proc. n. 1846/09 R.G.N.R.), issued on 21 June 2012; Tribunale di Catanzaro, Sezione GIP-GUP, *Sentenza*, issued on 17 May 2013.
128 Procura della Repubblica di Palermo, Direzione distrettuale antimafia, *Richiesta per l'applicazione di misure cautelari*, Proc. n. 16676/01, R.G.N.R.

129 Similarly, Allum and Marchi reads the presence of women at top level in the Camorra as linked to the clan's necessity status, Allum and Marchi, *Analyzing the Role of Women in Italian Mafias*.
130 Irene is a pseudonym.
131 This seems to suggest that female access to mafia power was similar to the model of women's access to power in undeveloped countries. Here, in fact, women in power were always daughters, sisters or widows of men who had been in power. Blok reported the case of Indira Ghandi in India, Benazir Bhutto in Pakistan and Cory Aquino in the Philippines; Blok, *Honour and Violence*, p. 221.
132 Dino and Principato, *Mafia donna*.
133 Ibid., p. 86.
134 Siebert, *Secrets of Life and Death*, p. 14.
135 Blok, *Honour and Violence*, p. 220.
136 Ibid., p. 220.
137 Alessandra Dino, 'Narrazioni al femminile di Cosa Nostra', in 'Donne di mafia', *Meridiana. Rivista di storia e scienze sociali*, 67 (2011), p. 67.
138 Ibid.
139 Ibid.
140 Massari and Martone, *Mafia Violence*.
141 Siebert, *Mafia Women: The Affirmation of a Female Pseudo-Subject*, pp. 40–1.
142 Alessandra Dino, *Unpublished Relation at the Summer School on Organized Crime Mafia and Women*, University of Milan, September 2019.
143 Evelyn Fox Keller, *Reflections on Gender and Science* (New Haven, 1985).
144 Mackenzie and Stoljar (eds.), *Relational Autonomy*, pp. 9–10.
145 Ibid., p. 9.

Chapter 6

1 Thomas Casadei, 'La vulnerabilità in prospettiva critica', in G. Orsetta and B. Pastore, *Vulnerabilità. Analisi multidisciplinare di un concetto* (Rome, 2018).
2 Martha Albertson Fineman and Anna Grear (eds.), *Vulnerability. Reflections on a New Ethical Foundation for Law and Politics* (Furnam, 2013), p. 20.
3 Carol Levine *et al.*, "The Limitations of 'Vulnerability' as a Protection for Human Research Participants', in *American Journal of Bioethics*, 4 (3) (2004), p. 47.
4 Florencia Luna, 'Elucidating the Concept of Vulnerability. Layers not Labels', in *International Journal of Feminist Approaches of Bioethics*, vol 2, N 1 (2009).
5 Florencia Luna, 'Identifying and Evaluating Layers of Vulnerability – a Way Forward', *Developing world. Biothetics*, vol.19, n.2 (2019), p. 89. It has to consider that Luna discusses the concept of vulnerability in the context of bioethics research. Therefore,

she wonders about the problems underlying rigid classification of vulnerability in relation to subjects participating to experimental research study.
6 Casadei, *La vulnerabilità in prospettiva critica*, p. 79.
7 bell hooks, *Feminist Theory. From Margin to Center* (Cambridge, MA, 2000).
8 Casadei, *La vulnerabilità in prospettiva critica*, p. 77.
9 Judith Butler, Zeynep Gambetti and Leticia Sabsay (eds.), *Vulnerability in Resistance* (Durham, 2016), p. 25.
10 The South Africa Truth and Reconciliation Commission drew inspiration from Italian witness programmes in order to organize the protection of those people who spoke out, Priscilla B. Hayner, *Unspeakable Truths. Facing the Challenge of Truth Commission* (London, 2002), p. 246.
11 Salvatore D'Amico, *Il collaboratore della giustizia* (Rome, 1995).
12 Maurizio Romenelli, *I collaboratori di giustizia: l'esperienza italiana* (Zurich, 2003), p. 361.
13 Ibid., p. 363.
14 Ibid.
15 Longrigg, *Mafia Women*, p. 231.
16 Marco Amenta, Documentary *Diario di una siciliana ribelle* (Rome, 1998).
17 Sandra Rizza, *Rita Atria. Una ragazza contro la mafia* (Palermo, 1993), p. 130.
18 Ibid., p. 128.
19 Ibid., p. 137.
20 Robin Pickering-Iazzi, *The Mafia in Italian Lives and Literature: Life Sentences and Their Geographies* (Toronto, 2015).
21 Interview with Rosa N., Milan, 28 April 1998.
22 Bourdieu, *Masculine Domination*, p. 38.
23 All the quotations of the interview are from Interview with Rosa N., Milan, 28 April 1998.
24 Longrigg, *Mafia Women*, p. 228.
25 For exploring the relationship between mafia women and prison, see Panzarasa, *Donne di mafia e carcere*.
26 Interview with Public Prosecutor, DDA Palermo, Palermo, 5 July 2001.
27 Dino, *Narrazioni al femminile*, p. 69.
28 Ibid., p. 66.
29 Ibid., p. 68.
30 Abbate, *Fimmini ribelli*, p. 55.
31 Prestipino and Pignatone, *Il contagio*, p. 146.
32 Stefanelli, Mareso, *Loro mi cercano ancora*.
33 The quotations relating to Maria Concetta's case are from the following judicial files: Tribunale di Palmi, *Sentenza* n. 6357/15, issued on 11 May 2017, Tribunale di Palmi, *Sentenza* n. 612/15, issued on 24 May 2015.

34 Bourdieu, *Masculine Domination*, p. 37.
35 Ibid., p. 23.
36 The letter is a cry for help that it is given in its entirety in the appendix.
37 Anna Sergi, 'Widening the Antimafia Net: Child Protection and the Socio-Cultural Transmission of Mafia Behaviours in Calabria', in *Youth Justice*, 18 (2) (2018), p. 10.
38 Roberto Di Bella and Monica Zapelli, *Liberi di scegliere. La battaglia di un giudice minorile per liberare i ragazzi delle 'ndrangheta* (Milan, 2019).
39 Ibid.
40 ONU, Convention on the Rights of the Child, Adopted and opened for signature, ratification and accession by General Assembly resolution 44/25 of 20 November 1989, entry into force 2 September 1990, in accordance with article 49, https://www.ohchr.org/en/professionalinterest/pages/crc.aspx.
41 Ibid.
42 Sergi, *Widening the Antimafia Net*, p. 7.
43 Roberto Di Bella and Giuseppina Maria Patrizia Surace, *Liberi di scegliere. La tutela dei minori di 'ndrangheta nella prassi giudiziaria del Tribunale per i minorenni di Reggio Calabria* (Soveria Mannelli, 2019), pp. 71–2.
44 Some of these stories are narrated in Giovanni Tizian, *Rinnega tuo padre* (Rome-Bari, 2018).
45 Interview with lawyer, Modena 18 July 2019.
46 For a critical view on this concept of autonomy see Martha Fineman, *The Autonomy Myth: A Theory of Dependency* (New York, 2004).
47 Abbate, *Fimmini ribelli*, p. 79.
48 Ingrascì, *Confessioni di un padre*, pp. 137–8.
49 Interview with Giuseppe C., 2 April 2004.
50 Diana T. Meyers, *Self, Society, and Personal Choice* (Columbia, 1989).
51 Meyers, *Gender in the Mirror*, p. 4.
52 Meyers, *Self, Society, and Personal Choice*, p. xi.
53 Mackenzie and Stoljar, *Relational Autonomy*, p. 18.
54 Interview with Rosa N., Milan, 28 April 1998.
55 Ibid.
56 Ibid.
57 For watching the trial in which Denise testified as a witness, see Raiplay, *Un giorno in pretura. Sangue lava sangue*: https://www.raiplay.it/video/2016/04/Lea-Garofalo-Sangue-lava-sangue---Un-giorno-in-pretura-del-17042016-fb319132-7203-4095-8ccd-b517fbca1cb1.html.
58 Annalisa Tota, 'Storia di Lea Garofalo e di sua figlia Denise', *Rivista di Studi e Ricerche sulla Criminalità Organizzata*, 3 (2017).

59 Ombretta Ingrascì, *Le donne in Cosa nostra e nella 'Ndrangheta*, in E. Ciconte, F. Forgione, and I. Sales, *Atlante delle mafie volume secondo* (Soveria Mannelli, 2013), p. 431.
60 Ruddick, *Maternal Thinking. Towards a Politics of Peace.*
61 Ibid., p. 22.
62 Di Bella and Surace, *Liberi di scegliere.* pp. 71–2.
63 Ibid.

Bibliography

Aase, Tor (ed.), *Tournaments of Power, Honour and Revenge in the Contemporary World* (Ashgate, 2002).
Abbate, Lirio, *Fimmine ribelli* (Milan, 2013).
Acker, Joan, Kate Barry and Johanna Esseveled, 'Objectivity and Truth. Problems in Doing Feminist Research', in M. M. Fonow and J. A. Cook (eds.), *Beyond Methodology. Feminist scholarship as lived research* (Indiana, 1991).
Albera, Dionigi, Anton Blok and Christian Bromberger (eds.), *L'anthropologie de la Méditerranée. Anthropology of the Mediterranean* (Paris, 2001).
Allum, Felia and Irene Marchi, 'Analyzing the Role of Women in Italian Mafias: the Case of the Neapolitan Camorra', in *Qualitative Sociology*, 41 (2018), pp. 361–80.
Allum, Felia, Isabella Clough Marinaro and Rocco Sciarrone, *Italian Mafias Today. Territory, Business and Politics* (Cheltenham, Northampton, 2019).
Amenta, Marco, *Diario di una siciliana ribelle*, documentary (Rome, 1998).
Anderson, Tammy, 'Dimension of Women's Power in the Illicit Drug Economy', in *Theoretical Criminology*, 9(4) (2005), pp. 371–400.
Anthias, Floya, 'The Material and the Symbolic in Theorizing Social Stratification', in *British Journal of Sociology*, 52(3) (2001), pp. 367–90.
Archivio italiano, *Testo integrale della Relazione della Commissione Parlamentare d'inchiesta sul fenomeno della mafia*, Volume terzo doc. 2332, 476 (Rome, 1973).
Arlacchi, Pino, *Addio Cosa Nostra* (Milan, 1994).
Arlacchi, Pino, *Mafia Business* (Oxford, 1988).
Armao, Fabio, *Il sistema mafia. Dall'economia-mondo al dominio locale* (Turin, 2000).
Aymard Maurice and Giuseppe Giarrizzo (eds.), *La Sicilia* (Turin, 1987).
Balbo, Laura, 'La doppia presenza', in *Inchiesta*, 32 (1978).
Balbo, Laura, M. Pia May and Giuseppe A. Micheli, *Vincoli e strategie nella vita quotidiana* (Milan, 1990).
Banfield, Edward, *The Moral Basis of a Backward Society* (Chicago, 1958).
Barbacetto, Gianni and Davide Milosa, *Le mani sulla città. I boss della 'Ndrangheta vivono tra noi e controllano Milano* (Milan, 2011).
bell hooks, *Feminist Theory. From Margin to Center* (Cambridge, MA, 2000).
Bellavia, Enrico and Maurizio De Lucia, *Il cappio* (Milan, 2009).
Bellavia, Enrico and Salvo Palazzolo, *Voglia di mafia* (Rome, 2004).
Berger, Peter L. and Thomas Luckmann, *The Social Construction of Reality: A Treatise in the Sociology of Knowledge* (New York, 1966).

Berger, Peter L., Brigitte Berger and Hansfried Kellner, *The Homeless Mind* (London, 1974).
Bertaux, Daniel, *L'enquête et ses méthodes: le récit de vie* (Paris, 2000).
Bettio, Francesca and Alina Verashchagina, *Gender Segregation in the Labour Market: Roots, Implications and Policy Responses*, Denmark Report to European Commission, Directorate-General for Employment, Social Affairs and Equal Opportunities, Unit G. 1 (September 2008).
Bettio, Francesca, *The Sexual Division of Labour. The Italian Case* (Oxford, 1988).
Bimbi, Franca, 'Three Generations of Women: Transformations of Female Identity Models in Italy', in M. Cicioni and N. Prunster (eds.), *Vision and Revision* (Oxford, 1993).
Blando, Antonino and Gabriele Licciardi, *I nemici della Repubblica. Mafia e terrorismo 1969–1993* (Catania, 2019).
Blando, Antonino, 'La normale eccezionalità. La mafia, il banditismo, il terrorismo e ancora la mafia', in *Meridiana. Rivista di storia e scienze sociali*, 87 (2016).
Blando, Antonino, 'L'avvocato del diavolo', in *Meridiana. Rivista di storia e scienze sociali*, 63 (2008).
Block, Anton, *East Side, West Side: Organizing Crime in New York 1930–1950* (Cardiff, 1980).
Blok, Anton, *Honour and Violence* (Oxford, 2001).
Blok, Anton, *The Mafia of a Sicilian Village 1860–1960* (New York, 1975).
Bolzoni, Attilio and Giuseppe D'Avanzo, *Il capo dei capi. Vita e carriera criminale di Totò Riina* (Milan, 1993).
Bolzoni, Attilio, 'Le signore del crimine nuovi boss della mafia', in *la Repubblica* (28 May 2002).
Bolzoni, Attilio and Giuseppe D'Avanzo, *La giustizia è cosa nostra* (Palermo, 2018).
Bourdieu, Pierre, *Masculine Domination* (Stanford, 2001).
Butler, Judith, Zeynep Gambetti and Leticia Sabsay (eds.), *Vulnerability in Resistance* (Durham, 2016).
Butler, Judith, *Gender Trouble. Feminism and the Subversion of Identity* (New York and London, 1999).
Cabras, Federica and Nando dalla Chiesa, *Rosso Mafia* (Milan, 2019).
Cagnetta, Franco, *Bandits d'Orgosolo* (Paris, 1954).
Calabrò, Antonio, *I mille morti di Palermo. Uomini, denaro e vittime nella guerra di mafia che ha cambiato l'Italia* (Milan, 2016).
Calderoni, Francesco, 'The Structure of Drug Trafficking Mafias: The 'Ndrangheta and Cocaine', in *Crime, Law and Social Change*, 58, 3 (2012), pp. 321–49.
Caldwell, Lesley, *Italian Family Matters. Women, Politics and Legal Reform* (London, 1991).
Camassa, Alessandra, 'Lo psichismo mafioso femminile. Una testimonianza', in G. Lo Verso, *La mafia dentro. Psicologia e psicopatologia di un fondamentalismo* (Milan, 1998).

Campbell, Howard, 'Female Drug Smugglers on the U.S.–Mexico Border: Gender, Crime and Empowerment', in *Anthropological Quarterly*, 81 (1) (2008), pp. 233–67.

Capizzi, Giovanna, *Essere donna in Sicilia* (Palermo, 1996).

Caplan, Paula J., *The New Don't Blame Mother. Mending the Mother-daughter Relationship* (London, 2000).

Caruso, Alfio, *Da cosa nasce cosa* (Milan, 2000).

Casadei, Thomas, 'La vulnerabilità in prospettiva critica', in O. Giolo and Baldassarre Pastore, *Vulnerabilità. Analisi multidisciplinare di un concetto* (Rome, 2018).

Casarrubea, Giuseppe and Pia Blandano, *L'educazione mafiosa* (Palermo, 1991).

Cascio, Anna and Anna Puglisi (eds.), *Con e contro. Le donne nell'organizzazione mafiosa e nella lotta contro la mafia*, Centro siciliano di documentazione Giuseppe Impastato (Palermo, 1987).

Catanzaro, Raimondo, *Il delitto come impresa. Storia sociale della mafia* (Milan, 1988).

Catino, Maurizio, 'Colletti bianchi e mafie. Le relazioni pericolose nell'economia del Nord Italia', in *Stato e Mercato*, 112 (2018).

Catino, Maurizio, *Mafia Organisations. The Visible Hand of Criminal Enterprises* (Cambridge, 2019).

Catino, Maurizio et al., 'Blood(y) Relationships: Interfamily Marriages and Kinship Networks in 'Ndrangheta', Unpublished paper presented at SISEC Conference (Turin, 20 January 2020).

Cerreti, Alessandra, *Unpublished Relation at the Summer School on Organized Crime Mafia and Women*, University of Milan, September 2019.

Cerreti, Alessandra, 'Il coroggio della venita', in E. Ciconte, F. Forgione and I. Sales, *Atlante delle mafie volume secondo* (Sovenia Mannelli, 2013)

Chianese, Gloria, *Storia sociale della donna in Italia (1800–1890)* (Napoli, 1980).

Ciconte, Enzo, ''Ndrangheta: A (Post-)Modern Mafia with Ancient Roots', in F. Allum, I. Clough Marinaro and R. Sciarrone, *Italian Mafias Today. Territory, Business and Politics* (Cheltenham, Northampton, 2019).

Ciconte, Enzo, *'Ndrangheta. Dall'Unita a oggi* (Rome-Bari, 1992).

Ciconte, Enzo, *Dall'omertà ai social. Come cambia la comunicazione della mafia* (Pavia, 2017).

Ciconte, Enzo, *Processo alla 'Ndrangheta* (Bari, 1996).

Colaprico, Piero and Luca Fazzo, *Manager Calibro 9* (Milan, 1995).

Coletti, Alessandro, 'The Welfare System of Italian Mafias', in F. Allum, I. Clough Marinaro and R. Sciarrone, *Italian Mafias Today. Territory, Business and Politics* (Cheltenham, Northampton, 2019).

Colombi, Alessio, 'L'invenzione del familismo amorale', in AA.VV., *Dopo il familismo*

Connell, Robert W., *Masculinities* (Berkeley, 2005).

Cordaro, Alessio and Salvo Palazzolo, *Se muoio, sopravvivimi. La storia di mia madre che non voleva essere più la figlia di un mafioso* (Milan, 2012).

Corso, Paola, 'Alle donne non è consentita l'aggressività', in VV., AA., *Dal materno al mafioso – Ruoli delle donne nella cultura delle mafie*, Quaderni di CLD – Cultura Legalità Democratica, n. 1 (Firenze, 1996).

Cortese, Irene, Sara Di Bella and Cinzia Paolillo, *Sdisonorate. Le mafie uccidono le donne*, Associazione da Sud (Rome, 2011).
Cozza, Michela and Francesca Gennai, *Il genere nelle organizzazioni* (Rome, 2009).
Crenshaw, Kimberlé, W. *On Intersectionality: Essential Writing* (New York, 2017).
Crisantino, Amelia, *Della segreta e operosa associazione. Una setta all'origine della mafia* (Palermo, 2000).
Cross, Università degli Studi di Milano, *Secondo rapporto trimestrale sulle aree settentrionali, per la presidenza della Commissione parlamentare d'inchiesta sul fenomeno mafioso* (Milan, 2015).
Cross, Università degli Studi di Milano, *Primo rapporto trimestrale sulle aree settentrionali, per la presidenza della Commissione parlamentare d'inchiesta sul fenomeno mafioso* (Milan, 2014).
Cutrufelli, Maria, *Disoccupata con onore. Lavoro e condizione della donna* (Milan, 1975).
D'Amico, Salvatore, *Il collaboratore della giustizia* (Rome, 1995).
Dalla Chiesa, Nando, *Passaggio a Nord. La colonizzazione mafiosa* (Turin, 2016).
Deliziosi, Francesco, *Don Pino Puglisi. Vita del prete pugliese ucciso dalla mafia* (Milan, 2001).
Della Bella, Angela, *Il regime detentivo speciale del 41 bis: quale prevenzione speciale nei confronti della criminalità organizzata?* (Milan, 2012).
Demaria, Marika, *La scelta di Lea. La ribellione di una donna alla 'ndrangheta* (Milan, 2013).
Di Bella, Roberto and Giuseppina Maria Patrizia Surace, *Liberi di scegliere. La tutela dei minori di 'ndrangheta nella prassi giudiziaria del Tribunale per i minorenni di Reggio Calabria* (Soveria Mannelli, 2019).
Di Bella, Roberto and Monica Zapelli, *Liberi di scegliere. La battaglia di un giudice minorile per liberare i ragazzi delle 'ndrangheta* (Milan, 2019).
Di Giovine, Marisa, *Mafia Princess. They're Lawless, They're Criminal, They're Family* (UK, 2010).
Di Lello, Giuseppe, *Giudici* (Palermo, 1994).
Di Maria, Franco, 'Identità e sentire mafioso. Percorsi per leggere le trasformazioni', in G. Lo Verso, *La mafia dentro. Psicologia e psicopatologia di un fondamentalismo* (Milan, 1998).
Dickie, John, *Blood Brotherhoods: A History of Italy's Three Mafias* (London, 2014).
Dickie, John, *Cosa Nostra. A History of the Sicilian Mafia* (London, 2004).
Dino, Alessandra, 'Narrazioni al femminile di Cosa Nostra', in 'Donne di mafia', *Meridiana. Rivista di storia e scienze sociali*, 67 (2011).
Dino, Alessandra, *Mutazioni. Etnografia del mondo di Cosa Nostra* (Palermo, 2002).
Dino, Alessandra, 'Waiting for a New Leader: Eras and Transitions in Cosa nostra', in F. Allum, I. Clough Marinaro and R. Sciarrone (eds.), *Italian Mafias Today. Territory, Business and Politics* (Cheltenam, Elgar, 2019).

Dino, Alessandra, *Criminalità dei potenti e metodo mafioso* (Milan, 2009).
Dino, Alessandra, *Unpublished Relation at the Summer School on Organized Crime Mafia and Women*, University of Milan, September 2019.
Dolci, Alessandra, *Unpublished Relation at the Summer School on Organized Crime Mafia and Women*, University of Milan, September 2019.
Dominijanni, Ida, 'Un/Domesticated Feminism', in *Soft Power. Revista euro-americana de teoría e historia de la política y del derecho*, 4(2) (June–December 2017).
Duby, Georges and Michelle Perrot, *A History of Women in the West. Toward a Cultural Identity of Women in the Twentieth Century* (London, 1993).
Duggan, Christopher, *Fascism and the Mafia* (London, 1989).
Dunnage, Jonathan, *Twentieth Century Italy: a Social History* (London, 2002).
Esposito, Nicholas J., *Italian Family Structure* (New York, 1989).
Eures, *Ricerche economiche e sociali, Femminicidio e violenza di genere in Italia* (Rome, 2019).
European Institute for Gender Equality, *Gender Equality Index 2019: Italy* (Vilnius, 2019).
Falcone, Giovanni, 'Che cosa è la mafia', in Giovanni Falcone, *Interventi e proposte (1982-1992)* (Milan, 1994).
Fava, Giuseppe, *Mafia* (Rome, 1984).
Fineman, Martha A. and Anna Grear (eds.), *Vulnerability. Reflections on a New Ethical Foundation for Law and Politics* (Furnam, 2013).
Fineman, Martha A., *The Autonomy Myth: A Theory of Dependency* (New York, 2004).
Fiume, Giovanna (ed.), *Onore e storia nelle società mediterranee* (Palermo, 1989).
Fiume, Giovanna, 'Ci sono donne nella mafia?', in *Meridiana*, n. 7-8 (1990).
Fiume, Giovanna, 'Making Women Visible in the History of the Mezzogiorno', in E. Dal Lago and R. Halpernn (eds.), *The American South and the Italian Mezzogiorno* (London, 2002).
Foot, John, *The Archipelago:Italy since 1945* (London, 2018).
Forgacs, David and Robert Lumley, *Italian Cultural Studies: An Introduction* (Oxford, 1996).
Forgione, Francesco, *'Ndrangheta. Boss luoghi e affari della mafia più potente al mondo. La relazione della Commissione Parlamentare Antimafia* (Milan, 2009).
Foucault, Michelle, *Microfisica del potere. Interventi politici* (Turin, 1977).
Frari, Manuela (ed.), *Sociologia della famiglia, sull'emancipazione femminile* (Milan, 1979).
Fuochi, Giulia, Letizia Mencarini and Cristina Solera, 'I padri coinvolti e i mariti egalitari: per scelta o per vincoli? Uno sguardo alle coppie italiane con figli piccoli', in *About Gender. International Journal of Gender Studies*, 3, 6 (2014), pp. 54–86.
Gambetta, Diego, *The Sicilian Mafia. The Business of Private Protection* (Cambridge, 1993).
Garofalo, Anna, *L'Italiana in Italia* (Bari, 1956).
Garofalo, Sabrina and Ludovica Ioppolo, *Onore e dignitudine. Storie di donne e di uomini in terra di 'ndrangheta* (Cosenza, 2015).

Gelsthorpe, Loraine and Allison Morris, *Feminist Perspectives in Criminology* (Milton Keynes, 1990).

Ghigi, Rossella and Roberta Sassatelli, *Corpo, genere e società* (Bologna, 2018).

Gill, Aisha K., C. Carolyn Strange and Karl Roberts (eds.), *Honour Killing and Violence: Theory, Policy and Practice* (UK, 2014).

Gilmore, David D., *Manhood in the Making. Cultural Concepts of Masculinity* (New Haven, 1990).

Gilson, Erinn C., *The Ethics of Vulnerability. A Feminist Analysis of Social Life and Practice* (London, 2014).

Ginsborg, Paul, *A History of Contemporary Italy: 1943–1980* (London, 1990).

Ginsborg, Paul, *Italy and its Discontents* (London, 2001).

Goddard, A. Victoria, *Gender, Family and Work in Naples* (Oxford, 1996).

Gonzales, Maria Jose, Teresa Jurado and Manuela Naldini (eds.), *Gender Inequalities in Southern Europe, Women, Work and Welfare in the 1990s* (London, 2000).

Goody, Jack, *The Development of the Family and Marriage in Europe* (Cambridge, 1983).

Gratteri, Nicola and Antonio Nicaso, *Fratelli di sangue* (Cosenza, 2006).

Gratteri, Nicola and Antonio Nicaso, *Oro bianco* (Milan, 2015).

Gribaudi, Gabriella, 'Familismo e famiglia a Napoli e nel Mezzogiorno', *Meridiana*, n. 17 (1993).

Gribaudi, Gabriella, 'The Use of Violence and Gender Dynamics within Camorra Clans', in M. Massari and V. Martone, *Mafia Violence. Political, Symbolic, and Economic Forms of Violence in Camorra Clans* (London, 2019).

Gribaudi, Gabriella, 'Donne di camorra e identità di genere', in *Meridiana: Rivista di storia e scienze sociali*, 67 (2010).

Grzyb, Magdalena A., 'An Explanation of Honour-Related Killings of Women in Europe through Bourdieu's Concept of Symbolic Violence and Masculine Domination', in *Current Sociology*, 64 (7) (2016), pp. 1036–53.

Hayner, Priscilla B., *Unspeakable Truths. Facing the Challenge of Truth Commission* (London, 2002).

Hess, Henner, *Mafia* (Bari, 1973).

hooks, bell, *Feminist Theory. From Margin to Center* (Cambridge, MA, 2000).

Ianni, Francis A.J., *A Family Business. Kinship and Social Control in Organised Crime* (New York, 1972).

Ingrascì, Marina, *Le responsabilità penali nel diritto di famiglia* (Turin, 2004).

Ingrascì, Ombretta, 'Organised Crime's Lawyers, from Lawful Defence to the "Bridge Function": The Case of the Sicilian Mafia', in P. Van Duyne *et al.*, *Criminal Defiance in Europe and Beyond, From Organized Crime to Crime-Terror Nexus*(The Netherlands, 2020).

Ingrascì, Ombretta, 'Le fonti giudiziarie nello studio delle mafie. Riflessioni per un dibattito', in *Rivista di Studi e Ricerche sulla Criminalità Organizzata*, 4 (4) (2018), pp. 28–40.

Ingrascì, Ombretta, '*'Ndrangheta Women in Contemporary Italy: Between Change and Continuity*, in N. Serenata (ed.), *The 'Ndrangheta and Sacra Corona Unita. The*

History, Organization, and Operations of Two unknown Mafia Groups (New York, 2014).

Ingrascì, Ombretta, *Confessioni di un padre. Il pentito Emilio Di Giovine racconta la 'Ndrangheta alla figlia* (Milan, 2013).

Ingrascì, Ombretta, *Le donne in Cosa nostra e nella 'Ndrangheta*, in E. Ciconte, F. Forgione and I. Sales, *Atlante delle mafie volume secondo* (Soveria Mannelli, 2013).

Ingrascì, Ombretta, 'Donne, 'ndrangheta, 'ndrine. Gli spazi femminili nelle fonti giudiziarie', in *Meridiana. Rivista di Storia e Scienze Sociali*, n. 67 (2011), pp. 35–54.

Ingrascì, Ombretta, *Donne d'onore. Storie di mafia al femminile* (Milan, 2007).

Ingrascì, Ombretta, 'Women in the 'Ndrangheta: the Serraino-Di Giovine Case', in G. Fiandaca (ed.), *Women and the Mafia: Female Roles in Organised Crime Structure* (New York, 2007).

Ingrascì, Ombretta, *Mafia Women in Contemporary Italy. The Changing Role of Women in the Italian Mafia since 1945*, PhD thesis (London, 2006).

Ingrascì, Ombretta, 'Operazione Gemini e i collaboratori di giustizia', in *Omicron /38* (2002).

Ingrascì, Ombretta, 'Como: il clan dei Mazzaferro', in *Omicron/35*, 10/11 (2001).

Ingrascì, Ombretta, *Le donne, la mafia: nuove ipotesi di ricerca*, laurea thesis (Milan 1998-9).

Kahn, Milka and Anne Véron, *Women of Honour. Madonnas, Godmothers and Informers in the Italian Mafia* (London, 2018).

Kandiyoti, Deniz, 'Bargaining with Patriarchy', in *Gender and Society*, 2, (3) (Sep., 1988), pp. 274–90.

Keller, E. Fox, *Reflections on Gender and Science* (New Haven, 1985).

Leguil, Clotilde *L'essere e il genere. Uomo/donna dopo Lacan* (Turin, 2019; original and first edition: *L'etre et le genre*, Paris, 2015).

Levine, Carol, *et al.*, 'The Limitations of "Vulnerability" as a Protection for Human Research Participants, in *American Journal of Bioethics* 4 (3) (2004), pp. 44–9.

Lindisfarne, Nancy, 'Variant Masculinities, Variant Virginities: Rethinking "Honour and Shame"', in A. Cornwall and N. Lindisfarne (eds.), *Dislocating Masculinity: comparative ethnography* (London, 1994).

Lo Forte, Guido, 'The Sicilian Mafia: A Profile Based on Judicially Confirmed Evidence', in *Modern Italy*, 9 (1) (May 2004).

Lodato, Salvatore, *Quarant'anni di mafia. Storia di una guerra infinita* (Rome, 2012).

Lombardi Satriani, Luigi M. and Mariano Meligrana, *Il ponte di San Giacomo* (Milan, 1987).

Longrigg, Clare, *Mafia Women* (London, 1997).

Luna, Florencia, 'Elucidating the Concept of Vulnerability: Layers Not Labels', in *The International Journal of Feminist Approaches to Bioethics* (1) (2009), pp. 121–39.

Luna, Florencia, 'Identifying and Evaluating Layers of Vulnerability – a Way Forward', in *Developing World Bioethics*, 19 (2019), pp. 86–95.

Lupo, Salvatore, 'La mafia: definizione e uso di un modello virilista', in *Genesis*, II/1 (2003).
Lupo, Salvatore, *Storia della mafia dalle origini ai giorni nostri* (Rome, 2004; first edition 1996).
Mackenzie, Catriona and Natalie Stoljar (eds.), *Relational Autonomy. Feminist Perspectives on Autonomy, Agency, and the Social Self* (New York and Oxford, 2000).
Mackenzie, Catriona, Wendy Rogers and Susan Dodds, *Vulnerability: New Essays in Ethics and Feminist Philosophy* (Oxford, 2014).
Madeo, Liliana, *Donne di mafia. Vittime, complici, protagoniste* (Milan, 1994).
Mafai, Simona (ed.), *Essere donna in Sicilia* (Rome, 1976).
Mancina, Claudia, *Oltre il femminismo* (Bologna, 2002).
Marino, Giuseppe Carlo, *Storia della mafia* (Rome, 2000).
Masini, Vincenzo, *Sociologia di Sagunto* (Milan, 1984).
Massari, Monica and Roswitha Breckner, 'Biography and Society in Transnational Europe and Beyond. An Introduction', in *Rassegna italiana di Sociologia*, 1 (2019).
Massari, Monica and Vittorio Martone, *Mafia Violence. Political, Symbolic, and Economic Forms of Violence in Camorra Clans* (London, 2019).
Meger, Donald, *Sex and Power. The Rise of Women in America, Russia, Sweden and Italy* (Middletown, 1983).
Merlino, Rossella, '*Pizzini*: Sicilian Mafia Culture between Continuity and Change', in F. Allum, I. Clough Marinaro and R. Sciarrone (eds.), *Italian Mafias Today. Territory, Business and Politics* (Cheltenam, Elgar, 2019).
Mete, Vittorio and Rocco Sciarrone, 'The Boundaries of Mafias: Relationships and Business in the "Grey Area"', in S. Carnevale, S. Forlati and O. Giolo (eds.), *Redefining Organised Crime: A Challenge for the European Union?* (Oxford, 2017).
Meyers, Diana T., *Gender in the Mirror. Cultural Imagery and Women's Agency* (Oxford, 2002).
Meyers, Diana T., *Self, Society, and Personal Choice* (Columbia, 1989).
Minicuci, Marina, *Qui e altrove. Famiglie di Calabria e di Argentina* (Milan, 1994).
Mori, Cesare, *Con la mafia ai ferri corti* (Milan, 1932).
Nussbaum, Martha, *Sex and Social Justice* (New York, Oxford. 1999).
Nye, Joseph S., *Soft Power: The Means to Success in World Politics* (New York, 2004).
Nye, Joseph S., *Bound to Lead: The Changing Nature of American Power* (New York, 1990).
O'Reilly, Andrea (ed.), *From Motherhood to Mothering* (New York, 2004).
O'Reilly, Andrea, *Rocking the Cradle. Thoughts on Motherhood, Feminism, and Empowered Mothering* (Albany, 2006).
Oliva, Ernesto and Salvo Palazzolo, *L'altra mafia* (Soveria Mannelli, 2001).
Ortner, Sherry B., *Making Gender: The Politics and Erotics of Culture* (Boston, 1996).
Osservatorio regionale contro la violenza di genere, *Primo rapporto sulla violenza di genere in Calabria e documentazione* Consiglio Regionale della Calabria (2019).

Palazzolo, Salvo, 'Messina Denaro ritratto di famiglia "Noi casta di nobiltà"', in *la Repubblica* (11 May 2017).
Palazzolo, Salvo, 'E la mafia sentenziò "Tradisce il marito boss quella donna va uccisa"', in *la Repubblica* (10 February 2016).
Palazzolo, Salvo, 'Messina Denaro, liti senza fine a casa del boss', *la Repubblica* (25 November 2014).
Palazzolo, Salvo and Michele Prestipino, *Il codice Provenzano* (Rome, 2008).
Pantaleone, Michele, *The Mafia and Politics* (London, 1966).
Panzarasa, Martina, *Donne di mafia e carcere. Cultura, esperienze e pratiche in una sezione di alta sicurezza*, Università degli Studi di Milano, Università degli Studi di Turin, PhD thesis (Milan, Turin, 2018).
Paoli, Letizia, *Mafia Brotherhoods: Organized Crime, Italian Style* (Oxford, 2003).
Parca, Gabriella, *I sultani, mentalità e comportamento del maschio italiano* (Milan, 1965).
Parca, Gabriella, *Le italiane si confessano* (Florence, 1959).
Passerini, Luisa, 'The Women's Movement in Italy and the Events of 1968', in M. Cicioni and N. Prunster (eds.), *Vision and Revision, Women in Italian Culture* (Oxford, 1993).
Pescarolo, Alessandra, *Il lavoro delle donne nell'Italia contemporanea* (Rome, 2019).
Pezzino, Paolo, 'Stato violenza società. Nascita e sviluppo del paradigma mafioso', in M. Aymard and G. Giarrizzo (eds.), *La Sicilia* (Turin, 1987).
Pezzino, Paolo, *Mafia: industria della violenza* (Florence, 1995).
Piccone Stella, Simonetta (ed.), *Genere. La costruzione sociale del femminile e del maschile* (Bologna, 1996).
Piccone Stella, Simonetta, *Ragazze del Sud* (Rome, 1979).
Pickering-Iazzi, Robin, *The Mafia in Italian Lives and Literature: Life Sentences and Their Geographies* (Toronto, 2015).
Pigliaru, Antonio, *La vendetta barbaricina come ordinamento giuridico* (Nuoro, 2000; first edition: Milan, 1959).
Pino, Marina, *Le signore della droga* (Palermo, 1998).
Pitch, Tamar, *Un diritto per due. La costruzione giuridica di genere, sesso e sessualità* (Milan, 1998).
Portelli, Alessandro, 'Oral History as Genre', in M. Chamberlain and P. Thompson (eds.), *Narrative and Genre* (London, 1998).
Prestipino, Michele and Giuseppe Pignatone, *Il contagio. Come la 'Ndrangheta ha infettato l'Italia* (Rome-Bari, 2012).
Principato, Teresa and Alessandra Dino, *Mafia donna. Le vestali del sacro e dell'onore* (Palermo, 1997).
Principato, Teresa, 'La donna nell'universo mafioso', in *Segno*, 183 (1997).
Pristinger, Flavia, 'Il lavoro delle donne: passato e presente', in S. Ulivieri (ed.), *Educazione e ruolo femminile: la condizione delle donne in Italia dal dopoguerra a oggi* (Scandicci, 1992).
Puglisi, Anna, *Donne, mafia e antimafia*, CSD appunti, Quaderni 7–8 del Centro Impastato (Palermo, 1998).

Raffaele, Giovanni, 'Il concetto di onore in alcune tipologie criminali nella Sicilia rurale dell'Ottocento', in Fiume, *Onore e storia*.

Ravaioli, Carla, *Maschio per obbligo* (Milan, 1979).

Reddy, Rupa, 'Domestic Violence or Cultural Tradition? Approaches to "Honour Killing" as Species and Suspecies in English Legal Practice', in A. K. Gill, C. Strange and K. Roberts, *'Honour' Killing and Violence: Theory, Policy and Practice* (London, 2014).

Reeder, Linda, *Women in White. Migration and Transformation of Rural Italian Women, 1880–1920* (London, 2003).

Restaino, Franco and Adriana Cavarero, *Le filosofie femministe* (Turin, 1999).

Rew, Martin, Geetanjali Gangoli and Aisha K. Gill, 'Violence between Female In-Laws in India', in *International Journal of Women Studies*, 14(1) (2013), pp. 147–60.

Rizza, Sandra, *Rita Atria. Una ragazza contro la mafia* (Palermo, 1993).

Romenelli, Maurizio, *I collaboratori di giustizia: l'esperienza italiana* (Zurich, 2003).

Ruddick, Sandra, 'Maternal Thinking', in A. O'Reilly (ed.), *Maternal Theory. Essential Readings* (Brafford, Canada, 2007).

Ruddick, Sandra, *Maternal Thinking. Towards a Politics of Peace* (Boston, 1995).

Ruggiero, Vincenzo, *Crime and Markets. Essays in Anti-Criminology* (Oxford, 2001).

Santino, Umberto, *La mafia dimenticata. La criminalità organizzata in Sicilia* (Milan, 2017).

Santino, Umberto, *La mafia interpretata. Dilemmi, stereotipi, paradigmi* (Soveria Mannelli, 1995).

Santoro, Marco, 'Introduzione', in M. Santoro (ed.), *Riconoscere le mafie* (Bologna, 2015).

Santoro, Marco, *La voce del padrino. Mafia, cultura, politica* (Verona, 2007).

Saraceno, Chiara, 'The Italian Family from the 1960s to the Present', in *Modern Italy*, 9, (1) (May 2004).

Saraceno, Chiara, *Sociologia della famiglia* (Bologna, 1988).

Sassoon, Donald, *Contemporary Italy* (London, 1997).

Sassoon, Donald, *One Hundred Years of Socialism* (London, 1997).

Sen, Pura, 'Crimes of Honour: Value and Meaning', in L. Welchman and S. Hossain (eds.), *Honour: Crimes, Paradigms and Violence Against Women* (London, 2005).

Schneider, Jane and Peter Schneider, *Culture and Political Economy in Western Sicily* (London, 1976).

Sciarrone, Rocco, *Mafie vecchie, mafie nuove. Radicamento ed espansione* (Rome, 1998).

Sciarrone, Rocco (ed.), *Alleanze nell'ombra. Mafie ed economie locali in Sicilia e nel Mezzogiorno* (Rome, 2011).

Sciarrone, Rocco and Storti Luca, 'Complicità trasversali tra mafia ed economia. Servizi, garanzie e regolazione', in *Stato e Mercato*, 3 (2016), pp. 353–90.

Sciarrone, Rocco, ''Ndrangheta: A Reticular Organization', in N. Serenata (ed.), *The 'Ndrangheta and Sacra Corona Unita: The History, Organization and Operations of Two Unknown Mafia Groups* (New York, 2014).

Sciarrone, Rocco, 'The Economic Dimension of Mafias, Social Capital and the 'Grey Area', in F. Allum, I. Clough Marinaro and R. Sciarrone (eds.), *Italian Mafias Today. Territory, Business and Politics* (Cheltenham, Northampton, 2019).

Selmini, Rossella, 'Women in Organized Crime', in M. Tonry and P. Reuter, *Organizing Crime: Mafias, Markets and Networks, Crime and Justice*, vol. 49 (Chicago and London, 2020).

Sen, Purna, 'Crimes of Honour: Value and Meaning', in L. Welchman and S. Hossain (eds.), *Honour: Crimes, Paradigms and Violence against Women* (London, 2005).

Sergi, Anna, 'Widening the Antimafia Net: Child Protection and the Socio-Cultural Transmission of Mafia Behaviours in Calabria', in *Youth Justice*, 18 (2) (2018).

Sergi, Anna and Anita Lavorgna, *'Ndrangheta: the Glocal Dimensions of the Most Powerful Italian Mafia* (London, 2016).

Sergi, Pantaleone, 'Agguato d'onore alla moglie del boss', in *la Repubblica* (6 August 1997).

Servizio Studi del Senato, *Violenza di genere e femminicidio: dalla ratifica della Convenzione di Istanbul all'istituzione di una Commissione di inchiesta ad hoc*, nota breve n. 153 (Rome, February 2017).

Siebert, Renate, 'Mafia Women: The Affirmation of a Female Pseudo-Subject. The Case of the 'Ndrangheta', in G. Fiandaca (ed.), *Women and the Mafia: Female Roles in Organised Crime Structure* (New York, 2007).

Siebert, Renate, *E' femmina però è bella, Tre generazioni di donne al sud* (Turin, 1991).

Siebert, Renate, *Secrets of Life and Death* (London, 1996; first edition *Le donne e la mafia*, Milan, 1994).

Simon, Rita, *Women and Crime* (MA, 1975).

Skarbek, David, *The Social Order of the Underworld: How Prison Gangs Govern the American Penal System* (Oxford, 2014).

Sonstang, Susan, *Regarding the Pain of Others* (New York, 2004).

Spierenburg, Pieter (ed.), *Men and Violence* (Columbus, 1998).

Spiro, Melford, *Gender Ideology and Psychological Reality: An Essay in Cultural Reproduction* (Yale Cambridge, 1997).

Stancanelli, Bianca, *A testa alta* (Turin, 2003).

Stefanelli, Maria and Manuela Mareso, *Loro mi cercano ancora. Il coraggio di dire no alla 'ndrangheta e il prezzo che ho dovuto pagare* (Milan, 2014).

Stille, Alexander, *Excellent Cadavers: The Mafia and the Death of the First Italian Republic* (London, 1996).

Storiacce, Television transmission, *Sposa-bambina, per patto di 'ndrangheta'*, Radio 24 (28 November 2015).

Sykes, Gresham M. and David Matza, 'Techniques of Neutralization: A Theory of Delinquency', in *American Sociological Review*, 22 (6) (1957).

Temkin, Jennifer, 'Women, Rape and Law Reform', in M. Evans (ed.), *The Woman Question* (London, 1994).

Thrasher, John James and Toby Handfield, 'Honor and Violence. An Account of Feuds, Duels, and Honor Killings', in *Human Nature*, 29 (2018), pp. 371–89.

Tizian, Giovanni, *Rinnega tuo padre* (Rome-Bari, 2018).
Tolosana, Carmelo Lisòn, 'The Ever-Changing Faces of Honour', in A. Dionigi, A. Blok and C. Bromberger (eds.), *L'anthropologie de la Méditerranée* (Paris, 2001).
Torre, Roberta, *Angela*, Rita Rusic Company, Movie Web, Sister Film (Italy, 2002).
Tota, Annalisa, 'Storia di Lea Garofalo e di sua figlia Denise', *Rivista di Studi e Ricerche sulla Criminalità Organizzata*, 3 (2017).
Tranfaglia, Nicola, *Mafia, politica e affari 1943–2000* (Rome-Bari, 1992).
Trasferri, Ada (ed.), *Donna. Women in Italian Culture* (Ottawa, 1989).
Tronto, Joan, 'Care as a Basis for Radical Political Judgments', in *Hypatia*, 10 (2) (1995), pp. 141–9.
Truzolillo, Fabio, 'La struttura unitaria della 'ndrangheta dalle origini', in *Meridiana*, N. 77 (2013).
Varese, Federico, *Mafia Life: Love, Death, and Money at the Heart of Organized Crime* (Oxford, 2018).
Vitale Giusy with Camilla Costanzo, *Ero cosa loro. L'amore di una madre può sconfiggere la mafia* (Milan, 2009).
VV. AA., *Dopo il familismo cosa?* (Milan, 1992).
VV. AA., *Il Novecento delle italiane* (Rome, 2001).
Wikan, Unni, *In Honour of Fadime: Murder and Shame* (Chicago and London, 2008).
Wilson, Stephen, *Feuding, Conflict and Banditry in Nineteenth-Century Corsica* (Cambridge, 1988).
Zagari, Antonio, *Ammazzare stanca* (Cosenza, 1992).

Judicial Sources

Corte d'appello di Catanzaro, Seconda sezione penale, *Sentenza*, issued on 20 July 2017.
Corte d'Assise di Cataniar, Seconda sezione, *Sentenza*, n. 33/96.
Corte d'Assise di Milano, Terza sezione, *Sentenza* n. 20/98, issued on 28 April 1998.
Corte d'Assise di Palmi, *Sentenza*, issued on 6 April 2016.
Corte d'Assise di appello di Reggio Calabria, *Sentenza*, issued on 1 February 2019.
Corte d'Assise di appello di Trapani, *Sentenza* n.5/96.
Corte d'Assise di Palmi, Prima sezione, *Sentenza*, issued on 13 July 2013.
Corte d'Assise di Palmi, Prima sezione, *Sentenza*, issued on 7 September 2019.
Corte d'Assise di Trapani, *Sentenza* n. 4/2001, issued on 17 May 2001.
Procura della Repubblica di Caltanissetta, Direzione Distrettuale Antimafia, *Richiesta per l'applicazione di misura cautelare*, Proc. n. 1409/18 R.G.N.R.
Procura della Repubblica di Catanzaro, Direzione Distrettuale Antimafia, *Verbale di sommarie informazioni*, Proc. n. 1846/2009 R.G.N.R.
Procura della Repubblica di Milano, Direzione Distrettuale Antimafia, *Richiesta di rinvio a giudizio*, Proc. n. 3760/93 R.G.N.R.
Procura della Repubblica di Palermo, Direzione Distrettuale Antimafia, *Richiesta delle misure di custodia cautelare in carcere*, Proc. n. 3157/98 R.G.N.R.
Procura della Repubblica di Palermo, Direzione Distrettuale Antimafia, *Richiesta per l'applicazione di misure cautelari*, Proc. n. 16676/01 R.G.N.R.
Procura della Repubblica di Reggio Calabria, Direzione Distrettuale Antimafia, *Decreto di fermo di indiziato di delitto*, Agostino Anna Maria + 155, 2010.
Tribunale di Bologna, Ufficio del giudice per le indagini preliminari, *Ordinanza di applicazione di misure cautelari* n. 17375, issued on 15 January 2015.
Tribunale di Caltanissetta, Sezione GIP-GUP, *Ordinanza di misure cautelari* (Proc. n. 109/2014 R.G.N.R), issued on 25 June 2018.
Tribunale di Catanzaro, Sezione GIP/GUP, *Sentenza*, issued on 17 May 2013.
Tribunale di Catanzaro, Ufficio del giudice per le indagini preliminari, *Ordinanza di custodia cautelare* (Proc. n. 1846/09 R.G.N.R.), issued on 21 June 2012.
Tribunale di Milano, *Sentenza* n. 16/94.
Tribunale di Milano, *Sentenza*, Proc. n. 8317/92 R.G.N.R.
Tribunale di Palermo, Sez. II Penale, *Sentenza* n. 2370/2001.
Tribunale di Palermo, Sezione dei giudici per le indagini preliminari, *Ordinanza di applicazione di misure cautelari personali e contestuale decreto di sequestro preventivo* (Proc. n. 10944/08 R.G.N.R.).

Tribunale di Palermo, Ufficio del giudice per le indagini preliminari, *Ordinanza di custodia cautelare in carcere* (Proc. n. 1942 R.G.N.R.), issued on 30 November 2011.

Tribunale di Palermo, Ufficio del giudice per l'udienza preliminare, *Sentenza*, issued on 27 November 2000.

Tribunale di Palermo, Ufficio del giudice per le indagini preliminari, *Sentenza a seguito di giudizio abbreviato*, issued on 27 September 2017.

Tribunale di Palmi, *Sentenza* n. 612/15, issued on 24 May 2015.

Tribunale di Palmi, *Sentenza* n. 6357/15, issued on 11 May 2017.

Tribunale di Reggio Calabria, Ufficio del giudice per le indagini preliminari, *Ordinanza di custodia cautelare* n. 3926/08.

Tribunale di Reggio Calabria, Sezione G.I.P.-G.U.P., *Ordinanza di custodia cautelare* n. 52/18 (Proc. n. 6089/2015 R.G.N.R.), issued on 6 November 2018.

Tribunale di Reggio Calabria, Ufficio del giudice per le indagini preliminari, *Ordinanza di applicazione di misure cautelari* n. 452/13, issued on 25 March 2013.

Index

abortion 33
adultery 33
　see also mistresses
agency of mafia women 2–3, 5, 7, 119–25,
　　127–30
Aiello, Piera 132–3, 139
Allegra, Michele 14
amoral familism 64
Angela (dir. Torre) 41
Annamaria, from Calabria 67
anomie theory 83–4, 85
antimafia legislation 16
arranged marriages 5, 56–61
　examples of 57–8
　feuds, ending of 59–60
　inheritance of power 58–9
　kinship and 56–7, 59
　purpose of 60–1
　weddings, opportunities of 60
Artemisia operation 76–7
associations *see* organizations
Atria, Rita 132, 133–5
autonomy of women 156–7

Badalamenti, Gaetano 15
Bagarella, Calogero 44, 58
Bagarella, Leoluca 17
Bagarella, Ninetta 58
Balbo, Laura 35
Banfield, Edward 64
Barbaro, Giuseppe 60
Battaglia, Serafina 75–6, 78, 79
Belgio operations 92
Bellocco, Antonio 53
Bellocco, Francesca xi, 53–4
Bellocco, Francesco xi, 53
Bellocco, Maria Rosa 53
Belnome, Antonino 40, 42
betrayals
　by mafiosi 74
　by women 42, 43, 53–5
　see also collaborators with justice

Betti, Francesca 24
Blok, Anton 74–5, 79, 122
blood alliances *see* arranged marriages
Boemi, Salvatore 73, 102
Bontate (Bontade), Stefano 15, 16
Borsellino, Paolo 16, 17, 133, 134–5, 139
Bourdieu, Pierre 136
Brancaccio *mandamento* 107, 120
brothers, oppression of women 43, 44
Buscetta, Tommaso 13–14, 16, 74, 131
business, mafia 10–11
Butler, Judith 130

Cacciola, Domenico 53, 54
Cacciola, Maria Concetta 50–2, 146,
　　147–50, 151–2, 155–6
calendarizzazione (calendarization) 75
Camassa, Alessandra 68, 75, 132–3,
　　133–4
Camorra, code of honour 37
Catholic Church 29, 32, 33
Cerreti, Alessandra 55, 69, 145–6
Chiara, from Gela 94
Chicago School of Sociology 83
childless women 67
children
　education of 63–71
　and leaving the mafia 151–4
　rights of 153
　use of 71
　see also arranged marriages; daughters;
　　sons
Christian Democrats 29
Cintorino, Antonino 109, 110
clothes, keeping of 79
Cloward, Richard 84
code of honour 5, 37–42
Cohen, Albert 84
collaborators with justice 131–50
　background 3, 131–2, 166 n.8
　difficulties of 146–50
　prison and 144–6

risks to 155, 159
vendettas against 74, 78–9
communications 101–7
Communist party 29
construction work 10, 20
consumerism 31
contraceptive pill 32
control mechanisms *see* code of honour
Convention on the Rights of the Child 153
coordination bodies 15
Corleone 15
Cosa Nostra
    arranged marriages 58
    business of 10, 11
    characteristics of 3
    code of honour 37, 40
    collaborators with justice 132–5
    communications 104–6
    drug trade 81–3
    economic crimes 95–8
    family terms 63
    honour killings 49–50
    leadership positions 107–17, 120
    oppression of women 43, 47
    organization of 12, 13–18
    vendetta, use of 74, 76
Cosco, Carlo xi, 52–3
Cosco, Denise 158
cousins 43, 56–7, 59
criminal involvement of women 6
criminality, theories of 83–4
Crimine-Infinito investigation 21
cultural attitudes 25
cultural systems, transmission of 65–6
Cupola 15, 16

Daria, from Caltanissetta 115–17
daughters
    honour killings 49, 50
    oppression of 42–3, 47
    relationships with mothers 67
    supporting mothers 157–8
    see also arranged marriages
death penalty *see* honour killings
defectors *see* collaborators with justice
Denaro, Matteo Messina 18, 47, 105–6
Denaro, Patrizia Messina 98
Di Bella, Roberto 151, 152, 153–4

Di Giovine, Emilio 44, 60, 68–9, 71, 91, 92–3, 155
Di Giovine, Marisa 94, 121
Di Giovine, Rita 155
Di Matteo, Giuseppe 74
differential opportunity theory 84
Dino, Alessandra 17, 122–3
disowning of women 155
divorce 32, 33
domestic labour 25, 26, 27
domestic violence *see* honour killings
Donne d'onore operation 88
doppia presenza (dual role of women) 28, 35–6
drug trade 6, 10, 81–93
    awareness of women 89–90, 91
    Cosa Nostra 81–3
    drug dealing 86–8
    drug smuggling 82–3, 85
    drug trafficking 10, 25, 81, 89, 91–2
    motivation of women 84–5
    'Ndrangheta 88–93
    sociological theories 83–4
Durkheim, Emile 83

economic crimes 6, 93–101
    extortion 98–9
    female professionals 100–1
    money laundering 93–7
    women's dependency on men 97–8
economy of Italy 24, 30
education 63–72
    in the absence of fathers 67–8
    effect of 28, 32, 34
    family relationships 63–5, 67
    primary socialization 65
    restriction of 42
    transmission of cultural systems 65–6
    by women 5–6, 63, 66–7
Eleanora, from Palermo 111–13
Elisa, from Rosarno 44–5
emancipation of women 7–8, 23, 34, 100–1, 129
    see also pseudo-emancipation
employment of women 23–9
enterprise syndicates 10
'European 'Ndrangheta connection' operation 88–9

exploitation of women 25-6
extended family 70-1
external work 24-5
extortion 9, 20, 98-9

factories 24, 25
Falcone, Giovanni 16, 17, 49, 59
Families 14
familism 64
family law 33
family memory 75
family relationships 63-5, 67, 70-1
family terms 63
family ties *see* kinship
family units 30-1
fathers
　absent 67-8
　role of 33, 64, 67
　surrogate 133
femicides 35
　see also honour killings
feminist movement 29, 30, 32, 33, 35
feuds 20, 59, 73
　see also vendettas; warfare
Filippello, Giacoma 78-9, 139
Fineman, Martha 127
Foucault, Michel 72
fugitives 102, 105-6
funerals 73

Gallace, Antonio 55
Garofalo, Anna 29-30
Garofalo, Lea xi, 52-3, 146, 150, 158, 161-3
Gemini investigation 94
gender relations 29, 31, 32, 35, 47, 124
Ghiaccio operation 107
Giampà, Francesco 102
Giampà, Giuseppe 102-4, 107
Gill, Aisha, *et. al.* 48-9
Gilmore, David D. 68
Ginsborg, Paul 30-1
Giuseppe C. 44
Golden Market operation 107
Golem II operation 98
Goody, Jack 56, 58
grandparents 69, 70
Graviano, Nunzia 97-8, 124
Greco, Michele 16

health-care investments 96
Hermes tasks 101-7
hierarchical structures 14, 15, 18-19, 21
homosexuality 44
honour, code of 5, 37-42
honour killings 5, 48-56
　Cosa Nostra 49-50
　cultural context 48-9
　as deterrent 55
　Francesca Bellocco 53-4
　Lea Garofalo 52-3
　Maria Concetta Cacciola 50-2
　of men 55-6
　motives 49
　other examples 54-5
hooks, bell 129
housewives 26

identities
　changing of 140-4
　of children 65, 66
　of men 9, 13, 14, 39, 40
　of women 28, 30, 33, 35-6, 125
indirect female participation 5
industry in Italy 24, 25
infame 74
informants *see* collaborators with justice
inheritance of power 58-9
initiation ceremonies 13
intersectionality approach 2
Inzerillo, Salvatore 58
Irene, from Rosarno 120-1

juvenile delinquents 151

kidnapping 16
killings *see* honour killings; murders
kinship 18, 56-7, 59, 63-4, 118

La Licata, Francesco 78, 79
labour market 4-5, 23-9
L'Ala, Natale 78, 79
Lamezia Terme 77, 90, 99
Lavinia, from Lamezia Terme 77-8, 117-19, 121
laws 16, 33, 93, 131
leadership positions 6, 107-19, 119-25
　Daria, from Caltanissetta 115-17
　Eleanora, from Palermo 111-13

Giuseppina Vitale 108–9
Lavinia, from Lamezia Terme 117–19
Maria Filippa Messina 109–11
Santina, from Palermo 113–14
leaving the mafia
   children and 151–4
   collaborators with justice 131–50
   ethical impact of 154–60
legislation 16, 33, 93, 131
lesbians 44
letters from women 29–30
Libera (NGO) 151
liberation of women 32, 33
   see also emancipation of women; pseudo-emancipation
Liggio (Leggio), Luciano 15, 79
Lima, Salvo 17
Lipari, Giuseppe, daughter of 96, 104–5, 121
Lo Piccolo, Salvatore 18
Longrigg, Clare 83, 95, 139
Lucchese, Giuseppe 49–50
Lupo, Salvatore 14
Luppino, Giuseppe 14
Luzza, Pino Russo 55

Mackenzie, Catriona 156
'*mafia rosa*' (pink mafia) 94
mafia system 1–2
mafia tax (*pizzo*) 9
   see also extortion
managers, female 122
Mannoia, Francesco 49, 59, 74
Marchese, Giuseppe 58
Marchese, Pino 49–50
Marcianò, Calogero 19
marginalization of women 24
marriage rates 34
marriages see arranged marriages
masculine ideology 68
masculinity of female power 121, 122–3
masculinity, performance of 40, 68–9, 76
Medusa investigation 102
memory, family 75
Merton, Robert 83
messengers, women as 101–7
Messina, Leonardo 59
Messina, Maria Filippa 109–11
Meyers, Diana T. 156

Milan 52–3, 85, 91–2
mistresses 42, 59
money laundering 11, 93–7
Morabito, Saverio 44, 57
morality 30, 31
Morello, Maria 19
mothers
   drug trade 82–3, 85, 86–7, 89–90
   relationships with sons 67, 69–70
   role of 27, 33, 64, 149–50
   supported by daughters 157–8
   teaching by 66, 67–8, 158–9
   vendetta and 75–6
multi-belonging identities 125
murders 16, 17, 35
   see also honour killings

Naffine, Ngaire 84
Navarra, Michele 15
'Ndrangheta
   arranged marriages 57–8, 60
   business of 10, 11
   characteristics of 4
   code of honour 37, 40, 42
   collaborators with justice 134–44
   communications 101–4
   drug trade 88–93
   economic crimes 94–5, 98–100
   education by women 66, 67, 68
   female membership of 13
   honour killings 49, 50–5
   leadership positions 117–19, 120–1
   oppression of women 42, 43, 44–5
   organization of 12, 18–21
   performing masculinity 68–9
   relationships of sons and mothers 69–70
   rituals of 13
   vendetta, use of 73, 74, 75, 76–8
   Youth Court and leaving the mafia 151–2
New York 83–4
normality, notion of x, 46, 71, 139–40
nostalgia 140–1

Ohlin, Lloyd 84
Onorato, Francesco 50
oppression of women 5, 42–8
   homosexuality 43

segregation of women 42–3
widows 43–4
wives of prisoners 46
by women 44–5, 47
see also honour killings; submission of women
organizations
characteristics of 1–2, 4
Cosa Nostra 13–18
'Ndrangheta 18–21
structures and rituals 11–13
violence, power and business 9–11

Palazzolo, Salvo 96
Palermo
drug trade 82, 85, 86–8
extortion 99
maxi-trial 16–17
structure of organizations 14
warfare 15, 16
Panepinto, Lorenzo 73
Paola, from Naples 89, 90
Papalia, Domenico 44
Parca, Gabriella 30, 31
Parole di donne (Women's Words) 29
Pasolini, Pier Paolo 32
patriarchal ideology 31–4, 66, 67–8
Pelle, Elisa 60
pentiti law 131
Pesce, Giuseppina (Giusy) 43, 54, 69, 70, 145–6, 152, 154–5
Petralia, Margherita 40
Pino, Marina 82, 85, 86
political protection 17
pornography 35
power, mafia 9
delegation of power to women 108–9, 109–10, 113–14, 115–17, 121–2
inheritance of 58–9
masculinity of female power 121, 122–3
soft power 6, 79–80
Prestipino, Michele 57
primary socialization 65
Principato, Teresa 94
prisoners
children of 67–8, 71
collaborators with justice 144–6

communications of 102–3, 104–5, 105–6
delegation of power to women 108–9, 109–10, 113–14, 115–17, 121–2
financial dealings of 97
gangs 177 n.16
wives of 46
Pristinger, Flavia 25
professional jobs 27–8, 100–1
protection 9
see also extortion
protest movements 31–2
Provenzano, Bernardo 15, 17–18, 96, 104
pseudo-emancipation 7–8, 124–5
pseudo-subjects, female 124–5
public officials, trust in 138–9
public sector employment 27
Puglisi, Pino 65

racketeering *see* extortion
ragionamento (reasoning) 41
rape 34–5
real estate businesses 94, 95
Rebus operation 113–14
recruitment 12–13
Reggio Calabria 20–1
rejecting the mafia *see* leaving the mafia
relationships 11, 63–5, 67, 69–70
reputation 38–9, 40, 68
revenge 135–6
see also vendettas
Ribisi, Grazia 59, 74
rights of children 153
rights of women 30, 32, 33, 34
Riina, Arcangela 44, 58
Riina, Totò 15, 16, 17, 44, 58
rituals 13, 19, 75, 79
Rizzotto, Placido 79
Rognoni-La Torre law 16, 93
roles of women, in the mafia system x–xi, 2, 4–5
Romenelli, Maurizio 92, 131
Rosa, from Africo 38
Rosa N. 3
collaboration of 134–44
on communications 101–2
daughter, support of 157–8
on mothers 66, 67, 70

on vendetta 74, 75
on weddings 60
Ruddick, Sara 66, 68
Russo, Angela 86–8

Sangiorgi, Ermanno 14
Santina, from Palermo 113–14
Satriani, Lombardi 79
Scaglione, Pietro 16
Sciarrone, Rocco 12
Second World War 23, 29
segregation of women 25, 42
sentences 87, 92, 94, 98, 110, 137
separation from the mafia *see* leaving the mafia
Serraino, Ciccio 73
Serraino, Maria 91–3, 120
Serraino-Di Giovine clan 94
service sector employment 26, 27
sexual behaviour
    abuse 83
    adultery 32–3
    homosexuality 44
    rape of women 34–5
    of women 30, 38, 39–40, 41–2
Sicily *see* Cosa Nostra
Siebert, Renate 67, 78, 124
Siino, Angelo 104
Simon, Rita 100–1
smuggling 82–3, 85
social customs 4–5, 29–36
social protection *see* welfare system
socialization 65
sociological theories 83–4
soft power 6, 79–80
sons
    drug dealing 86
    education of 68–9, 70–1
    relationships with mothers 67, 69–70
    vendetta and 75–6
    see also arranged marriages
sorella d'omertà (sister of silence) 19
sources ix, 3–4
speaking out against mafias *see* collaborators with justice
Stefanelli, Maria 46, 55, 146
Stoljar, Natalie 156
strage di viale Lazio 44, 58
strain theory 83–4, 85

structures 11–12, 14–15
student movements 32
subcultures 84
subjects, female 124–5
submission of women 136, 149
    see also oppression of women
Sugamiele, Gaspare 40

Terranova, Cesare 14
terrorism 17
Theorema (dir. Pasolini) 32
theories of criminality 83–4
Tolosana, Carmelo Lisòn 37
Torre, Roberta 41
Torretta 83
transformative agency 127–30
trust
    in mafia organizations 12, 38, 57, 120, 122
    in public officials 138–9

uncles 70–1
unregulated work 24–5
urbanization, impact on women 25–6

vendetta trasversale 74
vendettas 6, 72–80
    betrayals and 74
    distribution of 74–5
    memory and 75
    ritual practices 79
    timing of 75
    use of 72–3
    women and 73–4, 75–80
victimization of women 83
violence 9–10, 34–5, 124
    see also honour killings; murders; vendettas
virginity 30, 31, 56, 59–60
Vitale, Giuseppina (Guisy) 43, 108–9, 122–3, 124, 144–5
Vitale, Leonardo 14, 108, 109
Vitale, Vito 71, 108
vote, right to 29
vulnerability of women 7, 127–30, 160

wages 27–8
warfare 15, 16
    see also feuds; vendettas

weakness of women 24, 25
welfare state 27
welfare system 10–11
widows 44–5
witness programme 131–2
witnesses *see* collaborators with justice

women's liberation 32, 33
women's rights 30, 32, 33, 34
work *see* labour market

Youth Court 151–4, 159

Zagari, Antonio 19

www.ingramcontent.com/pod-product-compliance
Lightning Source LLC
Chambersburg PA
CBHW062221300426
44115CB00012BA/2170